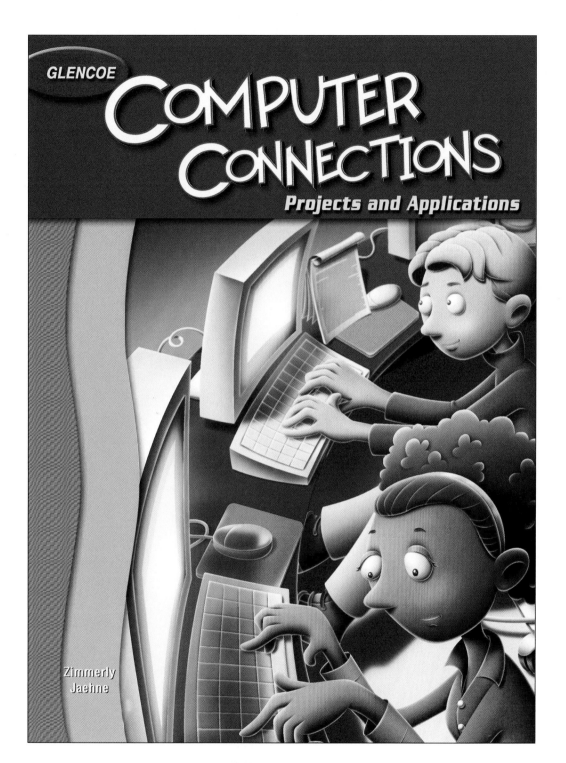

GLENCOE

COMPUTER CONNECTIONS

Projects and Applications

Zimmerly
Jaehne

Glencoe

New York, New York
Columbus, Ohio
Chicago, Illinois
Peoria, Illinois
Woodland Hills, California

ABOUT THE AUTHORS

Arlene Zimmerly is a professor at Los Angeles City College where she teaches a broad list of computer applications and office technology courses, to include keyboarding online, Web page design, and word processing. She is a co-author of the best-selling postsecondary keyboarding text in the country—*Gregg College Keyboarding & Document Processing*.

Julie Jaehne is an instructor in the College of Education at the University of Houston where she teaches a graduate course "Technology in the Classroom." She has extensive experience consulting schools in the use of technology in K–12 instruction and has written ten computer application textbooks and software tutorials.

Cover/Unit Opener Illustrator: Bernard Adnet

Photo Credits

Terry Sutherland, Sutherland Photodesign vi; vii; 2(inset); 4(inset); 5(t); 5(b); 9(inset); 11; 12; 13; 14; 16(inset); 58(inset); 163(inset); 212(inset); 248(inset); 300(inset); 318(inset).

Glencoe

The *McGraw-Hill* Companies

Glencoe Computer Connections: Projects and Applications

Printed in the United States of America.

Send all inquiries to:
Glencoe/McGraw-Hill
21600 Oxnard Street, Suite 500
Woodland Hills, CA 91367

ISBN 0-07-861399-X

1 2 3 4 5 6 7 8 9   027   09 08 07 06 05 04 03

CONTRIBUTORS

Jack E. Johnson, Ph.D.
Director of Business Education
Department of Management and
   Business Systems
State University of West Georgia
Carrollton, Georgia

Judith Chiri-Mulkey
Adjunct Teacher
Department of Computer Information Systems
Pikes Peak Community College
Colorado Springs, Colorado

Delores Sykes Cotton
Supervisor, Business Education
Detroit Public Schools
Detroit, Michigan

Carole G. Stanley, M.Ed.
Keyboarding and Computer Literacy
   Teacher, Retired
Rains Junior High School
Emory, Texas

REVIEWERS

Connie Buchanan
Roulhac Middle School
Chipley, FL

Laura de Wet
The Selwyn School
Denton, TX

Richard DiRenno
Feliz Festa Middle School
West Nyack, NY

Marc H. Doyle
Porter Middle School
Austin, TX

Beatrice Ellis
Parkman Junior High School
Woodland Hills, CA

Karen Finklestein
Pines Charter Middle School
Miramar, FL

Lee Mendenhall
Woodbrook Middle School
Lakewood, WA

Nancy Poncik
La Vernia Middle School
La Vernia, TX

Mary Reid
Mountain Shadows Middle School
Nuevo, CA

Jacque Schaffer
Clayton Middle School
Clayton, WI

Karen Sjoberg
Wauzeka-Steuben Schools
Wauzeka, WI

Jan F. Stark
Port Jervis Middle School
Port Jervis, NY

William A. Stenzel
Sierra Vista Junior High School
Canyon Country, CA

Dan Vasiloff
Stevenson Middle School
Westland, MI

Joan Wooten
Knox Middle School
Salisbury, NC

Jason Zuba
Lancaster Middle School
Akron, NY

TABLE OF CONTENTS

About the Authors   ii
Contributers and Reviewers   iii
About Your Book   vi
Reference Section   R1

UNIT 1 COMPUTER USAGE

Page

Focus on Good Keyboarding Habits   2

Section 1.1   Computer Usage   3

UNIT 2 COMPUTER ETHICS

Page

Focus on Good Keyboarding Habits   9

Section 2.1   Computer Ethics   10

UNIT 3 COMPUTER BASICS

Page

Focus on Good Keyboarding Habits   16

Section 3.1   Software Basics   17

Section 3.2   Manage Files   22

Section 3.3   Editing Basics   26

Section 3.4   Formatting Basics   33

Section 3.5   Internet Basics   39

Section 3.6   Data Collection   44

Review   53

Curriculum Portfolio   55

UNIT 4 WORD PROCESSING

Page

Focus on Good Keyboarding Habits   58

Section 4.1   Edit and Format Short Stories   59

Section 4.2   Format and Edit Poems   64

Section 4.3   Format a Journal Entry and
               Proof Text   69

Section 4.4   Create and Format Tables   73

Section 4.5   Format Outlines   79

Review   84

Curriculum Portfolio   85

Section 5.1   Format a Personal Letter   87

Section 5.2   Format a Business Letter
               With Envelope   94

Section 5.3   Format an E-Mail Message   103

Review   109

Curriculum Portfolio   110

Section 6.1   Format a One-Page Report   112

Section 6.2   Format a Report With
               a Bibliography   120

Section 6.3   Format a Title Page   128

Section 6.4   Format a Report With
               a Reference Page   132

Section 6.5   Format a Report With Footnotes
               or Endnotes   142

Section 6.6   Table of Contents   152

Review   157

Curriculum Portfolio   160

TABLE OF CONTENTS *(continued)*

UNIT 5 DESKTOP PUBLISHING

		Page
Focus on Good Keyboarding Habits		163
Section 7.1	Design Pages With Pictures and Objects	164
Section 7.2	Design Pages With Drawing Tools	168
Section 7.3	Create Newsletters	174
Section 7.4	Create Documents From Templates	180
Section 8.1	Create a Web Page	185
Section 8.2	Create a Table in a Web Page	192
Section 8.3	Create Hyperlinks for Web Pages	198
Review		208
Curriculum Portfolio		210

UNIT 6 PRESENTATIONS

		Page
Focus on Good Keyboarding Habits		212
Section 9.1	Presentation Basics	213
Section 9.2	Edit Slides	221
Section 9.3	Add Clip Art to Slides	230
Section 9.4	Add Animation	235
Review		240
Curriculum Portfolio		245

UNIT 7 SPREADSHEETS

		Page
Focus on Good Keyboarding Habits		248
Section 10.1	Spreadsheet Basics	249
Section 10.2	Create and Edit a Spreadsheet	256
Section 10.3	Use Simple Formulas	266
Section 10.4	Enter Functions	275
Section 10.5	Create Charts	284
Review		292
Curriculum Portfolio		297

UNIT 8 DATABASE

		Page
Focus on Good Keyboarding Habits		300
Section 11.1	Create Database Tables and Enter Data	301
Section 11.2	Sorts and Queries	306
Review		313
Curriculum Portfolio		315

UNIT 9 CAPSTONE PROJECTS

		Page
Focus on Good Keyboarding Habits		318
Section 12.1	Capstone Projects	319
Glossary		G1
Index		I1

ABOUT YOUR BOOK

Your book is divided into 9 Units. Each unit opens with Focus on Good Keyboarding Habits to demonstrate correct posture and position at the keyboard, Proofreading Warmup lines to begin each day, and a Making the Connection feature to introduce you to the projects and applications.

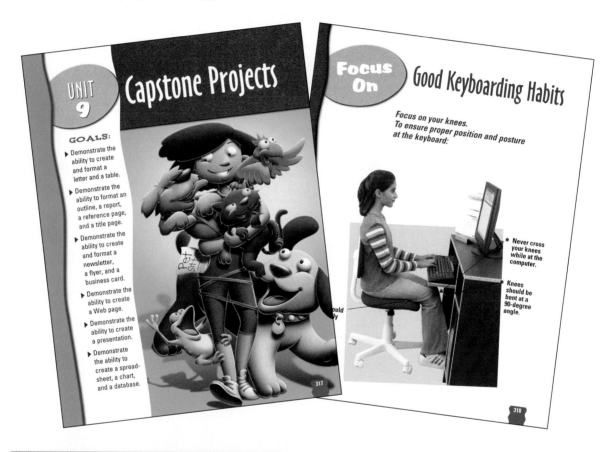

UNITS

Unit 1 introduces you to the care and operation of a computer. Unit 2 focuses on ethics, safety, and computer etiquette.

In Units 3 through 8 you will use your skills to create documents and to format them correctly. In addition, you will learn word processing features, Internet features, desktop publishing, presentations, spreadsheets, and databases.

In Unit 9 you will use all the skills you learned throughout the book in a capstone simulation of projects called "*The Pet Sitter*." In *The Pet Sitter*, you will create and format all the documents necessary to begin and successfully work for a business!

ABOUT YOUR BOOK *(continued)*

PROJECTS

Each unit is divided into sections. Every section begins with a Proofreading Warmup that you should begin keying as soon as you are settled at your keyboard. Making the Connection introduces you to projects.

The Projects are designed to be used with any software application or platform. While using various software applications, you will be able to create documents, spreadsheets, presentations, maintain data, and gather information and images from the Internet.

PROJECT 3
Continued

Reinforce

Create a Newsletter

2. Spell-check, proofread, and correct any errors.

3. Save the document as *urs*The Great Globe. Keep the file open for the next step.

4. Format the newsletter similar to the one illustrated below.

Create a masthead.

Enhance the headings.

The Great Globe

Issue XXV   1599

William Shakespeare

William Shakespeare produced plays since 1594. He worked as an actor and manager for many years in *The Chamberlain's Men*, the most popular acting company in London. He attained financial prosperity by making sound investments, and became part owner in *The Globe*, the most prestigious public playhouse in all of London.

Romeo and Juliet

Shakespeare's beloved work known to all is *Romeo and Juliet*. In this play, the city of Verona is split by a feud between two families - the Montagues and Capulets. Romeo is a young Montague, and Juliet, a Capulet. The most memorable scene takes place in the garden as Juliet stands at her balcony. The two star-crossed lovers pledge their deep and abiding love for each other.

Romeo and Juliet are wed in secret by a friar, but their bliss is not to last. In the end, Romeo believes Juliet is dead in the Capulet crypt, but she is in a deep, drugged sleep. In his despair, he poisons himself. Juliet awakens from her deep slumber and realizes her most precious Romeo is dead. In utter desperation, she also ends her life. Shakespeare's tragedy is one of his most moving and heartfelt works.

Insert appropriate clip art.

5. Save the changes. Print and close the file.

Focus On

Good Keyboarding Habits

Practice perfect posture:

- Distance your abdo... approximately one span from the key...

- Center your body in front of the keyboard (body directly in front of the "J" key).

- Keep your spine and abdomen straight.

Focus on Good Keyboarding Habits is where you have a chance to review your posture and position at the keyboard. You can compare the way you sit at the keyboard to students with good keyboarding technique.

2

ABOUT YOUR BOOK *(continued)*

PROJECTS

PROJECT 2 · Practice

Cut and Paste Text

A quick way to change text is to use the Cut and Paste commands. When text is cut, it is stored in the **clipboard**. The **clipboard** is a temporary storage area in your software. The text on the clipboard can be placed in another location.

In order to move text, you must first select a portion of the document you want to change. An easy way to **select text** is to use the "click-Shift-click" method.

Your Turn

Symbol	Draft Copy	Final Copy
move ⌐⌐→Move text	9. Lauren (carefully) swam	Lauren swam

1. In Sentence 9, position the insertion point before in the word "carefully."

2. Hold down the SHIFT key and move the insertion the letter "y" in "carefully." The entire word is h shown in the illustration below.

Selected text is text that is highlighted by a colored or shaded box. ⟶ 9. Lauren carefully swam.

3. Choose the **Cut** command. The word "carefully"

4. Position the insertion point after the letter "m" "swam."

If you accidentally remove more text than you want to delete, be sure to use the Undo command immediately.

5. Choose the **Paste** command. The word "caref again.

6. Choose the **Undo** command until the word "c in its original position.

7. Save the changes. Keep the file open for Pro

Editing Basic

> **Practice Projects** will help you practice new features and improve your skills.

> **Proofreading Warmup** activities prepare you for work.

> **Color Coding** helps you identify instructions. Instructions are coded in **blue**. Naming a file to be saved is coded in **green**. New skills are coded in **red**. Glossary terms and illustration labels are coded in **black** bold.

> **Making the Connection** prepares you for new learning and gets you involved in the lesson at the very beginning.

SECTION 3.1 · Software Basics

GOALS: Demonstrate the ability to:
- ▶ Open a new document.
- ▶ Identify menu commands, shortcut keys, and function keys.
- ▶ Use the Help feature.
- ▶ Save and close a document.

PROOFREADING WARMUP

In a word processing document, key each line 3 times. Proofread your work.

Set your goals, and then make plans to achieve those goals.
messes make some moms mad; half a dome; for his risk; mills
he reads ahead; his middle silo is filled; more old mirrors

Making the Connection

An easy way to learn software is to explore and use the features. You can learn about many software features by using the online Help feature.

Your Turn

1. Open a new word processing document.

2. Key a list of all the software features that you find. For example, can you find the button for Bold? Do you see the word Help?

3. Keep the document open for Project 1.

LIST OF SOFTWARE FEATURES

Bold
Help

INDEX *(continued)*

SUM function
    spreadsheet, 276
Switch windows, 46

T

Tab stops
    table of contents, 153
Table
    database, 302–303
    on Web pages, 192–194
    shading, 193–194
    (project), 74, 75, 76, 192–193, 194–195
Table of contents, 152–155
    (project), 152, 154–155
Template
    business cards, 181–182
    calendar, 183
    presentation, 218
    defined, 180
Text box, 165
Theme, 187
Thesaurus, 66
Timeline, 172
Title
    in reports, 113
    in presentations, 216
Title page, 128–130, 165–166
    (project), 129–130, 165, 166, 329

U

Underline, 34
Undo, 30
URL, 46–48

V

Vertical alignment, 129
View
    presentations, 214–215

W

Web page
    applying themes, 187
    creating, 185–186
    hyperlinks, 199–203
    inserting photos and graphics, 188
    photos and captions, 195–196
    saving document as, 186
    tables, 192–193, 194–195
Web page (project), 186–188, 189–190, 334–336
Web site
    definition, 202
Word processing features
    alignment, 35
    bold, 34, 60
    clipboard, 29
    close document, 20
    cut/copy/paste, 29, 30, 115
    find and replace, 118
    font, 20, 34
    grammar, 20, 36
    italic, 34
    margins, 113
    open document, 20
    outline numbered list, 81
    page numbers, 121
    paste, 29–30
    print, 20
    print preview, 34
    Save, 20
    scroll, 20
    select, 29–30
    Spelling, 20, 36
    thesaurus, 66
    toolbar button, 20
    underline, 34
    undo, 29, 30
    vertical alignment, 129
Works Cited page, 137
    (project), 137, 140
Write On!, 72, 78, 102, 108, 119, 127, 131, 141, 151

ABOUT YOUR BOOK *(continued)*

PROJECTS

Projects include a variety of special features. The following pages show samples of these features.

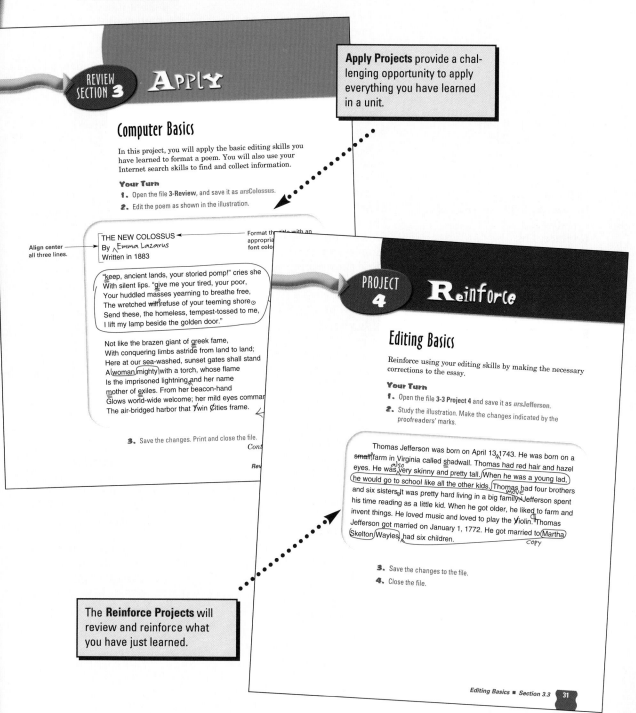

Apply Projects provide a challenging opportunity to apply everything you have learned in a unit.

REVIEW SECTION 3 APPLY

Computer Basics

In this project, you will apply the basic editing skills you have learned to format a poem. You will also use your Internet search skills to find and collect information.

Your Turn

1. Open the file **3-Review**, and save it as *urs*Colossus.
2. Edit the poem as shown in the illustration.

Align center all three lines.

THE NEW COLOSSUS
By Emma Lazarus
Written in 1883

Format the title with an appropriate font color.

"keep, ancient lands, your storied pomp!" cries she
With silent lips. "give me your tired, your poor,
Your huddled masses yearning to breathe free,
The wretched will refuse of your teeming shore
Send these, the homeless, tempest-tossed to me,
I lift my lamp beside the golden door."

Not like the brazen giant of greek fame,
With conquering limbs astride from land to land;
Here at our sea-washed, sunset gates shall stand
A woman mighty with a torch, whose flame
Is the imprisoned lightning, and her name
mother of exiles. From her beacon-hand
Glows world-wide welcome; her mild eyes comman
The air-bridged harbor that Twin Cities frame.

3. Save the changes. Print and close the file.

Cont

Rev

The **Reinforce Projects** will review and reinforce what you have just learned.

PROJECT 4 Reinforce

Editing Basics

Reinforce using your editing skills by making the necessary corrections to the essay.

Your Turn

1. Open the file **3-3 Project 4** and save it as *urs*Jefferson.
2. Study the illustration. Make the changes indicated by the proofreaders' marks.

Thomas Jefferson was born on April 13, 1743. He was born on a small farm in Virginia called shadwall. Thomas had red hair and hazel eyes. He was very skinny and pretty tall. When he was a young lad, he would go to school like all the other kids. Thomas had four brothers and six sisters. It was pretty hard living in a big family. Jefferson spent his time reading as a little kid. When he got older, he liked to farm and invent things. He loved music and loved to play the violin. Thomas Jefferson got married on January 1, 1772. He got married to Martha Skelton Wayles, had six children.

3. Save the changes to the file.
4. Close the file.

INDEX *(continued)*

Proofreading Warmup, 3, 10, 17, 22, 26, 33, 39, 44, 59, 64, 69, 73, 79, 87, 94, 103, 112, 120, 128, 132, 142, 152, 164, 168, 174, 180, 185, 192, 198, 213, 221, 230, 235, 249, 256, 266, 275, 284, 301, 306, 319

Q

Query
  database, 306–311
  filter, 310
  multiple sort, 309
  simple sort, 308

R

Reference, 137
Reference page (project), 137, 140, 328
Replace, 116
Report
  bibliography, 123, 124–126
  body, 113
  bound, 121–123
  byline, 113
  citations, 133–134, 138–140
  footnotes, 143–145, 148, 150
  multi-page with bibliography, 124–126
  multi-page with citations, 138–140
  multi-page with footnotes and endnotes, 143–145, 148–150
  multi-page with reference page, 132
  one-page, 112–116, 117–118
  page numbers, 122
  side headings, 121
  title, 113
Results, Internet search, 40, 42
Return address
  envelope, 90
  letter, 88
Row
  spreadsheet, 250
  table, 74

S

Salutation
  business letter, 95
  personal letter, 88–89
Search
  for files, 24
  Internet/Web, 40–41
  results, 40, 42
Search engine, 40
Select
  database field, 307
  editing, 29, 30
  on Web page, 46
Shading
  in tables, 193–194
Shadows, 165
Short stories
  editing, 59–61
Short story (project), 61
Shortcut keys, 19
Side heading, 121–122
Simple sort, 308
Slide show view
  presentation, 214, 218
Slide sorter view
  presentation, 215
Slide view, 215
Slides, 214
  adding and deleting, 224–226
  editing, 221, 222–223
  order, 224–226
  proofing tools, 222–223
  sorting, 215
  with clip art, 230–231
Software features
  drop-down menu, 18
  filename, 23
  files, 23
  find file, 24
  folders, 23
  function key, 19
  Help, 19
  insertion point/cursor, 18
  menu, 18
  menu bar, 18
  navigate, 19
  Save as, 19, 23
  scroll, 19
  shortcut key, 19
  switch, 46
  title bar, 18
  toolbar, 18

Sort
  database, 306, 307–308, 309
Sort
  spreadsheet data, 261
Sound
  presentation, 237
Spelling feature, 20, 36
Spreadsheet, 249
  alignment, 254
  AVERAGE function, 277
  bar, 251
  bar chart, 285
  cell, 250
  cell reference, 281
  change column width, 257–258
  charts, 284–291
  column, 250
  create new, 256–258
  definition, 250
  deleting/inserting columns and rows, 259
  division formula, 272
  Fill Right/Down command, 280–281
  format and edit data, 258
  formula bar, 267
  formulas, 266, 267–274
  functions, 279–281
  line chart, 287–288
  MAXIMUM function, 278–279
  MINIMUM function, 278–279
  multiplication formula, 270–271
  navigating, 251
  number/pound ## symbols, 258
  parts, 250–251
  pie chart, 289–290
  row, 250
  sorting data, 261
  subtraction formula, 269
  SUM function, 276
  (project), 249, 250–252, 257–258, 259–260, 262–264, 267–269, 270–271, 272, 273, 276, 277, 278–279, 280–281, 282, 285–286, 287–288, 289–290, 291, 292–296, 337
Subtraction
  spreadsheet, 269

ABOUT YOUR BOOK *(continued)*

SPECIAL FEATURES

Check Your Understanding ✓

1. Open a new word processing document.
2. Describe how a business letter differs from a personal letter.
3. Describe the parts of a business letter that are different from those of a personal letter.
4. Explain why your return address is included at the top of a business letter.
5. Explain the purpose of an enclosure notation.
6. Save the document as *ursLetterinfo*. Print and close the file.

Check Your Understanding is where you can find out if you have learned the main ideas or if you need to go back and review.

interNET CONNECTION

In this lesson you learned to format a business letter to be mailed within the United States. What if your letter were to be mailed outside of the United States? What information would you need to include on the envelope? Would you need to format the envelope differently?

1. Open your Web browser and search for information on how to address envelopes for international addresses properly. Choose an international location.
2. Open a new word processing document and key an example of the inside address you would create for the letter. Then add any additional information that should be included on the envelope.
3. Save the document as *ursInternational Addresses*. Print and close the file.

Write On!

1. Open your journal and position the insertion point at the end of the document. Enter today's date to create a new journal entr[y]
2. Write at least one paragraph about a fo[rmal event] that you have attended or wish you coul[d attend] (a wedding, an awards banquet, or a soc[ial event] in your community). Describe how you w[ould] dress for the event and the proper etiqu[ette that] would be expected of you.
3. Save the changes to your journal. Clos[e]

Write On! activities give you the chance to use the computer to write your thoughts as you are learning.

Format a Business Letter With Envelope ■

COMPLETING UNIT 3

ENRICH

Curriculum Portfolio

Use the word processing skills you have learned to help you create your curriculum portfolio project. Choose from one of the following topics.

SCIENCE:

Compose a paragraph describing fossils.

What are living fossils? Use the Internet to find at least two examples. Compose a paragraph describing the fossils. Add a title. Be sure to cite your sources at the end of the paragraph.

SOCIAL STUDIES:

Compose two paragraphs about citizenship.

Persons born in the United States are citizens. Others, through naturalization, can become citizens and enjoy the same privileges and responsibilities. Use the Internet to find facts about the steps a person must take to successfully emigrate to the United States. Be sure to answer the following questions.

1. Who is a citizen?
2. If a person is not born in the United States, how can he or she become a citizen?
3. How does a person become a citizen?
4. What are the rights and duties of a citizen?
5. How can a citizen lose his or her citizenship?

Add a title. Be sure to cite your sources at the end of the paragraphs.

Each **Internet Connection** has fun search tips, great ideas for surfing the Web, and information about the Internet.

Curriculum Portfolios are projects in the curriculum areas of Math, Social Studies, Science, and Language Arts. The **Portfolios** give you the chance to demonstrate that you have mastered the concepts and skills as they apply to a computer application.

Continued on next page

Curriculum Portfolio ■ Unit 3 **55**

About Your Book **x**

INDEX *(continued)*

K

Keyword, 40

L

Landscape page orientation, 169
Legend, 285
Letter
    block-style, 88–89, 91–92,
        95–96, 98–99, 100–101
    body, 88–89, 95–96
    business, 94–101
    closing, 89, 96
    date, 88, 95
    delivery address, 90
    enclosure notation, 96
    inside address, 88, 95
    letterhead, 95
    personal, 87–92
    return address, 88, 90
    salutation, 88, 95
    with return address, 98–99,
        100–101
Letterhead, 95
Line chart
    spreadsheet, 287–288

M

Making the Connection, 3, 10,
    17, 22, 26, 33, 39, 44, 59, 64, 69,
    73, 79, 87, 94, 103, 112, 120,
    128, 132, 142, 152, 164, 168,
    174, 180, 185, 192, 198, 213,
    221, 230, 235, 249, 256, 266,
    275, 284, 301, 306, 319
Margins
    in reports, 113
    table of contents, 153
Masthead, 176, 178
MAXIMUM function
    spreadsheet, 278–279
MINIMUM function
    spreadsheet, 278–279
Multipage report (project),
    124–126, 132–137, 138–140,
    157–159
Multiple sort, 309
Multiplication
    spreadsheet, 270–271

N

Navigating
    presentation, 214
    spreadsheet, 253
    general, 18–19
Newsletter
    creating, 174–178
    masthead, 176
    (project), 175–176, 177–178,
        330–331
Newspaper-style columns, 175
Normal view
    presentation, 214
Number/pound ## symbols
    spreadsheet, 258

O

Object
    tables, 303
    title pages, 165
Objects, 164–171
One-page report (project),
    112–116, 117–118
Outline
    formatting, 79–81
    (project), 80–82
    numbered list, 81
Outline view
    presentations, 215
Overtype mode, 27

P

Page break
    before Works Cited page, 137
Page design
    with drawing tools, 168
Page orientation, 169
Paste, 29, 46
Personal letter (project), 88–89,
    91–92, 320–321
Photographs
    in presentations, 232–233
    on Web pages, 188, 195–196
Pictures
    in presentations, 232–233
Pie chart, 289–290
Poem (project), 64–65, 66, 67

Portrait page orientation, 169
    arms and elbows, 163
    eye distance, 16
    feet, 300
    head and neck, 58, 248
    knees, 318
    wrists, 212
Presentation (project), 216–218,
    219, 227–228, 231–233,
    236–237, 238, 240–244,
    338–340
Presentation software features
    adding and deleting slides,
        224–226
    adding pictures and
        photographs, 232–233
    animation, 236
    changing animation order, 237
    changing slide order, 224–226
    clip art, 230–231
    editing, 221
    Insert Picture, 231–233
    inserting clip art, 231
    inserting slides, 216–217
    navigating, 215
    proofing tools, 222–223
    resizing, 232–233
    Slide Layout command, 231
    sound, 237
    templates, 218
    Title Slide Layout command,
        216
    views, 214–215
Print preview, 34
Proofing
    journal entries, 70–71
Proofing tools, 36
Proofreaders' marks
    add period, 60
    add space, 60
    capital letter, 60
    capitalize, 28
    copy text, 30
    delete, 27, 60
    double-space, 60
    insert, 27
    insert a comma, 28, 60
    insert a period, 27
    lowercase, 28, 60
    move text, 29
    new paragraph, 28, 60
    transpose, 27, 60

ABOUT YOUR BOOK *(continued)*

VISUAL AIDS

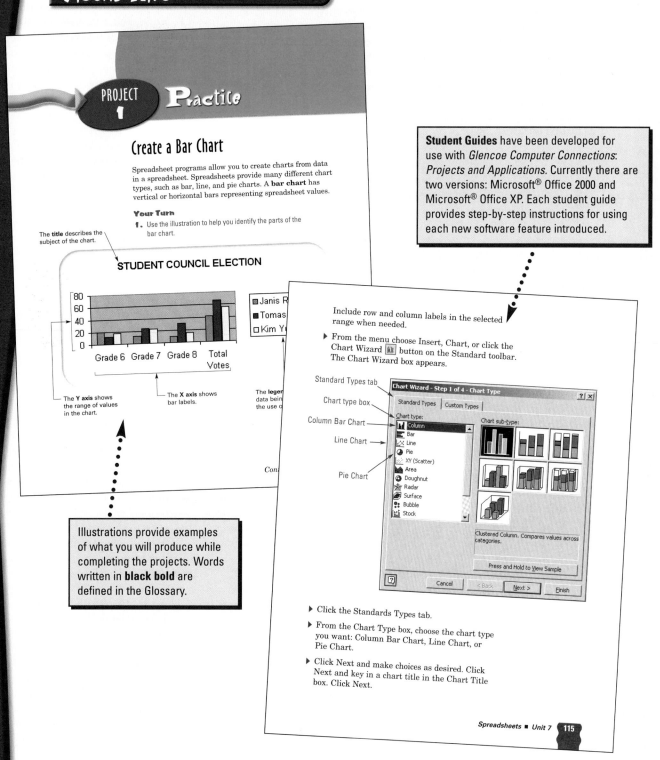

Student Guides have been developed for use with *Glencoe Computer Connections: Projects and Applications.* Currently there are two versions: Microsoft® Office 2000 and Microsoft® Office XP. Each student guide provides step-by-step instructions for using each new software feature introduced.

Create a Bar Chart

Spreadsheet programs allow you to create charts from data in a spreadsheet. Spreadsheets provide many different chart types, such as bar, line, and pie charts. A **bar chart** has vertical or horizontal bars representing spreadsheet values.

Your Turn

1. Use the illustration to help you identify the parts of the bar chart.

The **title** describes the subject of the chart.

STUDENT COUNCIL ELECTION

☐ Janis R
■ Tomas
☐ Kim Y

Grade 6 Grade 7 Grade 8 Total Votes

The **Y axis** shows the range of values in the chart.

The **X axis** shows bar labels.

The **lege**
data bein
the use o

Illustrations provide examples of what you will produce while completing the projects. Words written in **black bold** are defined in the Glossary.

Include row and column labels in the selected range when needed.

▸ From the menu choose Insert, Chart, or click the Chart Wizard button on the Standard toolbar. The Chart Wizard box appears.

Standard Types tab
Chart type box
Column Bar Chart
Line Chart
Pie Chart

Chart Wizard - Step 1 of 4 - Chart Type
Standard Types | Custom Types
Chart type:
- Column
- Bar
- Line
- Pie
- XY (Scatter)
- Area
- Doughnut
- Radar
- Surface
- Bubble
- Stock

Chart sub-type:

Clustered Column. Compares values across categories.

Press and Hold to View Sample

Cancel | < Back | Next > | Finish

▸ Click the Standards Types tab.

▸ From the Chart Type box, choose the chart type you want: Column Bar Chart, Line Chart, or Pie Chart.

▸ Click Next and make choices as desired. Click Next and key in a chart title in the Chart Title box. Click Next.

Con

INDEX *(continued)*

E-mail
   address, 104
   attachment, 104–107
   emoticon, 105
   header form, 104
   message, 103
   shorthand, 105
   subject, 104
   (project), 104–105, 106–107
Emoticon, 105
Enclosure notation, 96
Endnote, 146–150
Envelope
   business letter, 97
   personal letter, 90
Errors
   grammar, 71

F

Favorite, 41
Field, database
   defined, 303
   select, 307
Field name, 302
Field type
   database, 302
File
   managing, 23–25
Filename, 23
Fill
   spreadsheet, 280–281
Fill colors, 165
Filter
   database, 310–311, 312,
      313–314
Find and replace, 116
Flyer (project), 208–209, 332
Folder, 23
Font, 34
Footer, 135–136
Footnote, 143–147
   converting to endnotes,
      146–147
Format
   alignment, 65
   bibliography, 123
   block style letter, 88–89,
      91–92
      bound report, 121–123
   business cards, 181–182

business envelopes, 96–97
business letters, 95–96, 98–99,
   100–101
citations, 133–134, 138–140
e-mail message, 104–107
endnotes, 146, 148–150
envelopes, 90, 97
font, 34, 65
footer/header, 135–136
footnotes and endnotes,
   143–150
header, 135–136
hyperlinks, 199–203
journal entries, 70–71
line spacing, 65
multi-page report with
   bibliography, 124–126
multi-page report with
   citations, 138–140
newsletter, 174–178, 330–331
one-page report, 112–113,
   117–118
outlines, 79–81, 82–83
personal letter, 88–89,
   91–92, 320–321
poems, 64–65
reference page, 123, 132, 137
short stories, 59
spreadsheets, 252, 258
table of contents, 152–153,
   154–155
tables on Web pages, 193–194
title page, 129–130
using templates, 180
Web pages, 185–190
works cited page, 137
presentation, 213
Formula bar
   spreadsheet, 267
Formula, spreadsheet
   AVERAGE, 277
   division, 272
   Fill Right/Down, 280–281
   MAXIMUM, 278–279
   MINIMUM, 278–279
   multiplication, 270–271
   subtraction, 269
   SUM, 276
Function keys, 19

G

Good Keyboarding Habits, 2,
   9, 16, 58, 163, 212, 248, 300, 318
Grammar check feature, 20,
   36, 71
Graphics
   on Web pages, 188
Grid, 287

H

Hanging indent, 123
Header/footer, 135–136
Heading
   column, 75
   side, 121–122
Help, 19
Hyperlink, 41
   creating, 199–203
   graphic, 206
   to another Web page location
      on same Web page,
      202–203
   using text, 205
   to location on the same Web
      page, 199–201

I

Indent
   outlines, 79–80
Insert key, 27
Inside address
   business letter, 95
   personal letter, 88
Internet
   search steps, 41
   search (project), 42
   data collection, 44–45
Internet browser, 40
Internet Connection, 43, 52, 63,
   68, 77, 83, 93, 102, 108, 119,
   127, 131, 141, 151, 156, 167,
   173, 179, 184, 191, 234, 239
Italic, 34

J

Journal entry (project), 70, 71
Justification, in columns, 175

REFERENCE SECTION *Table of Contents*

PROJECT SAMPLES

Personal Letter R2
Business Letter R2
Personal Business Letter R2
Outline R2
One-Page Report R3
Multi-Page Report R3
Works Cited R3
Title Page R4
Multi-Page Reports With Side Headings R4
Bibliography R4
Format for Envelopes R5
Boxed Table R6
Contents R6
Proofreaders' Marks R6
Punctuation and Usage R7
Punctuation R7
Grammar R10
Mechanics R12
Number Expression R13
Abbreviations R13

INDEX

A

Alignment, 35
  columns, 175
  spreadsheet, 250
Animation
  defined, 236
  in presentations, 235–237
Apply Design Template
  presentation, 218
Arrow keys
  navigating spreadsheets, 253
AVERAGE function
  spreadsheet, 277

B

Backspace key, 27–28
Bar chart
  spreadsheet, 285
  (project), 337
Bibliography (project), 123–126
Block-style letter, 89–90, 95–96
Body
  business letter, 95–96
  personal letter, 89–90
Bold, 60
Bookmark, 41
Boolean operators, 40
Borders
  objects, 165
  tables, 75
Bound report (project), 121–123
Bulleted list
  presentation, 217
Business cards
  (project), 181–182, 333
Business letter, 94–101
  (project), 95–96, 98–99,
     100–101, 109
Byline, 113

C

Calendar (project), 183
Callout, 171
Caption
  on Web page, 195–196
Cell
  spreadsheet, 250
  table, 74

Cell reference
  spreadsheet, 281
Chart
  create, 284
  (project) bar chart, 285–286,
     287–288, 289–290, 291, 296
Check Your Understanding
  7, 14, 21, 25, 32, 38, 43, 52, 63,
    68, 72, 77–78, 83, 93, 102, 108,
    127, 131, 141, 151, 156, 167,
    173, 179, 184, 191, 197, 207,
    220, 229, 234, 239, 255, 265,
    274, 283, 311
Citation, 133–134
  Internet, 46–48
  Internet image, 49–50
  works cited page, 146
Clip art, 165
  business cards, 182
  slides, 230–231
  Web page, 188
Clipboard, 29
Closing
  business letter, 96
  personal letter, 89
Column heading, 75
Column
  spreadsheet, 250, 259
  table, 74
Copy
  from Web page, 46
  proofreaders' marks, 30
Copy and paste
  between documents, 114–115
Criteria box, filter
  database, 311
Curriculum Portfolio, 55–56,
  85–86, 110–111, 160–161, 210,
  245–246, 297–298, 315–316
Cut/copy/paste, 29

D

Data label, 288
Database
  data entry, 304
  defined, 302
  field, 302
  filter, 310–311
  query, 306, 308–309

  search, 307
  sort, 306, 310–311
  table, 302
  (project), 302–303, 304, 305, 306,
    307–308, 309, 310–311, 312,
    313–314, 341
Date
  business letter, 95
  personal letter, 88
Delete key, 28
Delete/insert
  spreadsheet, 259
Delivery address
  envelope, 90
Designing pages
  with objects, 164, 168
Desktop publishing
  business cards, 181–182
Desktop publishing documents
  calendar, 183
  flyers, 208–209
  newsletters, 174–178
  Web pages, 185–190
Desktop publishing features
  borders, 165
  clip art, 165
  columns, 174–175
  drawing tools, 168–169
  fill, 165
  insert, 165
  line style, 169
  line tool, 169
  objects, 164–165
  page design, 164, 168
  pictures, 164–165
  shadows, 165
  templates, 180–182
  text boxes, 165
Division
  spreadsheet, 272
Document
  print, 34
  saving as Web page, 186
Dot leader, 153
Drawing tools, 168

E

Editing
  presentation, 221–223

REFERENCE SECTION *(continued)*

PERSONAL LETTER

1719 Lakeview Drive
Fontana, WI 53125
March 21, 20-- ↓ 4x

Ms. Susan Yu, Director
Turtle Creek Animal Shelter
2023 North Lake Shore Drive
Fontana, WI 53125 ↓ 2x

Dear Ms. Yu: ↓ 2x

I am interested in volunteering at your animal shelter. I love animals, and I have pets of my own, including a dog and a cat. I can help you feed, groom, and exercise the animals in your shelter. ↓ 2x

I am available to help you on weekdays after school and on weekends. I would be willing to work up to six hours a week. I can start working next week. ↓ 2x

Please call me at 555-6978 and let me know how I can help. ↓ 2x

Sincerely, ↓ 4x

Your Name

BUSINESS LETTER

LINCOLN MIDDLE SCHOOL
6021 Brobeck Street • Flint, MI 48532
Phone: 810-555-9001 • Fax: 810-555-9004

Today's Date ↓ 4x

Mr. Anthony Martinez
Cyber Foundation
4092 Barnes Avenue
Burton, MI 48529 ↓ 2x

Dear Mr. Martinez: ↓ 2x

My friends and I at Lincoln School want to help your organization. ↓ 2x

Our district is replacing our computers with new ones. Our computer technology teacher Mrs. Jones explained that your organization recycles computers to help developing countries keep up with technology. We want our school district to consider donating our computers. ↓ 2x

I am enclosing a copy of the specs for the computers in my classroom at our school. These computers are going to be replaced in the next six months. Can you please let me know if your organization would be interested in recycling these computers? If they can be recycled, my teacher will give the information to the administrators in our school district. ↓ 2x

Sincerely, ↓ 4x

Steve Rach ↓ 2x

Enclosure

PERSONAL BUSINESS LETTER

5419 Mirra Loma Drive
Reno, NV 89502
Today's Date ↓ 4x

Mainstream Music, Inc.
270 Clara Street
San Francisco, CA 94107 ↓ 2x

Ladies and Gentlemen: ↓ 2x

About four weeks ago, I mailed you an order for a DVD movie package. I purchased DVD package #41-809 from page 5 of your catalog. The total cost of the order was $47.35. ↓ 2x

Today I saw a package at my door. I was so excited that my order had finally arrived. But I was really disappointed when I opened it and saw that you sent me the wrong DVDs. ↓ 2x

I am returning the DVD package with this letter and I am enclosing the order return form. I am asking for a full refund of $47.35. And I also want to be reimbursed for the $5.00 it cost me to ship the DVD package back to you. Please send the refund to me at the above address. ↓ 2x

Sincerely, ↓ 4x

Martine Pico ↓ 2x

Enclosure

OUTLINE

↓ 1 inch

OCEAN WATER AND LIFE

I. WAVES AND TIDES
   A. *Waves*
      1. How waves move
      2. How waves form
   B. *Tides*
      1. The gravitational pull of the moon
      2. Spring and neap tides
   C. *Life in the intertidal zone*

II. OCEAN CURRENTS
   A. *Definition of currents*
   B. *Surface currents*
   C. *Density currents*
   D. *Upwellings*

GLOSSARY *(continued)*

Theme Consists of design elements and color schemes. (Section 8.1)

Title Bar The top of a window where the title of the document is displayed. (Section 3.1)

Title Page A page of information displaying the title of a document, the author's name and date. (Section 6.3)

Toolbar A series of selectable buttons on a word processing screen or desktop. (Section 3.1)

Transpose A mark made by a proofreader to correct letters or words that are in reverse order. (Section 3.3)

U

Undo A software command that reverses the last action taken. (Section 3.3)

URL (Uniform Resource Locator) The address of a Web site that starts with the abbreviation http://. (Sections 3.6, 8.1, 8.2)

V

View A software feature you use to look at a document in different ways or to display or hide software features on the screen. (Section 9.1)

Visual Theme Set of design elements and color schemes that can be applied to Web pages. (Section 8.1)

W

Web Page An electronic page on the Internet that is formatted to look like a page in a magazine, except it might have sound clips, video clips, and hyperlinks to other pages. (Sections 8.1, 8.2)

Web Site Two or more related Web pages. (Section 8.3)

Window A framed portion of the screen displayed while you are working in a software program or document.

Word Processing Software A program you use to create, edit, and print documents. (Section 3.1)

Works Cited Page A page located at the end of a document with a list of sources specifically mentioned in a paper. (Section 6.4)

Worksheet A spreadsheet form that enables you to input data and formulas.

X

X-Axis A horizontal bar-chart scale that displays a range of values. (Section 10.5)

Y

Y-Axis A vertical bar-chart scale that displays a range of values. (Section 10.5)

REFERENCE SECTION *(continued)*

ONE-PAGE REPORT

↓ 1 inch default margin

ALL THE CHOCOLATE YOU CAN EAT!

By Rachelle Cantin

I read the book *Charlie and the Chocolate Factory*. The author of the book is Roald Dahl. The book is 155 pages long, and it was published by Puffin.

Charlie Bucket is a poor boy who lives in a tiny house with his parents. Both sets of grandparents also live with Charlie in that tiny house. Charlie didn't have any money, but he found a dollar bill in the street. He used the money to buy a Wonka candy bar. The Willy Wonka Chocolate Company held a contest. When Charlie opened the candy bar, he found a golden ticket. He was one of five winners.

The other four winners were Augustus Gloop, Violet Beauregarde, Veruca Salt, and Mike Teavee. Charlie went on the tour of the chocolate factory with his Grandpa Joe. The other four winners were there with their parents. They saw lots of amazing things, and they met the Oompa-Loompas. The Oompa-Loompas were the tiny people who lived and worked in the factory.

The other four kids behaved very badly on the tour. When they didn't follow directions, Mr. Wonka punished them. Funny things happened to them that made them disappear. Charlie was kind and polite. Mr. Wonka liked Charlie, and he knew he could trust Charlie. At the end of the tour, Charlie was the only kid left, and Mr. Wonka gave him the chocolate factory. Charlie and his family could live at the factory, and they could have all the chocolate they could eat!

My favorite part about this book was when the other four kids didn't follow directions and Mr. Wonka punished them. Charlie followed directions, and Mr. Wonka rewarded him for that.

MULTIPAGE REPORT

(MLA Style)

↓ .5 inch
Last Name 1

Your First and Last Name
↓ 1x
Your Teacher's Name ↓ 1x
Class
↓ 1x
Current Date
↓ 1x

King of the Wild Frontier ↓ 1x

ds

"Be always sure you are right, then go ahead" (Lofaro 1148d). You're probably wondering what that means. Well, a guy named Davy Crockett used to say that. It is one of his best known quotes. Read on to find out more about this legendary person.

1 inch

Actually, his name was David Crockett. He was born in a small cabin in Tennessee on August 17, 1786. (*Davy Crockett*). His family lived in a cabin on the banks of the Nolichucky River. Davy had eight brothers and sisters. Four were older and four were younger.

1 inch

Davy lived with his family in Tennessee until he was 13. He went to school, but he didn't like it. He skipped school a lot. He ran away from home because he knew his dad was going to punish him for playing hooky. He joined a cattle drive to make money. He drove the cattle to Virginia almost 300 miles away. He stayed in Virginia and worked a lot of jobs for over two years. He returned to his family in Tennessee when he was 16 (*Davy Crockett Biography*).

When Davy returned home his dad was in debt. Now Davy was 6 feet tall and he could do a man's work. Davy went to work for Daniel Kennedy. Davy's dad owed Daniel 76 dollars and Davy worked for one year to pay the debt (The Texas State Historical Association).

In 1806 Davy married Polly Finley. They had two sons, John Wesley and William. Then Davy went to fight for the Tennessee Volunteer Militia under Andrew Jackson in the Creek Indian War. When he returned home from the war, he found his wife very ill. She died in 1815 (Davy Crockett Birthplace Association).

MULTIPAGE REPORT CONTINUED

(MLA Style)

↓ .5 inch
Last Name 2

Davy then married Elizabeth Patton in 1817. She was a widow and she had two children of her own, George and Margaret Ann (The Texas State Historical Association).

Davy was well known in Tennessee as a frontiersman. He was a sharpshooter, a famous Indian fighter, and a bear hunter. In 1821, he started his career in politics as a Tennessee legislator. People liked Davy because he had a good humor and they thought he was one of their own. He was re-elected to the Legislature in 1823, but he lost the election in 1825.

In 1827 Davy was elected to Congress. He fought for the land bill. The land bill allowed those who settled the land to buy it at a very low cost. He was re-elected to Congress in 1829 and again in 1833, but he lost in 1836 (Lofaro, 1148d).

1 inch

Many Americans had gone to Texas to settle. In 1835, Davy left his kids, his wife, his brothers, and his sisters to go to Texas. He loved Texas. When the Texans were fighting for their independence from Mexico, Davy joined the fight. He was fighting with a group of Tennessee volunteers defending the Alamo in San Antonio on March 6, 1836 (The Texas State Historical Association). He was 49 years old.

1 inch

WORKS CITED

↓ .5 inch
Last Name 3

Works Cited

Author Unknown. "Davy Crockett Biography." 6 April 2002.
   <http://www.infoporium.com/heritage/crockbio.shtml>.

ds

"Davy Crockett." *Microsoft Encarta Online Encyclopedia 2002*. <http://encarta.msn.com>.

Davy Crockett Birthplace Association. "American West-Davy Crockett." 6 April 2002.
   <http://www.americanwest.com/pages/davycroc.htm>.

Lofaro, Michael A. "Davy Crockett." *The World Book Encyclopedia 2002*. Chicago: World
   Book, Inc., Vol. 14, pp. 1148d-1149.

The Texas State Historical Association. *The New Handbook of Texas-Online.* "Davy Crockett
   (1786-1836)-Biography." 6 April 2002. <http://www.alamo-de-
   parras.welkin.org/history/bios/crockett/crockett.html>.

GLOSSARY *(continued)*

Q

Query A database feature that enables you to locate records that meet certain criteria. (Section 11.2)

R

Range A group of spreadsheet cells. (Section 10.4)

Record A group of fields that contain the data that makes up a file. (Section 11.1)

Reference Number A raised number inserted automatically by the footnote feature in word processing software; matches the footnote number at the bottom of the page or endnote at the end of a report. (Section 6.5)

Reference Page A page at the end of a report in which the sources of information are listed, such as a bibliography or a list of citations. (Sections 6.2, 6.4)

Report A summary of information you arrange in an attractive, organized, easily understandable format. (Sections 6.1, 6.2, 6.4)

Resize A software feature you use to change the size of an object like a drawing, picture, or textbox. (Section 7.1)

Return Address The sender's address keyed in a specific location on a personal or business correspondence. (Section 5.1)

Right Justification A software feature used to align copy at the right. (Sections 7.2, 7.3)

Row Information arranged horizontally in a table; in a spreadsheet, rows are identified by numbers such as 1, 2, or 3. (Section 4.4)

Row Height The distance between the top and bottom borders of a cell. (Section 4.4)

S

Salutation The greeting of a personal or business letter. (Sections 5.1, 5.2)

Save A software feature you use to store data on a hard drive, floppy disk, or CD. (Section 3.1)

Save As A software feature you use to store a file under a different name. (Section 3.2)

Saved Search A software feature you use to save the results of database search in a database file. (Section 11.2)

Scrolling The activity of moving text up and down or left and right to reveal additional copy on your screen. (Section 3.1)

Search A software feature that enables you to look for text or formats within a document.

Search Engine A software program on the Internet that looks for word matches based on keywords you key in the search window. (Section 3.5)

Select A software feature you use to highlight text in order to change it in some way. (Section 3.3)

Shading A software feature used to add fill to cells or boxes to add visual interest.

Shortcut Key A function key or key combinations. (Section 3.1)

Side Heading The major subdivisions or major topics of a report. (Section 6.2)

Sort A software feature that enables you to rearrange data in a particular order, such as in a table, a spreadsheet, or database. (Sections 10.2, 11.2)

Slide Contains design templates, color schemes, and animation scheme for Powerpoint Presentations. (Section 9.1)

Spelling A software feature that checks the spelling of words in a document. (Sections 3.1, 3.4)

Spreadsheet A software program that enables you to perform various calculations on the data. (Section 10.1)

Spreadsheet Function A built-in formula in a spreadsheet. (Section 10.4)

Standard Punctuation Punctuation that consists of a colon after the salutation and a comma after the complimentary close.

Status Line A line displayed at the bottom of the screen that provides the page number, section number, vertical position in inches, and line number of a document as well as the horizontal position of the insertion point.

SUM Function A built-in spreadsheet formula that adds a range of cells. (Section 10.4)

Switch Screens/Windows A software feature you use to move from one open document or program to another. (Section 3.6)

T

Tab Set A software feature you use to define the position of the insertion point on a line of text when you press the tab key.

Table A grid of rows and columns that intersect to form cells into which information can be keyed. (Sections 4.4, 8.2)

Table of Contents A guide that lists topics and page numbers. (Section 6.6)

Template A predefined document format. (Section 7.4)

Textbox A created box that can contain text or art. (Sections 7.1, 9.1)

Table A grid of rows and columns that intersect to form cells into which information can be keyed. (Sections 4.4, 8.2)

REFERENCE SECTION *(continued)*

TITLE PAGE

↓ center vertically

THE STAR-SPANGLED BANNER ↓ 13x

Prepared by ↓ 2x
Hallie Thompson
La Mesa Valley School ↓ 13x

Prepared for ↓ 2x
Ms. Gibson
Social Studies--5th Hour ↓ 2x
Today's Date

MULTIPAGE REPORT

(left bound with side headings)

↓ 1 inch default margin

THE STAR-SPANGLED BANNER

By Hallie Thompson

The Story Behind the Flag

During the War of 1812, Americans knew that the British would likely attack the city of Baltimore. In the summer of 1813, Major George Armistead was the commander at Fort McHenry at the Baltimore harbor. He asked Mary Young Pickersgill to make a flag for the fort. Armistead wanted the flag to be so big that the British would be sure to see it from a distance.

Mary's 13-year-old daughter Caroline helped her make the flag. They cut 15 stars. Each star was two feet long from point to point. They also cut eight red stripes and seven white stripes. Each stripe was two feet wide. It took them several weeks to make the flag. When they sewed everything together, the flag measured 30 feet by 42 feet. The flag weighed 200 pounds.

Francis Scott Key's Point of View

Francis Scott Key was 35 years old and he was a well-known and successful lawyer in Georgetown, Maryland. He opposed the War of 1812, but in 1814 he had to get involved. His long-time friend Dr. William Beanes was being held prisoner on a British warship.

On September 3, 1814, Key and a government agent named John S. Skinner boarded a ship that flew a flag of truce. They went to the British warship and negotiated the release of Beanes. On September 7, the British agreed to let Beanes go, but by then Key, Skinner, and Beanes knew too much about the planned attack on the city of

1

MULTIPAGE REPORT CONTINUED

(left bound with side headings)

Baltimore. So the British held all three Americans as prisoners on the warship while they attacked Baltimore.

On September 13, the three American prisoners watched from the warship as the British battleships fired upon Fort McHenry. They knew it would be difficult for the American soldiers to fight off the British. The battle continued through the night, and they feared the American soldiers would surrender.

The Story Behind the Song

When the sun rose the next morning, they saw a big American flag flying over the fort. It was the flag Pickersgill had made. The Americans had survived the battle.

Oh! Say, can you see, by the dawn's early light,

What so proudly we hailed at the twilight's last gleaming?

Whose broad stripes and bright stars, through the perilous fight,

O'er the ramparts we watched were so gallantly streaming?

And the rocket's red glare, the bombs bursting in air,

Gave proof through the night that our flag was still there.

Oh! Say, does that Star-Spangled Banner yet wave

O'er the land of the free and the home of the brave.

2

BIBLIOGRAPHY

↓ 1 inch default margin

BIBLIOGRAPHY

Armed Forces Collections. "Star-Spangled Banner and the War of 1812." 10 May 2002. <http://www.si.edu/resource.faq/nmah/starflag.htm>. ↓ 2x

Author Unknown. "Francis Scott Key." 10 May 2002. <http://www.usflag.org.francis.scott.key.html>. ↓ 2x

Goertzen, Valerie Woodring. "Star-Spangled Banner." *The World Book Encyclopedia 2002*. Chicago: World Book, Inc., Vol. 18, pp. 853-854. ↓ 2x

"Star-Spangled Banner." *Microsoft Encarta Online Encyclopedia 2002*. <http://encarta.msn.com/encnet/refpages/refarticle.aspx?refid=761575047>.

GLOSSARY *(continued)*

Leader A line or a row of characters that points to something on the page, such as the row of dots in a table of contents which leads the reader's eye to the page number, or a line drawn between part of a graphic and its defining text. (Sections 6.6, 7.3)

Left Justification A feature that aligns text at the left margin. (Sections 7.2, 7.3)

Legend A guide on a chart that explains the symbols, colors, etc., used to represent categories of data. (Section 10.5)

Letterhead Stationery that has information such as the company name, address, and telephone number printed at the top. (Section 5.2)

Level headings One or more lines of text that appears at the top of a document.

Line Chart A chart that uses points on a grid connected by lines to represent values in a spreadsheet. (Section 10.5)

Line Draw A software feature that enables you to draw a variety of lines in a document. (Section 7.2)

Line Spacing A software command that enables you to set the amount of space between lines of text. (Section 4.1)

M

Margins The blank space at the top, bottom, left, and right sides of a document. (Section 6.1)

Masthead The title of a newsletter usually with an issue number and a date. (Section 7.3)

MAX Function A built-in formula in a spreadsheet that determines the largest or maximum number in a cell range. (Section 10.4)

Menu A list of commands or options from which you can choose. (Section 3.1)

Menu Bar Usually at the top of the active window, a list of commands or options. (Section 3.1)

MIN Function A built-in formula in a spreadsheet that determines the smallest or minimum number in a cell range. (Section 10.4)

MLA Style A format standard developed by the Modern Language Association.

N

Navigate To move around in a document electronically using arrow keys or the cursor. (Section 3.1)

New Document A software feature you use to create a new, blank document. (Section 3.1)

New Folder A software feature you use to create a name for a collection of files and documents. (Section 3.2)

O

Object A graphic representation or clip art. (Sections 7.1, 7.2)

Open A software command that enables you to retrieve a file that was previously created and saved. (Section 3.1)

Outline A listing of main topics and subtopics arranged in a hierarchy. (Section 4.5)

Outline Numbered List A list where terms of importance are treated by indenting and numbering. (Section 4.5)

Overtype Mode An input mode in which the existing text is replaced as new text is added. (Section 3.3)

P

Page Break A manually inserted page break that does not change regardless of the changes made within the document. (Section 6.2)

Page Numbering A software command that automatically numbers the pages of a document. (Section 6.2)

Page Orientation The direction (portrait or landscape) in which information is printed across the paper. (Section 7.2)

Paste To copy text or objects to a file. (Section 6.1)

Percentage Label A label that indicates what percentage is indicated. (Section 10.5)

Personal Letter A letter from an individual to another individual. (Section 5.1)

Pie Chart A graphic illustration of spreadsheet data that compares the sizes of pieces to a whole. (Section 10.5)

Point Size A reference to the size of font; 72 points equal one inch. (Section 3.4)

Portrait Orientation The printing of information across the short edge of a paper so that the page layout is tall. (Section 7.2)

Presentation A word processing software using visual aids, such as slides. (Section 9.1)

Print A software feature you use to produce hard copies of documents on paper. (Section 3.1)

Print Preview A software feature that enables you to view an entire document before it is printed. (Section 3.4)

Proofing Re-reading text. (Section 4.3)

Proofing Tools Software features, such as the spelling and grammar checks, which enable you to find errors in the text of a document. (Sections 3.4, 4.3)

Proofreaders' Marks A set of standard symbols used by an editor or proofreader to mark corrections and changes to a document. (Sections 3.3, 4.1)

REFERENCE SECTION *(continued)*

FORMAT FOR ENVELOPES

A standard large (No. 10) envelope is 9½ by 4⅛ inches. A standard small (No. 6¾) envelope is 6½ by 3⅝ inches. The format shown is recommended by the U.S. Postal Service for mail that will be sorted by an electronic scanning device.

Your Name
4112 Bay View Drive
San Jose, CA 95192

Mrs. Maria Chavez
1021 West Palm Blvd.
San Jose, CA 95192

 **LINCOLN MIDDLE SCHOOL**
6021 Brobeck Street • Flint, MI 48532

Mr. Anthony Martinez
Cyber Foundation
4092 Barnes Avenue
Burton, MI 48529

HOW TO FOLD LETTERS

To fold a letter for a small envelope:
1. Place the letter *face up* and fold up the bottom half to 0.5 inch from the top edge of the paper.
2. Fold the right third over to the left.
3. Fold the left third over to 0.5 inch from the right edge of the paper.
4. Insert the last crease into the envelope first, with the flap facing up.

To fold a letter for a large envelope:
1. Place the letter *face up* and fold up the bottom third.
2. Fold the top third down to 0.5 inch from the bottom edge of the paper.
3. Insert the last crease into the envelope first, with the flap facing up.

GLOSSARY *(continued)*

Fill Right A spreadsheet feature you use to copy cell contents to a range of cells to the right of the active cell. (Section 10.4)

Fill Handle The small box in the lower right corner of an active spreadsheet cell that can be dragged to create the desired fill. (Section 10.4)

Find and Replace A software command that enables you to search for and replace specific text, formatting commands, or special attributes. (Section 6.1)

Find File A software feature used to locate a file using the name of the document. (Section 3.2)

Flush Right Alignment of text at the right margin. (Section 4.2)

Folder On a computer drive, a collection of files and documents linked by a common name. Folders are arranged in a hierarchy. (Section 3.2)

Font A set of type characters of a particular design and size. Also, a software feature you use to change the style of the text in a document. (Sections 3.4, 4.2)

Footer Repetitive information or text that is repeated at the bottom of a page throughout a section of a document. See also headers. (Section 6.4)

Footnote At the bottom of a page, a note that identifies the source of information in a report. (Section 6.5)

Format The appearance of information such as bold or italics on a page or in a computer document; in a spreadsheet displaying commas, dollar signs, percent signs, or decimal places. (Section 4.2)

Formula A mathematical expression entered into a cell of a spreadsheet that solves a problem (for example, adding, subtracting, multiplying, dividing, or averaging) using data from other cells. (Section 10.3)

Full Justification An alignment feature that aligns text at the left and right margins by adding space between characters. (Section 7.3)

F

Functions Built-in formulas on a spreadsheet. (Section 10.4)

G

Grammar A software feature that locates grammar inconsistencies. (Sections 3.1, 3.4, 4.3)

Graphics Pictures, clip art, bar graphs, pie charts, or other images available on or created on a computer. (Sections 7.4, 8.1)

Gridlines The lines appearing around the cells in a table. (Section 4.4)

H

Hanging Indent A temporary left margin that indents all lines but the first line of the text. (Section 6.2)

Header Repetitive information or text that is repeated at the top of each page of a section or a document. (Section 6.4)

Help On-screen information about how to use a program and its features. (Section 3.1)

Home-Key Position (Keypad) The row where fingers are to be placed on the numeric keypad. (Section 2.8)

Hyperlink Text or a graphic on a Web page that you can click on to jump or go to information on another Web page, a location on the same Web page, or a file. (Sections 3.5, 8.3)

I

Insert A software command that enables you to add text, page and column breaks, graphics, tables, charts, cells, rows, columns, formulas, dates, time, fields, and so on, to a document. (Sections 4.1, 10.2)

Insertion Mode An input mode in which the existing text moves to the right as new text is added. (Section 3.1)

Inside Address In a personal or business letter, the address for the recipient of the letter. (Sections 5.1, 5.2)

Internet A global network connecting millions of computers. (Section 3.5)

Internet Browser A software application used to locate and display Web pages. (Section 3.5)

Italic A special font attribute in which the characters are slanted used to emphasize text. (Section 4.2)

J

Justification The alignment of text. (Sections 7.2, 7.3)

K

Keyword One or more words keyed in a search box in order to search for matches on the Internet. (Section 3.5)

L

Landscape Orientation Page orientation in which the printing of information runs across the long edge of the paper so that the page layout is wide. (Section 7.2)

Launch To open. (Section 10.1)

Layer To place an object or graphic close to another object or graphic. (Section 7.2)

REFERENCE SECTION *(continued)*

BOXED TABLE

Dogs for Adoption

Name	Date Arrived in Shelter	Description
Jack	April 11	5-year-old male; shepherd/lab mix; about 70 pounds; house-trained; good watchdog; great with kids.
Autumn	April 16	3-year-old female; golden retriever; about 75 pounds; house-trained; high energy; needs plenty of exercise.
Tigger	April 16	6-year-old male; terrier mix; about 20 pounds; sweet, friendly, and obedient; good with other dogs; loves to play.
Jasmine	April 18	9-year-old female; sheltie; about 25 pounds; gentle and calm; needs daily exercise and a quiet environment.
Max	April 20	3–4-year-old male; dalmatian mix; about 70 pounds; loves to play with other dogs and needs an area to run and play.
Billy Bob	April 21	5–6-year-old male; beagle; about 30 pounds; a very bright dog; house-trained, active, and good around kids.
Sophie	April 22	1–2-year-old female; collie; about 40 pounds; well-mannered; loves to run and play; short-to-medium hair and is a very pretty dog; gets along with dogs as well as cats.
Molly	April 23	1-year-old female; cocker spaniel mix; about 25 pounds; adorable and happy; playful and energetic; very bright and trainable.

CONTENTS

CONTENTS

INTRODUCTION 1

PROBLEM 1

HYPOTHESIS 1

RESEARCH 2

THE EXPERIMENT 5

Materials 5

Procedures 5

Results 7

CONCLUSION 8

BIBLIOGRAPHY 9

PROOFREADERS' MARKS

Proofreaders' Marks		Draft	Final Copy
⌒	Omit space	data base	database
∨ or ∧	Insert	if he's not going,	if he's not going,
≡	Capitalize	Maple street	Maple Street
ℓ	Delete	a final draft	a draft
#	Insert space	allready to	all ready to
when/if	Change word	and if you	and when you
/	Use lowercase letter	our President	our president
¶	Paragraph	¶ Most of the	Most of the
•••	Don't delete	a true story	a true story
O	Spell out	the only ①	the only one
∽	Transpose	they all see	they see all

Proofreaders' Marks		Draft	Final Copy
SS	Single-space	first line / second line	first line / second line
ds	Double-space	first line / second line	first line / second line
⌐	Move right	Please send	Please send
⌐	Move left	May I	May I
⁓	Bold	Column Heading	**Column Heading**
ital	Italic	*Time* magazine	*Time* magazine
u/ℓ	Underline	Time magazine readers	Time magazine readers
♂	Move as shown	readers will see	will see

GLOSSARY *(continued)*

Column Information arranged vertically. (Section 4.4)

Column Bar Chart A display of data represented in a graphic illustration. (Section 10.5)

Column Heading A vertical row of cells usually with enhanced formatting. (Section 4.4)

Computer Hardware The physical parts of a computer system such as the monitor, the keyboard, and the hard drive.

Computer Software Programs that tell the computer what to do. (Section 3.1)

Copy To duplicate text or data from one location to another. (Sections 3.3, 6.1)

Cursor See Insertion point. (Section 3.1)

Cut/Copy/Paste Computer software features that enable you to move or copy text from one place to another. (Sections 3.3, 6.1)

D

Data Label A label that provides information from the spreadsheet. (Section 10.5)

Database A software program used to organize, find, and display information. (Section 11.1)

Database Search A software feature that enables you to look for text or numbers in database fields according to certain criteria. (Section 11.2)

Database Table A collection of records organized into a table format containing fields. (Section 11.1)

Delete (File) To remove or erase a file from storage on the computer. (Section 3.2)

Delete Key A key which deletes one character at a time to the right of the insertion point. (Section 3.3)

Descending Order A sort of data in descending alphabetical (Z–A) or numerical (9–0) order. (Section 10.2)

Design Template A pre-formatted set of fonts and margins stored in a document. (Section 9.1)

Desktop Publishing Special software or software features that enable you to design and create documents such as newsletters, flyers, and brochures. (Sections 7.1–7.4)

Document A file created in a word processor which may contain text or graphics. (Section 3.2)

Dot Leader The same as a line of periods used to separate titles from page numbers. (Section 6.6)

Double Space An electronic method to add an additional space between lines of text. (Section 4.1)

Drawing Tool A software feature you use to draw objects like lines and shapes in a document. (Section 7.2)

E

Edit Using proofreaders' marks to indicate changes to a document, such as deleting, moving, or adding characters. (Sections 3.3, 4.1)

E-Mail An electronic message that usually includes the e-mail address, subject line, and body of the message. (Section 5.3)

E-Mail Address An electronic address that has two parts (user name and domain name) separated by the @ (at) symbol. (Section 5.3)

Emoticon An acronym for **emot**ion **icon**, a small icon composed of punctuation characters that indicate how an e-mail message should be interpreted (that is, the writer's mood). For example, a :-) emoticon indicates that the message is meant to be humorous and shouldn't be taken seriously. (Section 5.3)

Enclosure Notation A special notation at the end of a letter (usually the word Enclosure); indicates that an item(s) is included with the letter. (Section 5.2)

Endnote A software feature you use to create endnotes; notes at the end of a report that identify the source of information in a report. (Section 6.5)

Envelope Format A format for an envelope address in which all lines are keyed in all capital letters with no punctuation.

F

Favorite An Internet software feature used in *Internet Explorer* that allows you to save a Web site or Web page for future use. (Section 3.5)

Field A category of information in a database. (Section 11.1)

Field Name A name used to identify the contents of a field. (Section 11.1)

Field Type A designed space used for particular information. (Section 11.1)

File On a computer drive, a storage area that contains text or data. Files that contain text formatted using computer applications are called **documents**. Every file, or document, has a name and is organized in a folder, where it can be accessed. (Section 3.2)

Filename A unique name given to a document or file so that it can be saved and retrieved. (Section 3.2)

Fill Shading or patterns used to fill an area. In a spreadsheet, to enter common or repetitive values, or formulas, into a group of cells. (Section 10.4)

Fill Down A spreadsheet feature you use to copy cell contents to a range of cells below the active cell. (Section 10.4)

REFERENCE SECTION *(continued)*

PUNCTUATION AND USAGE

ALWAYS SPACE ONCE . . .

- After a comma.
  We ordered two printers, one computer, and three monitors.

- After a semicolon.
  They flew to Dallas, Texas; Reno, Nevada; and Rome, New York.

- After a period following someone's initials.
  Mr. A. Henson, Ms. C. Hovey, and Mr. M. Salisbury will attend the meeting.

- After a period following the abbreviation of a single word.
  We will send the package by 7 p.m. next week. [Note: space once after the final period in the "p.m." abbreviation, but do not space after the first period between the two letters.]

- Before a ZIP code.
  Send the package to 892 Maple Street, Grand Forks, ND 58201.

- Before and after an ampersand.
  We were represented by the law firm of Bassett & Johnson; they were represented by the law firm of Crandall & Magnuson.

- After a period at the end of a sentence.
  Don't forget to vote. Vote for the candidate of your choice.

- After a question mark.
  When will you vote? Did you vote last year?

- After an exclamation point.
  Wow! What a performance! It was fantastic!

- After a colon.
  We will attend on the following days: Monday, Wednesday, and Friday.

PUNCTUATION

COMMAS:

1. Use a comma between independent clauses joined by a conjunction. (An independent clause is one that can stand alone as a complete sentence.)
We requested Brown Industries to change the date, and they did so within five days.

2. Use a comma after an introductory expression (unless it is a short prepositional phrase).
Before we can make a decision, we must have all the facts.
In 1992 our nation elected a president.

GLOSSARY

A

Adjust Column Width A column is a vertical line extending from the top to the bottom of the screen. The size can be adjusted manually by hesitating the insertion point over the line and dragging the line to a new location. (Section 4.4)

Alignment A software feature you use to change the horizontal or vertical position of text such as left, right, or center. (Sections 3.4, 4.2, 6.3)

Anchor A home-key position of another finger that helps bring a reaching finger back to its home-key position. (Section 1.1)

Animation A simulation of movement created by displaying a series of pictures. (Section 9.4)

APA Style A formatting style standardized by the American Psychological Association.

Ascending Order A sort of data in alphabetical (A–Z) order or numerical (0–9) order. (Section 10.4)

Attachment A file attached to an e-mail message. (Section 5.3)

AVERAGE Function A built-in spreadsheet formula that adds and divides numbers. (Section 10.4)

B

Backspace Key A key that moves the insertion point backward one space at a time. The backspace key deletes text to the left of the insertion point one space at a time. (Sections 1.6, 1.7, 3.3)

Bar Chart A graphic illustration of spreadsheet data, in which vertical and horizontal bars, lines, or charts represent data values. (Section 10.5)

Bibliography An alphabetical listing of all the books, online sources, and articles consulted by the author of a report. (Section 6.2)

Block Style A letter style that has all lines, keyed at the left margin. (Sections 5.1, 5.2)

Body The main text of personal letter, business letter, or report. (Sections 5.1, 5.2)

Bold A print enhancement used to make characters appear darker than other text to add emphasis. (Section 4.2)

Bookmark An Internet software feature used in *Netscape Navigator* that allows you to place an electronic bookmark on a page so you can easily revisit the page. (Section 3.5)

Boolean operators The five Boolean operators refine and limit searches conducted on the Internet. (Section 3.5)

Borders A software feature (usually a line) you use to add an outline around a page, an object, or spreadsheet cells. (Section 4.4)

Bound Report A report with extra space added at the left margin to allow for pages to be placed in a notebook. (Section 6.2)

Bullets and Numbering A software feature you use to create a list in which each item begins with a number or a bullet—such as a circle, diamond, square, or triangle. (Sections 4.5, 9.1)

Business Card Personal or professional information including name and contact information formatted onto a card. (Section 7.4)

Business Letter A letter to a company or organization. (Section 5.2)

Byline The name of the author of a report keyed below the title. (Section 6.1)

C

Callout A textbox with a leader that points to something on the page. (Section 7.2)

Capitalization Uppercase treatment of alphabetic keys. (Section 2.8)

Caption The words or phrases that draw attention or emphasize a photo or graphic. (Section 8.2)

Cell The box formed at the intersection of a row and a column, either in a table or a spreadsheet. (Section 10.1)

Cell Reference The location (column letter and row number) of the active cell in a spreadsheet. (Section 10.4)

Center Alignment An alignment feature that centers text between margins. (Section 3.4)

Citation Usually the author's last name and page number in a report; used to give credit to the source of information. (Sections 3.6, 6.4)

Clip Art A gallery or collection of graphic images or pictures that you can add to documents. (Sections 7.1, 9.3)

Clipboard A special file or memory area where data is stored temporarily before being copied to another location. (Section 3.3)

Close File A software command that enables you to exit the current document without exiting from the program. (Section 3.1)

Closing An ending to a letter such as *Sincerely, Yours truly*, etc. before the signature line of a business or personal letter. (Sections 5.1, 5.2)

Colon Used to indicate a range of data to be included in a formula. (Section 10.4)

REFERENCE SECTION *(continued)*

PUNCTUATION

3. Use a comma before and after the year in a complete date.
We will arrive at the plant on June 2, 2003, for the conference.

4. Use a comma before and after a state or country that follows a city (but not before a ZIP Code).
Joan moved to Vancouver, British Columbia, in September.
Send the package to Douglasville, GA 30135, by express mail.

5. Use a comma between each item in a series of three or more.
There are lions, tigers, bears, and zebras at the zoo.

6. Use a comma before and after a transitional expression (such as therefore and however).
It is critical, therefore, that we finish the project on time.

7. Use a comma before and after a direct quotation.
When we left, James said, "Let us return to the same location next year."

8. Use a comma before and after a nonessential expression. (A nonessential expression is a word or group of words that may be omitted without changing the basic meaning of the sentence.)
Let me say, to begin with, that the report has already been finalized.

9. Use a comma between two adjacent adjectives that modify the same noun.
We need an intelligent, enthusiastic individual for this project.

SEMICOLONS:

1. Use a semicolon to join two closely related independent clauses that are not connected by a conjunction (such as and, but, or nor).
Students favored the music; teachers did not.

2. Use a semicolon to separate three or more items in a series if any of the items already contain commas.
Region 1 sent their reports in March, April, and May; and Region 2 sent their reports in September, October, and November.
The Home room class sent their reports in 1st, 2nd, 3rd, and 4th hour;
the history class sent their reports in 4th, 5th, 6th, and 7th hour.

HYPHENS:

1. Hyphenate compound adjectives that come before a noun (unless the first word is an adverb ending in *-ly*).
We reviewed an up-to-date report on Wednesday.
We attended a highly rated session on multimedia software.

APPLY

Create a Database

Your business has really grown. You now have several clients, and you want to organize the information you have gathered for each client.

Your Turn

1. Create a database table to maintain the following information:

Last Name	Phone	Pet Name	Pet Type	Notes
Karnowski	555-0181	Lucky	dog	
Jorgensen	555-9089	Pepper	cat	
Carmody	555-7866	Coco	dog	
Raez	555-3454	Duke	dog	keep on leash at all times
Miller	555-2421	Yoda	hamster	nocturnal
Sandell	555-0087	Shaggy and Scooby	parakeets	
Glomski	555-1334	Taffy	dog	
Hotchkiss	555-0755	Chloe	cat	
Butcher	555-4590	Ranger	dog	
Van Gilder	555-3391	Princess	cat	does not go outside

2. Save the database table as *urs*Clients.

3. Spell-check, proofread, and correct errors.

4. Sort the records in ascending order by client last name.

5. Add the following new record: Coretti, 555-9887, Haley, dog.

6. Sort the records again in ascending order by client last name.

7. Change Glomski's phone number to 555-4318.

8. If necessary, save the changes. Print and close the file.

REFERENCE SECTION *(continued)*

2. Hyphenate compound numbers (between twenty-one and ninety-nine) and fractions that are expressed as words.
We observed twenty-nine fumbles during the football game.
All teachers reduced their assignments by one-third.

3. Hyphenate words that are divided at the end of a line. Do not divide one-syllable words, contractions, or abbreviations; divide other words only between syllables.
To appreciate the full significance of rain forests, you must see the entire documentary showing tomorrow in the library.

APOSTROPHES:

1. Use 's to form the possessive of singular nouns.
The hurricane caused major damage to Georgia's coastline.

2. Use only an apostrophe to form the possessive of plural nouns that end in *s*.
The investors' goals were outlined in the annual report.

3. Use 's to form the possessive of indefinite pronouns (such as someone's or anybody's); do not use an apostrophe with personal pronouns (such as *hers, his, its, ours, theirs,* and *yours*).
She was instructed to select anybody's paper for a sample.
Each computer comes carefully packed in its own container.

COLONS:

Use a colon to introduce explanatory material that follows an independent clause. (An independent clause is one that can stand alone as a complete sentence.)
A computer is useful for three reasons: speed, cost, and power.

DASHES:

Use a dash instead of a comma, semicolon, colon, or parenthesis when you want to convey a more forceful separation of words within a sentence. (If your keyboard has a special dash character, use it. Otherwise, form a dash by typing two hyphens, with no space before, between, or after.)
At this year's student council meeting, the speakers—and topics—were superb.

PERIODS:

Use a period to end a sentence that is a polite request. (Consider a sentence a polite request if you expect the reader to respond by doing as you ask rather than by giving a yes-or-no answer.)
Will you please call me.

APPLY

Create a Presentation

Insert clip art. ⟶

Needs to Be Loved!

Contact
Turtle Creek Animal Shelter

2023 North Lake Shore Drive
Fontana, WI 53125
Telephone: 262-555-5050
www.AnimalShelter@tcas.org

2. Save the document as *urs***Pet of the Week**.

3. Spell-check, proofread, and correct errors.

4. Format slide transitions.

5. Save the changes. Print and close the file.

REFERENCE SECTION *(continued)*

QUOTATION MARKS:

1. Use quotation marks around the titles of newspaper articles, magazine articles, chapters in a book, reports, conferences, and similar items.

The best article I found in my research was entitled "Multimedia for Everyone."

2. Use quotation marks around a direct quotation.

Harrison responded by saying, "This decision will not affect our class."

ITALIC (OR UNDERLINE):

Italicize (or underline) the titles of books, magazines, newspapers, and other complete published works.

I read *The Pelican Brief* last month. I read <u>The Pelican Brief</u> last month.

AGREEMENT:

1. Use singular verbs and pronouns with singular subjects and plural verbs and pronouns with plural subjects.

I was pleased with the performance of our team.

Reno and Phoenix were selected as the sites for our next two meetings.

2. Some pronouns (*anybody, each, either, everybody, everyone, much, neither, no one, nobody,* and *one*) are always singular and take a singular verb. Other pronouns (*all, any, more, most, none,* and *some*) may be singular or plural, depending on the noun to which they refer.

Each employee is responsible for summarizing the day's activities.

Most of the workers are going to get a substantial pay raise.

3. Disregard any intervening words that come between the subject and verb when establishing agreement.

The box containing the books and pencils has not been found.

4. If two subjects are joined by *or, either / or, nor, neither / nor,* or *not only / but also,* the verb should agree with the subject nearer to the verb.

Neither the players nor the coach is in favor of the decision.

5. The subject a number takes a plural verb; *the number* takes a singular verb.

The number of new students has increased to six.

We know that a number of students are in sports.

Create a Presentation

Insert a photo or clip art. ——→

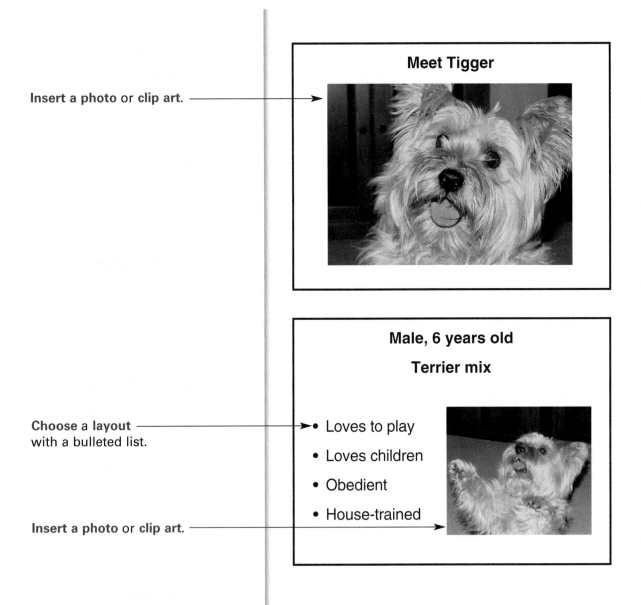

Meet Tigger

Male, 6 years old

Terrier mix

Choose a layout ——→
with a bulleted list.

- Loves to play
- Loves children
- Obedient
- House-trained

Insert a photo or clip art. ——→

Continued on next page

REFERENCE SECTION *(continued)*

6. Subjects joined by and take a plural verb unless the compound subject is preceded by *each, every,* or *many a (an).*
Every man, woman, and child is included in our survey.

7. Verbs that refer to conditions that are impossible or improbable (that is, verbs in the *subjunctive* mood) require the plural form.
If the total eclipse were to occur tomorrow, it would be the second one this year.

PRONOUNS:

1. Use nominative pronouns (such as *I, he, she, we,* and *they*) as subjects of a sentence or clause.
They traveled to Minnesota last week but will not return until next month.

2. Use objective pronouns (such as *me, him, her, us,* and *them*) as objects in a sentence or clause.
The package has been sent to her.

ADJECTIVES AND ADVERBS:

Use comparative adjectives and adverbs (*-er, more,* and *less*) when referring to two nouns; use superlative adjectives and adverbs (*-est, most,* and *least*) when referring to more than two.
Of the two movies you have selected, the shorter one is the more interesting.
The highest of the three mountains is Mt. Everest.

WORD USAGE:

Do not confuse the following pairs of words:

- *Accept* means "to agree to"; *except* means "to leave out."
  *We **accept** your offer for developing the new product.*
  *Everyone **except** Sam and Lisa attended the rally.*

- *Affect* is most often used as a verb meaning "to influence"; *effect* is most often used as a noun meaning "result."
  *Mr. Smith's decision will not **affect** our music class.*
  *It will be weeks before we can assess the **effect** of this decision.*

- *Farther* refers to distance; *further* refers to extent or degree.
  *Did we travel **farther** today than yesterday?*
  *We need to discuss our plans **further**.*

- *Personal* means "private"; *personnel* means "employees."
  *The letters were very **personal** and should not have been read.*
  *We hope that all **personnel** will comply with the new rules.*

APPLY

Create a Presentation

You still volunteer at the animal shelter a few hours each week. Each week the shelter chooses one of the animals as the "Pet of the Week." You offer to create a slide show to promote this week's pet.

Your Turn

1. Create and format the slides shown below.

Key the title and the subtitle on the first slide.

Choose and **apply a design** to all slides.

Pet of the Week

Turtle Creek Animal Shelter

Continued on next page

REFERENCE SECTION *(continued)*

GRAMMAR

- *Principal* means "primary"; *principle* means "rule."
  The **principal** means of research were interviewing and surveying.
  They must not violate the **principles** under which our country was founded.

- *Passed* means "went by"; *past* means "before now."
  We **passed** another car from our home state.
  In the **past**, we always took the same route.

- *Advice* means "to provide guidance"; *advise* means "help."
  The **advice** I gave her was simple.
  I **advise** you to finish your project.

- *Council* is a group; *counsel* is a person who provides advice.
  The student **council** met to discuss graduation.
  The court asked that **counsel** be present at the hearing.

- *Then* means "at that time"; *than* is used for comparisons.
  He read for a while; **then** he turned out the light.
  She reads more books **than** I do.

- *Its* is the possessive form of it; *it's* is a contraction for it is.
  We researched the country and **its** people.
  It's not too late to finish the story.

- *Two* means "one more than one"; *too* means "also"; *to* means "in a direction."
  There were **two** people in the boat.
  We wished we were on board, **too.**
  The boat headed out **to** sea.

- *Stationery* means "paper"; *stationary* means "fixed position."
  Please buy some **stationery** so that I can write letters.
  The **stationary** bike at the health club provides a good workout.

MECHANICS

CAPITALIZATION:

1. Capitalize the first word of a sentence.
  Please prepare a summary.

2. Capitalize proper nouns and adjectives derived from proper nouns. (A proper noun is the official name of a particular person, place, or thing.)
  Judy Hendrix drove to Albuquerque in her new car, a Pontiac.

PROJECT 10

APPLY

Create a Spreadsheet

You have been working for three months, and you kept notes about the money you earned. A spreadsheet will help you track your earnings.

Your Turn

1. Create a spreadsheet to track earnings, which are shown below.

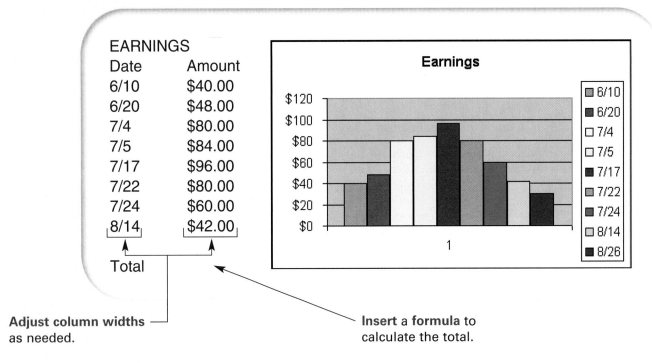

EARNINGS	
Date	Amount
6/10	$40.00
6/20	$48.00
7/4	$80.00
7/5	$84.00
7/17	$96.00
7/22	$80.00
7/24	$60.00
8/14	$42.00
Total	

Adjust column widths as needed.

Insert a formula to calculate the total.

2. Save the spreadsheet as *urs*Earnings.

3. Edit the spreadsheet by adding a new entry dated 8/26 for $30.00.

4. Spell-check, proofread, and correct errors. Save the changes to the document.

5. Create a bar chart to illustrate your summer's earnings.

6. Save the changes. Print and close the file.

REFERENCE SECTION *(continued)*

MECHANICS

3. Capitalize the names of the days of the week, months, holidays, and religious days (but do not capitalize the names of the seasons).
On Thursday, November 25, we will celebrate Thanksgiving, the most popular fall holiday.

4. Capitalize nouns followed by a number or letter (except for the nouns *line, note, page, paragraph,* and *size*).
Please read Chapter 5, but not page 94.

5. Capitalize compass points (such as *north, south,* or *northeast*) only when they designate definite regions.
The Crenshaws will vacation in the Northeast this summer.
We will have to drive north to reach the closest Canadian border.

6. Capitalize common organizational terms (such as *advertising department* and *finance committee*) when they are the actual names of the units in the writer's own organization and when they are preceded by the word *the*.
The quarterly report from the Advertising Department will be presented today.

7. Capitalize the names of specific course titles but not the names of subjects or areas of study.
I have enrolled in Accounting 201 and will also take a marketing course.

NUMBER EXPRESSION:

1. In general, spell out numbers 1 through 10, and use figures for numbers above 10.
We have rented two movies for tonight.
The decision was reached after 27 precincts had sent in their results.

2. Use figures for:
- Dates (use *st, d,* or *th* only if the day precedes the month).
  We will drive to the camp on the 23d of May.
  The tax report is due on April 15.

- All numbers if two or more related numbers both above and below ten are used in the same sentence.
  Mr. Carter sent in 7 receipts; Ms. Cantrell sent in 22 receipts.

- Measurements (time, money, distance, weight, and percentage).
  At 10 a.m. we delivered the $500 coin bank in a 17-pound container.

- Mixed numbers.
  Our sales are up 9½ percent over last year.

APPLY

Create a Web Page

5. Create a new Web page for your contact e-mail information.

Choose an appropriate layout and **apply a theme.**

Contact Information Page

A page displaying:
- Your contact information.
- A hyperlink to the home page.
- A hyperlink to the e-mail address.

Insert photos and/or **clip art.**

6. Save this page as *urs*Contact Page.

7. Open the home page, and create hyperlinks to the Fees Page and the Contact Page.

8. Spell-check, proofread, and correct errors.

9. Preview the Web pages, and test all hyperlinks. Make any necessary adjustments.

10. Save the changes. Print and close each file.

REFERENCE SECTION *(continued)*

MECHANICS

3. Spell out:

- Numbers used as the first word in a sentence.
  Seventy people attended the conference in San Diego last week.

- The smaller of two adjacent numbers.
  We have ordered two 5-pound packages for the meeting.

- The words millions and billions in even amounts (do not use decimals with even amounts).
  The lottery is worth 28 million this month.

- Fractions.
  About one-half of the audience responded to the questionnaire.

ABBREVIATIONS:

1. In nontechnical writing, do not abbreviate common nouns (such as *dept.* or *pkg.*), compass points, units of measure, or the names of months, days of the week, cities, or states (except in addresses).
The Sales Department will meet on Tuesday, March 7, in Tempe, Arizona.

2. In lowercase abbreviations made up of single initials, use a period after each initial but no internal spaces.
We will be including several states (e.g., Maine, New Hampshire, Vermont, Massachusetts, and Connecticut).

3. In all-capital abbreviations made up of single initials, do not use periods or internal spaces. (Exception: Keep the periods in most academic degrees and in abbreviations of geographic names other than two-letter state abbreviations.)
You need to call the EEO office for clarification on that issue.

Create a Web Page

3. Create a new page to describe the fees.

Choose an appropriate layout and **apply a theme.**

Fees Page

A page displaying:
- A table with the fees you will charge per day.
- A hyperlink to the home page.

Insert photos and/or clip art.

4. Save the document as a Web page, *urs*Fees Page.

Continued on next page

UNIT
1

Computer Usage

GOAL:

▶ Demonstrate proper care and operation of computer equipment.

APPLY

Create a Web Page

Your business is growing. Your parents have offered to help you with transportation if you should get pet-sitting jobs outside of your neighborhood. A Web site would be another good way to promote your business.

Your Turn

1. Using the information provided in Projects 7 and 8, create a home page to display important information about the business.

Choose an appropriate layout and **apply a theme**.

Format a **horizontal border**.

Insert photos and/or **clip art**.

Home Page

A page displaying:
- Name of the business.
- Business slogan.
- List of services available.

2. Save the document as a Web page, *urs*Home Page.

Continued on next page

Focus On

Good Keyboarding Habits

Practice perfect posture:

- Center your body in front of the keyboard (body directly in front of the "J" key).

- Distance your abdomen approximately one hand's span from the keyboard.

- Keep your spine and abdomen straight.

Create a Business Card

Several of your neighbors have expressed an interest in your pet-sitting services. In fact, you had your first job this week taking care of the neighbor's cat. You want to make it convenient for your neighbors to contact you when they need your help. You decide that a business card would be a good idea.

Your Turn

1. Use a template to create a business card. The business card should include information similar to that in the illustration.

Be creative and add borders and colors.

Home Alone Pet Care

While you're away,
I'll make sure your pets are okay.

Your Name
1719 Lakeview Drive
Fontana, WI 53125
Phone: 262-555-6978
E-mail: PetSitter@tyr.net

Insert clip art or photo.

2. Spell-check, proofread, and correct errors.

3. Save the document as *urs*Home Alone Cards. Print and close the file.

SECTION 1.1

Computer Usage

GOAL: To demonstrate proper care and operation of computer equipment.

In a word processing document, key each line 3 times.
Proofread your work.

```
jump free plum star yolk crab milk brag
exit pore zest only gate hump vest kiln
pet quo out who ink eat urn rid you tan
```

Making the Connection

How do you treat your personal equipment? For example, how would you feel if someone spilled his or her soda on your electronic games?

In this section, you will learn to properly care for and operate your school or home computer equipment.

Your Turn

1. Take out a blank sheet of paper.
2. List some of the steps to take care of the computer you are using.

The Computer

Your Name_____

1. Before turning on the computer make sure there are no diskettes in the computer's diskette drive.

2.

APPLY

Create a Flyer

You would like a summer job. You have decided to start a pet-sitting business. You decide to create a flyer that you can distribute in your neighborhood to promote your new pet-sitting business.

Your Turn

1. Design and create a flyer. The flyer should include information similar to that in the illustration.

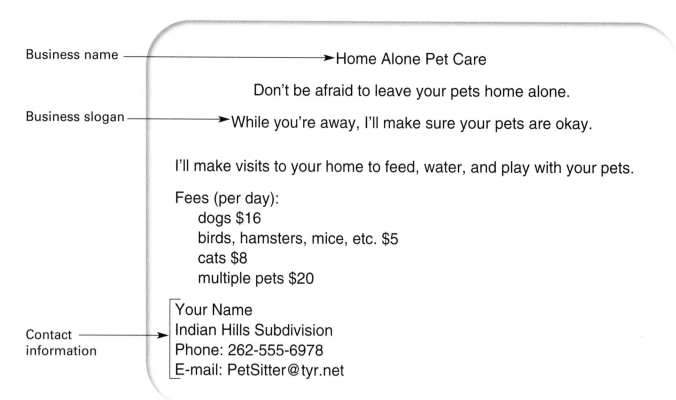

Business name → Home Alone Pet Care

Don't be afraid to leave your pets home alone.

Business slogan → While you're away, I'll make sure your pets are okay.

I'll make visits to your home to feed, water, and play with your pets.

Fees (per day):
dogs $16
birds, hamsters, mice, etc. $5
cats $8
multiple pets $20

Contact information →
Your Name
Indian Hills Subdivision
Phone: 262-555-6978
E-mail: PetSitter@tyr.net

2. Spell-check, proofread, and correct errors.

3. Save the document as *urs*Home Alone Flyer. Print and close the file.

Practice

Computer Usage

Treat your computer equipment carefully, as if it is your very own equipment.

Your Turn

1. Read the information below.

Food and drinks can ruin computer parts. Spilled drinks can cause electrical parts to short out. Food can get stuck in the keyboard and cause the keys and mouse to be sticky.

2. Discuss with your teacher why you should keep food and drinks away from your computer.

3. Check your computer work area to see if it is free from food and clutter.

Does it look similar to the photo?

Remember to keep your work area neat and free of clutter.

Create a Newsletter

Did you create a masthead at the top of the document?

Did you format a line between the columns?

Did you **insert** appropriate **clip art** or **photos**?

Did you **format** the two articles in two **columns** of equal width?

TURTLE CREEK ANIMAL SHELTER
2023 North Lake Shore Drive
Fontana, WI 53125

Telephone: 262-555-5050   *www.AnimalShelter@tcas.org*

VOLUNTEER OPPORTUNITIES

The success of Turtle Creek Animal Shelter relies on our volunteers to help manage the shelter and care for the animals. There are numerous areas where we need assistance in managing the shelter and caring for the animals.

Volunteer activities include the following:

- Adoption Day Volunteer
- Animal Foster Care Volunteer
- Fund-Raising Volunteer
- Grooming Volunteer
- Kennel Volunteer
- Lost and Found Volunteer
- Office Volunteer
- Pet Adoption Counselor
- Pet Pal Volunteer
- Special Events Volunteer
- Transportation Volunteer
- Volunteer Coordinator
- and much, much more!

You can schedule your volunteer hours at your convenience, and you determine how much time you want to contribute.

If you are interested in helping us, please contact Bonita at 555-4661 between 8 a.m. and 4 p.m., or e-mail us at AnimalShelter@tcas.org.

INTRODUCING THE NEW TEEN/JUNIOR PROGRAM

Teenagers have shown a great deal of interest in volunteering at TCAS. We recently established the Teen/Junior Program at TCAS to provide an opportunity for them to contribute. Students can choose from a variety of tasks, but they generally are most helpful socializing and playing with the animals. The animals really need this special attention, and it helps to prepare the animals for adoption.

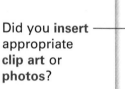

Students can volunteer after school and on weekends. Before volunteering, teens must first attend an orientation. The orientation is offered each Saturday from 9 a.m. to 10 a.m. at the TACS office. Parents/guardians must sign a waiver for children under 18 years of age.

---

4. Save the changes. Print and close the file.

Computer Usage

4. Read the information below.

Gently insert a disk into the drive. Disks are encased in a plastic or vinyl cover to protect them from fingerprints and dust. Once information has been saved on the disk, the disk can be removed from the computer disk drive and stored for later use.

5. Demonstrate with a partner the proper way to insert and eject a disk from your computer.

Insert the disk by holding onto the plastic casing.

6. Read the information below.

Gently insert a CD into the drive. When handling a CD, carefully avoid scratching the surface.

7. Demonstrate with a partner the proper way to insert and eject a CD.

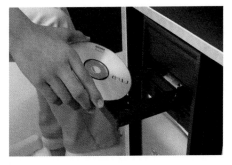

Hold the CD by the edges.

Create a Newsletter

Format a one-page newsletter.

Your Turn

1. Open the file **12-1 Project 6**, and save the document as *urs***Volunteer Newsletter**.

2. Format the document as indicated.

Create a masthead at the top of the document.

VOLUNTEER OPPORTUNITIES

The success of Turtle Creek Animal Shelter relies on our volunteers to help manage the shelter and care for the animals. There are numerous areas where we need assistance in managing the shelter and caring for the animals.

Volunteer activities include the following:
- Adoption Day Volunteer
- Animal Foster Care Volunteer
- Fund Raising Volunteer
- Grooming Volunteer
- Kennel Volunteer
- Lost and Found Volunteer
- Office Volunteer
- Pet Adoption Counselor
- Pet Pal Volunteer
- Special Events Volunteer
- Transportation Volunteer
- Volunteer Coordinator
- and much, much more!

You can schedule your volunteer hours at your convenience, and you determine how much time you want to contribute.

If you are interested in helping us, please contact Bonita at 555-4661 between 8 a.m. and 4 p.m., or e-mail us at AnimalShelter@tcas.org.

Format into two columns of equal width, with a line between columns.

Insert clip art or photos.

3. Compare your document with the illustration on the next page.

Continued on next page

Computer Usage

8. Read the information below.

> Before turning on the computer, make sure that there are no diskettes in the computer's diskette drive. Some computers take a minute or two to start. During the start-up process, your computer may display messages. Messages may prompt you to perform an action such as providing a user ID or password. After the computer has started, the desktop will appear on your screen.

9. What is the proper way to turn on your classroom computer?

10. Discuss and demonstrate to your teacher.

11. Read the information below.

> Before turning off the computer, make sure you have removed any disks from the diskette and CD-ROM drives. Make sure that all data is saved and all running programs are closed. Then proceed with the proper shutdown step for your computer system.

12. What is the proper way to turn off your classroom computer?

13. Discuss and demonstrate to your teacher.

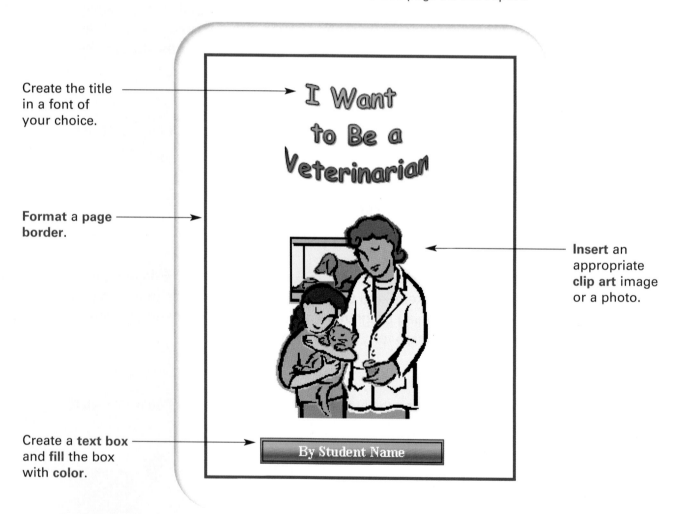

Create a Title Page

Include a title page for your report.

Your Turn

1. Open a new document.

2. Create an attractive title page for the report.

Create the title in a font of your choice.

I Want to Be a Veterinarian

Format a page border.

Insert an appropriate **clip art** image or a photo.

Create a **text box** and **fill** the box with **color**.

By Student Name

3. Save the document as *urs*Veterinarian Title Page. Print and close the file.

Computer Usage

14. Read the information below.

It is time-consuming and expensive to repair the damage done by a virus. You should protect your computer against computer viruses as insurance against damage to hardware, software, and data.

15. Discuss with your teacher how to scan disks for viruses.

Check Your Understanding

Discuss and answer the following with a partner:

1. Why should you keep food and drinks away from your computer?

2. Describe the proper way to take care of a disk and a CD.

3. Describe the proper way to turn on a computer.

4. Describe the proper way to turn off a computer.

5. How can you protect your computer from viruses?

Create a Reference Page

7. Position the insertion point at the end of the document and insert a new page. Create a bibliography listing all the sources you cited within the report.

List all references here, using an appropriate report style.

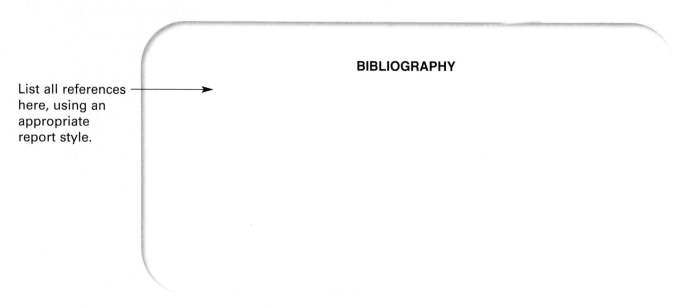

BIBLIOGRAPHY

8. Spell-check, proofread, and correct errors.

9. Save the changes. Print and close the file.

UNIT 2

Computer Ethics

GOAL:

▶ Demonstrate proper computer ethics, security, acceptable use, and etiquette.

Format a Report

5. Also search the Internet for information about the job outlook for veterinarians. You can search for information on any of the following topics:

- Number of veterinarians currently employed.
- Average salaries for veterinarians.
- Areas where veterinarians are needed.
- Job responsibilities of veterinarians.
- Advantages and disadvantages of a career in veterinary medicine.

Complete the report by writing at least two paragraphs to summarize what you have learned about the job outlook for veterinarians. Be sure to cite your sources.

Since it takes a long time to prepare to be a veterinarian, I wanted to be sure there is a need for veterinarians. Here's what I learned.

Insert the new paragraphs of text here. Be sure to cite your sources, using a style of your choice.

6. Save the changes. Keep the file open for the next step.

Continued on next page

Good Keyboarding Habits

Focus on your back.
To support your back:

- **The chair should support your upper and lower back.**

- **Your back should rest against the back of the chair.**

- **Your hips should be toward the back of the chair.**

- **Make sure your chair is adjustable.**

Format a Report

3. Save the changes. Keep the document open for the next step.

> Veterinarians can be very specialized in their work. For example, they can specialize in pet care or they can specialize in farm animals or exotic animals.
>
> **How to Bcoomo a Veterinarian**
>
> If you want to become a veterinarian, you must go to college. There are several colleges in the United States that will help you prepare to be a veterinarian. Each college has its own requirements, and so does each state. I researched the requirements in the state of XXXXXXX, and here is what I learned.

Indicate the state where you would choose to be a veterinarian.

4. Open your Web browser, and search the Internet for information about the educational requirements to become a veterinarian. Requirements will vary by state. Before you begin your search, choose a state where you would want to be a veterinarian. You can search for information about any of the following topics:
- Universities that offer programs for veterinary careers.
- Academic requirements for acceptance into veterinary programs.
- Number of years required to complete a veterinary program.
- Licensing for veterinary practice.
- Areas of specialty.

Then write at least two new paragraphs about what you have learned. Be sure to cite your sources.

Continued on next page

SECTION 2.1

Computer Ethics

GOALS: To demonstrate proper computer ethics, security, acceptable use, and etiquette.

PROOFREADING WARMUP

In a word processing document, key each line 3 times.
Proofread your work.

```
when they also glen wilt slam clan roam
exam dear ploy join jump plum wade quad
lend nape handy firms prowl gland kayak
```

Making the Connection

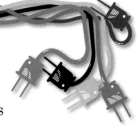

You have a responsibility to respect the property, rights, and privacy of others when you use computers at home and at school. You should find out about your school's rules for using computers.

Your Turn

Use a sheet of paper to list your school's rules for using the computers.

School's Rules for Computers

Your Name _____

1. No food near the computer.
2. No gum near the computer.
3.

APPLY

Format a Report

For as long as
~~Since~~ I can remember, I have ~~always~~ had a pet. When I was five years old, I had a dwarf hamster named Bubbles. ~~When I was~~ *Then at* six years old I ~~had~~ *got* a turtle and some gold fish. When I turned eight, we got a new puppy, and I named him Rocky. Rocky is *still* my best friend. We also have two cats, tiger and Sam. I guess you could say our whole family loves animals.

Insert page numbers. — 1

When I was ten years old, I was a member of the 4-H Club. For my state fair project I decided to raise a lamb. Before I selected my lamb, I had to learn a lot about the different breeds so I could make a good choice. I named my lamb Lolly. I fed her regularly, and I kept the water trough clean. I weighed Lolly every two weeks and kept a chart to monitor her growth. She weighed 110 pounds when we went to the fair. I groomed Lolly and showed her at the fair. I was so excited when Lolly ~~and~~ and I won a blue ribbon. All my hard work paid off. I learned about the livestock industry and animal agriculture. I also learned to be responsible.

I talked with our veterinarian Dr. Durocher, who owns her own animal clinic. Dr. Durocher said I would make a good veterinarian because I like animals and I like to take care of them. She said I need to study hard to be a veterinarian. She also said it would be a good idea if I volunteer at an animal shelter or a kennel. That way I can learn more about animal needs and how veterinarians help them.

Format all side headings bold. → **What a Veterinarian Does**

Veterinarians protect the health and happiness of animals. They take care of sick and injured animals. Veterinarians help control animal diseases, and they advise owners on how to take care of their pets and livestock.

Continued on next page

Practice

Acceptable Computer Use

Just as there are rules for how to treat the outside of a computer, there are general rules for how to treat information contained inside the computer.

Your Turn

1. Open a new word processing document.

2. Key the rule shown below:

> **1.** I will not damage the computer or network in any way.

3. Discuss with your teacher how to care for the computer. Use your list from Making the Connection.

The only thing that should be on the keyboard are your hands.

APPLY

Format a Report

You have started your report. You need to make some corrections and complete the report. Add information about educational requirements and job opportunities.

Your Turn

1. Open the file **12-1 Project 4**, and save the document as *ursVeterinarian*.

Change the left **margin** to 1.5 inches and the right margin to 1 inch.

2. Make the changes in the document as indicated below and on the next page.

I WANT TO BE A VETERINARIAN

Introduction

Format all side headings **bold**.

Have you ever wished you could play with a chimpanzee? Or have you ever thought about what it would be like to touch a crocodile? Well, I have I love to be around animals. When I watch shows on television about exotic animals, I wish I could be there, close to the animals, getting to know them, and learning all about them.

My Background

One of my most memorable experiences was ~~when I was~~ in second grade. *A farmer* ~~They~~ brought a llama named Charlie to our school. Charlie's face was fuzzy and he had big brown eyes. I got to pet Charlie. It was a really neat thing. When I touched Charlie's nose, I felt him blow in my face. Charlie's owner said ~~that~~ *it* was a llama kiss. *also* I learned ~~that day~~ that llamas are remarkably intelligent, and I knew then that some day I want *ed* to own a llama. I know it would be a lot of work to take care of a llama. But I still want to do it. I would like to learn about how to care for all kinds of animals. I want to do what I can to keep animals safe, healthy, and happy.

Continued on next page

Acceptable Computer Use

4. Key the rule shown below:

> **2.** I will not view or use other people's folders, files, or work without their permission.

5. Discuss with your teacher which files and folders are for student use on your school's computer.

Only view your own files and folders.

6. Key the rule shown below:

> **3.** I will not waste computer resources such as paper, ink, or disk space.

7. Discuss with your teacher how to use your classroom resources.

Create an Outline

One of your class assignments is to research and write a report about becoming a veterinarian. Prepare an outline for the report.

Your Turn

1. Key the outline shown below.

Center the title. → **I WANT TO BE A VETERINARIAN**

Level one heading. → **I. INTRODUCTION**

II. MY BACKGROUND

Level two heading. → A. *Interests*

Level three heading. → 1. Charlie the llama

2. My pets

B. *Skills and Abilities*

1. Lolly the lamb—4-H Project

2. Dr. Durocher and her animal clinic

III. WHAT A VETERINARIAN DOES

A. *Protect animals and people*

B. *Specialized care*

IV. HOW TO BECOME A VETERINARIAN

A. *Education requirements*

B. *Opportunities for employment*

2. Apply the **outline number feature** and choose an appropriate outline style.

3. Spell-check, proofread, and correct errors.

4. Save the document as *urs*Report Outline. Print and close the file.

Practice

Acceptable Computer Use

8. Key the rule shown below:

> **4.** I will not change any of the school's computer settings.

Do not change the display to add a screen saver to your school's computer.

9. Key the rule shown below:

> **5.** I will not check my personal e-mail account while in class.

10. Discuss with your teacher the school's policy regarding private e-mail and Internet research.

11. Key additional computer use rules you have discussed with your teacher.

12. Print the document.

13. Sign the rules and turn in to your teacher.

14. Close the file without saving.

PROJECT 2

APPLY

Create a Table

The Turtle Creek Animal Shelter welcomes your help. The office manager has asked you to create a list of all the dogs currently available for adoption from the shelter.

Your Turn

1. Create a table to organize the information shown below.

Center the table on the page horizontally.

Format the title and the column headings **bold** and **centered**.

Adjust the table to fit the contents.

Dogs for Adoption

Name	Date Arrived in Shelter	Description
Jack	April 11	5-year-old male; shepherd/lab mix; about 70 pounds; house-trained; good watchdog; great with kids.
Autumn	April 16	3-year-old female; golden retriever; about 75 pounds; house-trained; high energy; needs plenty of exercise.
Tigger	April 16	6-year-old male; terrier mix; about 20 pounds; sweet, friendly, and obedient; good with other dogs; loves to play.
Jasmine	April 18	9-year-old female; sheltie; about 25 pounds; gentle and calm; needs daily exercise and a quiet environment.
Max	April 20	3–4-year-old male; dalmatian mix; about 70 pounds; loves to play with other dogs and needs an area to run and play.
Billy Bob	April 21	5–6-year-old male; beagle; about 30 pounds; a very bright dog; house-trained, active, and good around kids.
Sophie	April 22	1–2-year-old female; collie; about 40 pounds; well-mannered; loves to run and play; short-to-medium hair and is a very pretty dog; gets along with dogs as well as cats.
Molly	April 23	1-year-old female; cocker spaniel mix; about 25 pounds; adorable and happy; playful and energetic; very bright and trainable.

2. Spell-check, proofread, and correct errors.

3. Save the document as *urs*Dog Details. Print and close the file.

Check Your Understanding

Discuss and answer the following with a partner:

1. What will damage a computer?

2. Why is it wrong to view other people's files?

3. When should you use computer resources?

4. Why is it wrong to change the school's computer settings?

5. Why is it wrong to check your personal e-mail account while in class?

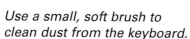
Use a small, soft brush to clean dust from the keyboard.

Create a Personal Letter

I am available to help you on weekdays after school and on weekends. I would be willing to work up to six hours a week. I can start working next week.

Please call me at 555-6978 and let me know how I can help.

Sincerely,

Your Name

2. Spell-check, proofread, and correct errors.

3. Save the document as *urs*Shelter Letter. Print the letter.

4. Print an envelope for the letter. Close the file.

UNIT 3

Computer Basics

GOALS:

▶ Demonstrate correct use of command, shortcut, and function keys.

▶ Demonstrate how to use the Help feature.

▶ Demonstrate how to create and organize electronic files and folders.

▶ Demonstrate basic editing skills.

▶ Demonstrate how to use search engines and collect and utilize data from the Internet.

15

Create a Personal Letter

After reading a newspaper article about animal shelters, you've decided to volunteer at an animal shelter in your community.

Your Turn

1. Create a personal letter in block style.

1719 Lakeview Drive
Fontana, WI 53125
March 21, 20--

Ms. Susan Yu, Director
Turtle Creek Animal Shelter
2023 North Lake Shore Drive
Fontana, WI 53125

Dear Ms. Yu:

I am interested in volunteering at your animal shelter. I love animals, and I have pets of my own, including a dog and a cat. I can help you feed, groom, and exercise the animals in your shelter.

Continued on next page

Good Keyboarding Habits

Focus on your eye distance from the monitor.
To avoid eyestrain:

- The distance from your eyes and the monitor should be between 20 inches and 24 inches.

- Eye gaze should be slightly down.

- Position the monitor slightly lower than the top of your head.

- Sit at a comfortable distance from the monitor.

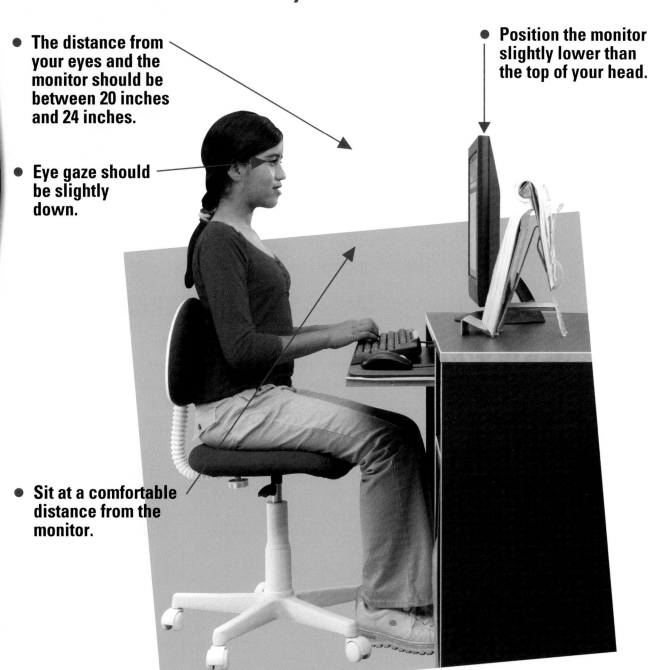

Capstone Projects

GOALS: Demonstrate the ability to:

▶ Format a personal letter, table, outline, report, newsletter, flyer, business card, Web page, spreadsheet, presentation, and database table.

PROOFREADING WARMUP

In a word processing document, key and complete the paragraph starter. Proofread your work.

```
I can't wait until I am 16 years old. When I am 16
I will...
```

Making the Connection

In this unit, you will apply all the skills you have learned throughout this course. You will create each project as if you were running your own pet-sitting business.

The Pet Sitter projects simulate realistic tasks when one is volunteering at an animal shelter, completing a research report for a school assignment, and starting a pet-sitting business. As you complete these tasks, you will apply what you have learned and you will demonstrate use of your keyboarding and computer skills for personal use.

SECTION 3.1

Software Basics

GOALS: Demonstrate the ability to:

▶ Open a new document.

▶ Identify menu commands, shortcut keys, and function keys.

▶ Use the Help feature.

▶ Save and close a document.

PROOFREADING WARMUP

In a word processing document, key each line 3 times. Proofread your work.

```
Set your goals, and then make plans to achieve those goals.
messes make some moms mad; half a dome; for his risk; mills
he reads ahead; his middle silo is filled; more old mirrors
```

Making the Connection

An easy way to learn software is to explore and use the features. You can learn about many software features by using the online Help feature.

Your Turn

1. Open a new word processing document.

2. Key a list of all the software features that you find. For example, can you find the button for Bold? Do you see the word Help?

3. Keep the document open for Project 1.

LIST OF SOFTWARE FEATURES

Bold
Help

Good Keyboarding Habits

Focus on your knees.
To ensure proper position and posture at the keyboard:

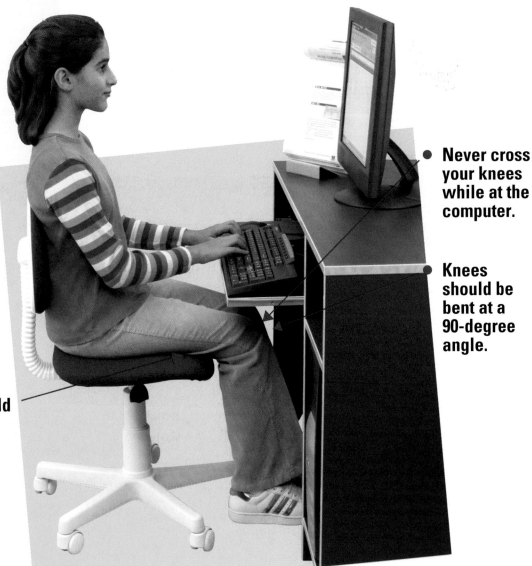

- **Never cross your knees while at the computer.**

- **Knees should be bent at a 90-degree angle.**

- **Thighs should slope gently downward.**

Identify Word Processing Software Functions and Use Software Commands

You will learn that no matter which software you use, you will become familiar with a core set of software features. Find the following screen parts (listed in bold) with a partner. You can find the bolded words in the glossary.

Your Turn

1. Find and point to the **title bar** on your screen.

2. Find and point to the **menu bar** on your screen.

3. Find and point to the **toolbar** on your screen.

4. Find and point to the **insertion point** on your screen.

5. Position the mouse pointer over the word File in the menu bar. Click 1 time.

   a. A drop-down menu appears. Each item in the menu indicates a different task.

   b. Find the command to open a new word processing document.

   c. Click anywhere outside the drop-down menu. The menu is no longer displayed.

6. Key your first and last name. Where is the insertion point? It should be at the end of your last name.

7. Use the mouse or the left arrow key on the keyboard to move the insertion point between your first and last name.

8. Key your middle name. Where is the insertion point? It should be at the end of your middle name.

9. Open the File menu, and select the Close command. When you are prompted to save the changes to your document, click No.

10. Open the File menu, and select the Open command to open a new document. Keep the document open for Project 2.

Capstone Projects

GOALS:

▶ Demonstrate the ability to create and format a letter and a table.

▶ Demonstrate the ability to format an outline, a report, a reference page, and a title page.

▶ Demonstrate the ability to create and format a newsletter, a flyer, and a business card.

▶ Demonstrate the ability to create a Web page.

▶ Demonstrate the ability to create a presentation.

▶ Demonstrate the ability to create a spread-sheet, a chart, and a database.

Practice

Use Help

You can learn many features of your word processing software by using online Help or the *Student Guide*. Important words and phrases that are listed in the Help feature or in the *Student Guide* are shown in red. Key the red word in your online Help; if you have a *Student Guide*, look up the words in red.

Your Turn

1. Open your online software Help.

2. Position the insertion point in the Help text window and key in **shortcut key** as shown below. If you are using the *Student Guide*, go to Unit 3 and look up the term **shortcut key**.

Look up words in **red** in the online Help feature or in the *Student Guide*.

> **shortcut key**

3. Read about shortcut keys. Click in your document to key your answer. Give an example of how a shortcut key is used.

4. Look up **print a document**. What are the steps to print a document? Key your answers.

5. Look up **navigate**. What are two ways to navigate or scroll in a document? Key your answers.

6. Look up keyboard **shortcuts**. What are two keyboard shortcuts that allow you to navigate through a document with the keyboard? Key your answers.

7. Look up **function keys**. What are the function keys? Find examples of function keys for the following: help, save, and check spelling.

8. Look up **Save As**. Read how to save a document.

9. **Save** the document **As** *urs***Help**. **Close** the document.

Replace **urs** with your own initials.

ENRiCh

Curriculum Portfolio

LANGUAGE ARTS:

Create a music database table.

Create a database table of music CDs. Create columns for your favorite types of music, favorite titles, and favorite artists.

MATH:

Create a monetary exchange rate database.

Create a database of the exchange rates of ten countries. Include the name of the country, the monetary unit of the country, and the exchange rate for one U.S. dollar. Then sort the database alphabetically by the name of the country.

Reinforce

Software Commands and Help

Your Turn

1. **Open** a new word processing document.

2. Key the sentence shown below in yellow.

When you see ——→ Franklin owned his own newspaper in Philadelphia.
words highlighted
in **yellow**, key the
words as shown.

3. Move the insertion point in front of the word Franklin, and key the word Ben.

4. Move the insertion point to the end of the line, and press ENTER 2 times.

5. Explore the command menus and the Help feature of your software to respond to the following questions. Key your answers.

   a. What menu name would you use to find the **Save** command?

   b. What menu name would you use if you wanted to change the **Font**?

   c. What shortcut keys would you use to **Open** a document?

   d. What does the Toolbar button look like for checking **Spelling and Grammar**?

   e. Describe what theToolbar button looks like to **print** a document.

6. **Save As** *urs*Software. **Close** the document.

COMPLETING UNIT 8

ENRICH

Curriculum Portfolio

Use the database skills you have learned to create your curriculum portfolio project. Choose from one of the following topics.

SCIENCE:

Create a database table about planets.

Create a table listing each of the planets in our solar system, the average temperatures, and the distance from our Sun.

SOCIAL STUDIES:

Create a parks and recreation address database.

Create a database of recreation areas or parks in your community. Contact the parks or recreation department to find out the names, addresses, phone numbers, e-mail, and operating hours for these places. Then sort the database alphabetically by the park and recreation department name.

Continued on next page

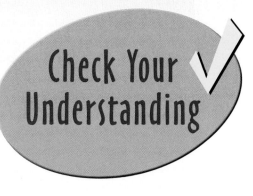

Check Your Understanding

1. Open a new word processing document.
2. Describe where on the screen you see the name of the document.
3. Describe where on the screen you see menu options.
4. Describe where on the screen you find shortcut keys and function keys displayed.
5. Name three different ways you can open a new word processing document.
6. Save the document as *urs*Screen. Close the file.

CD-ROMs store many forms of data, including text, music, audio, and full-motion video.

APPLY

Database Review

3. Alphabetize the database table as shown.

Sort the Last Name field in ascending order.

Review : Table

First Name	Last Name	Age
Jeff	Blessington	12
Paraskevi	Brunson	11
Sue	Cantor	11
Suzann	Connell	13
Patty	Cope	11
Alexander	D'Anca	13
Alissa	Hiraga	12
Deanna	Johnson	12
Mario	Leon	13
Jordan	Miller	12
Bethany	Schulenberg	11
Tiffany	Smith	11
Amy	Spears	29
Tashia	Stone	12
Bill	Thill	11
Rob	Wagman	13
		0

4. Edit Amy Spears' age to 11, and delete the record for Jordan Miller.

5. Add a new record for the following classmate:

Pat Young, age 12.

6. Create a query to filter all classmates who are age 11. Save the query as "Classmates Filter."

7. Save, print, and close the database.

Manage Files

GOALS: Demonstrate the ability to:

▶ Create a folder.
▶ Open an existing file.

▶ Find a file.
▶ Delete a file.

PROOFREADING WARMUP

In a word processing document, key and complete the paragraph starter. Proofread your work.

There are some things that make me happy. These are five things that make me happy and why they make me happy.

Making the Connection

Have you ever lost your homework? Putting your papers in folders for each class is similar to creating folders for your computer. You can store whatever documents you create and save them in folders on your computer.

Your Turn

1. Open a new word processing document.

2. Think about some tips that will help you organize your school papers. Key your ideas.

3. Keep the document open for Project 1.

ORGANIZING TIPS

Make one folder for each class.
Label each folder.

APPLY

Database Review

You will apply the skills you have learned to create and edit a database table.

Your Turn

1. Open a blank database file and name the table *urs*Classmates.

2. Key a database table, listing the first name, last name, and age of students in your class.

Name fields as shown. →

	First Name	Last Name	Age
	Bill	Thill	11
	Tashia	Stone	12
	Suzann	Connell	13
	Paraskevi	Brunson	11
	Jordan	Miller	12
	Bethany	Schulenberg	11
	Alexander	D'Anca	13
	Sue	Cantor	11
	Alissa	Hiraga	12
	Mario	Leon	13
	Jeff	Blessington	12
	Tiffany	Smith	11
∅	Patty	Cope	11
	Deanna	Johnson	12
	Rob	Wagman	13
*			0

Review : Table

List the first name, last name, and age of each student in your class.

Continued on next page

Practice

Organize Files and Create Folders

Documents you create using your software are called **files**. Use **folders** to organize files so you can find them easily.

To create a folder and save the file you created in *Making the Connection*, follow these steps:

Your Turn

1. Choose the **Save As** command.

2. Create a **New folder**.

3. Name the new folder Unit 3.

4. **Open** the **new folder**.

Replace **urs** with your own initials. →

5. Save the document with the filename *urs*Organizing.

6. **Close** the file.

7. Open the file **3-2 Project 1**, and read the paragraph.

The documents you create and use are called files. When you save the file, you save it to a drive—such as the hard drive, the network drive, or a floppy disk or CD—on your computer. To help you keep things neatly organized on the drives, you can create folders to store your files. To avoid losing your work, you should save changes you make to your document regularly.

8. Position the insertion point at the end of the paragraph; then key the highlighted sentence shown in the paragraph above.

9. Choose the Save As command and, if necessary, open the Unit 3 folder.

Notice the filename on the software Title Bar changes to *urs*File. →

10. Save the document as *urs*File.

11. Close the file.

Reinforce

Create a Table

In this project, you will sort the Presidents table, and then filter out any president with a first name other than George.

Your Turn

1. Open the database *urs*Presidents.

2. **Create a new query**, using the Presidents table, **sorting the table** by "First Name" ascending and then by "Last Name" ascending.

3. Save the query as "President Sort" and close design view.

4. Run the query and print the results.

5. **Create a new query**, using the Presidents table, **filtering** the table by "First Name," and setting the criteria to "George."

6. Save the query as "President Filter" and close design view.

7. **Run the query** and print the results.

8. Save and close your database.

Practice

Find and Delete Files

Sometimes you might forget where you saved your file. If this happens, you can locate the file by using the **Search** feature in the operating system software.

Your Turn

1. Choose the **Find** (or **Search**) command. (Use the command from your word processing or your operating system software.)

2. Find the file *urs*File.

3. When the filename appears, click on the filename 1 time and press the DELETE key.

4. Close the Find (or Search) feature.

If you do not know where your file is, choose the Find command from your word processing software.

Database Queries—Filter Queries

5. In the Criteria box underneath the Last Name field, type "Smith." In the Criteria box underneath State, type "NV." This tells the query to show records only where a person has a last name of Smith and lives in Nevada.

Field:	First Name	Last Name	City	State	E-Mai
Table:	Friends	Friends	Friends	Friends	Frien
Sort:					
Show:	☑	☑	☑	☑	
Criteria:		"Smith"		"NV"	
or:					

6. Close the query window.

7. Run the query.

8. Examine your results to ensure that the only information listed is people with the last name of "Smith" who live in "NV."

9. Close the query window and the database, saving changes.

Check Your Understanding

1. Open a word processing document and save as *urs*Sorting Basics.

2. Explain the difference between a simple sort and a multiple sort.

3. Explain the difference between a filter and a query.

4. Save the document. Print and close the file.

Reinforce

Manage Files

Reinforce what you have learned about managing files.

Your Turn

1. Find and open the file *urs*Organizing.

2. Save the file as *urs*Filetips in a new folder named Managing Files.

3. Keep the file open for Check Your Understanding.

4. Find and delete the file *urs*Organizing in the Unit 3 folder.

Check Your Understanding

1. Open a new word processing document.
2. Describe how to create a folder.
3. Describe how to use the Find command to find a file.
4. Save the document as *urs*Files.
5. Close the file.

Practice

Database Queries—Filter Queries

If you were searching a database for a specific set of criteria, there are faster ways to locate data than using multiple sorts. If you needed to locate all the people who live in Nevada who had a last name of "Smith," you could create a multiple sort by state and last name, then find the state section for "NV" and search down until you located the area that had last names of "Smith." A faster way of doing this is to ask our database to do the searching for us and display people *only* with a last name of "Smith" who live in "NV." Doing this creates a query known as a **Filter**. Here, we are going to filter our data to find all the Smiths who live in NV.

Your Turn

1. **Create a new query** by using the query wizard.

2. Select table Friends to be used in the query.

3. Select the fields to be used in the query. For this project, we will select all of the queries to be used.

4. Save the query as "Smith Filter" and choose the option to modify the query design after saving.

Continued on next page

SECTION 3.3

Editing Basics

GOALS: Demonstrate the ability to:

▶ Edit sentences with proofreaders' marks.

▶ Use the BACKSPACE, INSERT, and DELETE keys.

▶ Select text and insert text.

▶ Use the Cut, Copy and Paste commands, and the Undo command.

PROOFREADING WARMUP

In a word processing document, key each line 3 times.
Proofread your work.

```
I did not see her take the pencil, but I know that she did.
Taxi drivers are quick to zip by the huge jumble of wagons.
It's the secretary who accepted the stationery on Thursday.
```

Making the Connection

When you create your work in a word processing document, you will find that it is easy to correct your mistakes.

Your Turn

1. Open the file **3-3 Project 1**, and save it as *urs*Proofermarks.

2. Notice that your document contains ten sentences. These sentences require corrections. What kinds of errors do you see?

3. Keep the document open for Project 1.

PROOFREADERS' MARKS

1. The club officer is very busy.
2. He gave the final estimate for the bike repair.
3. They find all him funny.

Database Queries—Multiple Sorts

Congratulations! You have now created a Simple Sort. Now, let's try to do something a little more complicated. We are now going to sort our friends by the states in which they live, and then sort them by last name.

Your Turn

1. **Create a new query** by using the query wizard.

2. Select table Friends to be used in the query.

3. Select the fields to be used in the query. Once again, we will be using all of our fields, but we must be careful of the order in which we select them when constructing a multiple sort. Most database programs read from left to right, top to bottom. Sorting criteria is defined left to right, top to bottom. Select the state field first, then the last name field, then add the remaining fields using the ">>" button.

4. Save the query as "Friends Multiple Sort" and choose the option to modify the query design after saving.

Field:	State	▼	Last Name	First N
Table:	Friends		Friends	Friend
Sort:	Ascending		Ascending	
Show:	☑		☑	
Criteria:				
or:				

5. **Sort the data** contained within the State and Last Name fields in ascending order. These fields should resemble the diagram at the left.

6. Close the query window.

7. **Run the query.**

8. Examine your results to ensure that your list is sorted alphabetically by state, and then by last name. If you do not have more than one person in a state, it will appear to be sorted only by state. If everyone on your list is from the same state, it will appear to be sorted only by last name.

9. Close the query window, leaving the database open.

Practice

Insert and Delete Text

When you edit your work, you can use proofreaders' marks to show exactly how a document should be revised. **Proofreaders' marks** are symbols that are used to mark changes that need to be made.

Your Turn

PROOFREADERS' MARKS		
Symbol	**Draft Copy**	**Final Copy**
∧ Insert	1. The ‸student‸ club officer is very busy.	The student club officer is very busy.
⸕ Delete	2. He gave the ~~final~~ estimate for the bike repair.	He gave the estimate for the bike repair.
∽ Transpose	3. They find all him funny.	They all find him funny.

1. In Sentence 1, position the insertion point between "The" and "club" and key the text student.

2. In Sentence 2, position the insertion point after the letter "l" in the word "final." Press the **Backspace Key** until the entire word is erased. The **backspace key** erases the characters to the left of the insertion point.

3. In Sentence 3, position the insertion point before the letter "f" in the word "find." Press the **Insert Key** on your keyboard; this key is sometimes called the **Overtype key**. Key the text all find. The text is keyed over the existing words. Press Insert again to turn the feature off.

Continued on next page

Practice

Database Queries—Simple and Multiple Sorts

Field:	First Name	Last Name	City	State	Birthday	E-M
Table:	Friends	Friends	Friends	Friends	Friends	Frie
Sort:						
Show:	☑	☑	☑	☑	☑	
Criteria:						
or:						

You should now be able to view information about the query. The tables (complete with a listing of the fields contained within) should be displayed as well as the fields you specifically have selected for use in the sort. In addition, you should be able to modify the field name, table from which the field is selected, sorting criteria—whether or not the field is shown, and criteria for the fields.

6. **Sort the data** contained within the Last Name field in ascending order by selecting Ascending in the sort box underneath Last Name. When sorting alphanumeric data, ascending means A–Z, 0–9. Descending means Z–A, 9–0.

7. Close the query window.

8. **Run the query.**

9. Examine your results to ensure that your list is in fact sorted alphabetically by last name.

10. Close the query window, leaving the database open.

Practice

Insert and Delete Text

	Symbol	Draft Copy	Final Copy
PROOFREADERS' MARKS			
¶	New Paragraph	4. I can't wait to finish.¶They want to leave soon.	I can't wait to finish. They want to leave soon.
⊙	Insert a period	5. She left⊙He followed her.	She left. He followed her.
⋏	Insert a comma	6. If I go⋏so will he.	If I go, so will he.
=	Capitalize	7. president Lincoln was a tall man.	President Lincoln was a tall man.
/	Lowercase	8. Our club P̸resident met with the school staff.	Our club president met with the school staff.

4. In Sentence 4, position the insertion point between the period after "finish" and before "They." Press ENTER to create a new paragraph. If necessary, press TAB to indent the new paragraph.

5. In Sentence 5, position the insertion point after the word "left" and key a period.

6. In Sentence 6, position the insertion point after the word "go" and key a comma.

7. In Sentence 7, position the insertion point before the letter "p" in the word "president." Press the **DELETE KEY**. The **delete key** erases the characters to the right of the insertion point. Then key a capital P.

8. In Sentence 8, position the insertion point after the "P" in "President." Press BACKSPACE; then key a lowercase letter p.

9. **Save** the changes to the document. Keep the file open for Project 2.

Practice

Database Queries—Simple and Multiple Sorts

For a search in a random database of several hundred (or as is often the case, several hundred thousand) people, finding a specific person or group of people manually would be very difficult. To help us read and reference our Friends database more easily, we are going to sort our friends alphabetically by last name.

Your Turn

1. Open the database *urs*Friends created in Section 11.1 and open the Friends table.

2. **Create a new query** by using the query wizard.

3. Select the Friends table as the table/query to be used.

4. Select the fields to be used in the query. To select fields, choose the field to be used in the query and click the ">" button. For this project, select all fields to be used in the query.

5. Save the query as "Friends Simple Sort" and choose the option to modify the query design after saving.

Continued on next page

Practice

Cut and Paste Text

A quick way to change text is to use the Cut and Paste commands. When text is cut, it is stored in the **clipboard**. The **clipboard** is a temporary storage area in your software. The text on the clipboard can be placed in another location.

In order to move text, you must first select a portion of the document you want to change. An easy way to **select text** is to use the "click-Shift-click" method.

Your Turn

Symbol	Draft Copy	Final Copy
move ⬜→Move text	move 9. Lauren (carefully) swam	Lauren swam carefully.

1. In Sentence 9, position the insertion point before the letter "c" in the word "carefully."

2. Hold down the Shift key and move the insertion point to after the letter "y" in "carefully." The entire word is highlighted as shown in the illustration below.

Selected text is text that is highlighted by a colored or shaded box. ⟶ 9. Lauren **carefully** swam.

3. Choose the **Cut** command. The word "carefully" disappears.

4. Position the insertion point after the letter "m" in the word "swam."

If you accidentally remove more text than you want to delete, be sure to use the Undo command immediately. ⟶ **5.** Choose the **Paste** command. The word "carefully" appears again.

6. Choose the **Undo** command until the word "carefully" is back in its original position.

7. Save the changes. Keep the file open for Project 3.

SECTION 11.2

Sorts and Queries

GOALS: Demonstrate the ability to:

▶ Create a simple query.
▶ Use queries to do simple sorts.
▶ Use queries to do multiple sorts.
▶ Use queries to filter data sets.

PROOFREADING WARMUP

In a word processing document, key each line 3 times.
Proofread your work.

```
It was a good idea to start to write your report this week.
My ax just zipped through the fine black wood quite evenly.
The accident was distressing; however, no one was impaired.
```

Making the Connection

So far, you've entered data into something that feels a lot like a spreadsheet. What is it then that makes databases so special? In addition to storing vast amounts of data, databases have the ability to search this information and display a desired result. To do this, we construct what is known as a **query**. Queries are questions we ask our database.

In addition to queries, we can display the information a database contains in many different ways. For instance, we can print our list of friends alphabetically, by state, or alphabetically by state. When we sort based on a single criteria (alphabetically OR by state), we call this a **Simple Sort**. When we sort based on a number of criteria (alphabetically AND by state), we call this a **Multiple Sort**.

Copy and Paste Text

If you want the same text to appear in different places in a document, use the Copy and Paste commands. Copying text allows you to repeat information in your document without having to key the text again.

Your Turn

Symbol	Draft Copy	Final Copy
ᶜᵒᵖʸ ⤳ Copy text	10. The girl (is fast.) The boy ↴ ᶜᵒᵖʸ	The girl is fast. The boy is fast.

1. In Sentence 10, position the insertion point before the letter "i" in the word "is."

2. Hold down the SHIFT key and move the insertion point to after the period following the word "fast." The group of words is highlighted as shown in the illustration below.

Selected text ⟶ The girl **is fast.**

3. Choose the **Copy** command.

4. Position the insertion point after the letter "y" in the word "boy."

5. Choose the **Paste** command. The words "is fast." are copied.

If you change your mind ⟶ **6.** Choose the **Undo** command to delete the words "is fast."
about copying the text,
be sure to use the Undo **7.** Save the changes to the file.
command immediately.

8. Close the file.

Reinforce

Create and Edit Database Tables

Create a table about some of the presidents of the United States.

Field Name	Data Type
First Name	Text
Last Name	Text
Start	Text
End	Text

Your Turn

1. **Open a new database.** Name the database *urs*Presidents.

2. **Create a table** and name the fields as shown.

3. Enter the following data into the table.

Resize the columns so the data can be easily seen.

First Name	Last Name	Start	End
James	Polk	1845	1849
Theodore	Roosevelt	1901	1909
George	Bush	1989	1993
John	Adams	1797	1801
George	Washington	1789	1797
Woodrow	Wilson	1913	1921

4. Change the last name of George Bush to Bush, Sr.

5. **Add new records** for the following presidents:

Abraham Lincoln – 1861-1865; John Kennedy – 1961-1963

6. **Delete** the **record** about James Polk.

7. **Add a new field** after "End" and name it # President. Research the # Presidency for each person. For example, George Washington was the 1st.

8. Print the table. Save and close the database table.

PROJECT 4

Reinforce

Editing Basics

Reinforce using your editing skills by making the necessary corrections to the essay.

Your Turn

1. Open the file **3-3 Project 4** and save it as *urs*Jefferson.

2. Study the illustration. Make the changes indicated by the proofreaders' marks.

> Thomas Jefferson was born on April 13, 1743. He was born on a ~~small~~ farm in Virginia called shadwall. Thomas had red hair and hazel eyes. He was *also* very skinny and pretty tall. When he was a young lad, he would go to school like all the other kids. Thomas had four brothers and six sisters. It was pretty hard living in a big family. Jefferson spent his time reading as a little kid. When he got older, he liked to farm and invent things. He loved music and loved to play the violin. Thomas Jefferson got married on January 1, 1772. He got married to Martha Skelton Wayles. had six children. *copy*

3. Save the changes to the file.

4. Close the file.

Editing Basics ■ *Section 3.3*   **31**

Practice

Editing a Database

One of your friends has a new e-mail address and phone number. As information changes, you need to be able to delete old records and add new ones to a database.

Your Turn

1. Use the illustration to edit the database table.

First Name	Last Name	City	State	Birthday	E-Mail	Phone
Janet	Jones	Houston	TX	May 9	jjones@hotmail.com	(713) 555-3115
Sasha	Smith	Las Vegas	NV	March 10	sasha421@aol.com	(702) 555-0444
Bob	Thompson	Seattle	WA	July 12	kpxracer719@aol.com	(206) 555-0100
Edwin	Jones	Los Angeles	CA	August 8	eddiej@rr.com	(213) 555-7000

Add a new field, "Birthday."
Key the data shown.

2. Change the e-mail address of Janet Jones to jjones@rr.com.

3. Add a new record for a new friend as follows:

Jamie Kent lives in Austin, TX. His birthday is August 10. E-mail is kentj@hotmail.com. Phone # is (512) 555-8934.

4. Delete the **record** about Edwin Jones.

5. Fill in the Birthday field for your own friends you have added.

6. Print the table.

7. Save and close the database table.

1. Open *urs*Jefferson.

2. Check to see if you interpreted the proofreaders' marks correctly by comparing your edits to the illustration below.

3. Print and close the file.

Thomas Jefferson was born on April 13, 1743. He was born on a farm in Virginia called Shadwall. Thomas had red hair and hazel eyes. He was also very skinny and pretty tall. Thomas had four brothers and six sisters. It was pretty hard living in a big family. When he was a young lad, he would go to school like all the other kids. Jefferson spent his time reading as a little kid. When he got older, he liked to farm and invent things. He loved music and loved to play the violin.

Thomas Jefferson got married on January 1, 1772. He got married to Martha Wayles Skelton. Martha had six children.

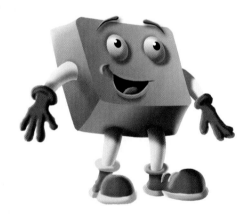

Practice

Create a Table and Enter Data

6. Use the illustration below to help you identify the parts of a database table. Add the following records to your database table.

A column or **field** is a specific category of information. Here, the fields (in order) are First Name, Last Name, City, State, E-Mail, and Phone.

First Name	Last Name	City	State	E-Mail	Phone
Janet	Jones	Houston	TX	jjones@hotmail.com	(713) 555-3115
Sasha	Smith	Las Vegas	NV	sasha421@aol.com	(702) 555-0444
Bob	Thompson	Seattle	WA	kpxracer719@aol.com	(206) 555-0100
Edwin	Jones	Los Angeles	CA	eddiej@rr.com	(213) 555-7000

A row or **record** is a group of fields that give information about a given topic, idea, or object. The first record in the example above gives Janet's name, the city and state where she lives, e-mail address, and telephone number.

When records are entered into fields, they form an object called a **table**. A table is a combination of the fields (First Name, City, State, etc.) and the records they contain (Janet's information, Sasha's information, etc.).

7. Enter the information you gathered about your friends in the Making the Connection section to your database table.

8. Resize the columns so the data can be easily seen.

9. Print the table.

10. Close the table.

SECTION 3.4

Formatting Basics

GOALS: Demonstrate the ability to:

▶ Format fonts, and font sizes and styles.

▶ Change alignment of text in a document.

▶ Preview and print a document.

▶ Use the spelling and grammar feature.

PROOFREADING WARMUP

In a word processing document, key and complete the paragraph starter. Proofread your work.

```
This is a list of my favorite TV programs.
They are my favorites because...
```

Making the Connection

Your friend Ryan has lost his dog, and he has asked you to help him make a sign that you can distribute around the neighborhood. You want to help Ryan create a sign that will grab people's attention. Begin creating the sign by determining how you will display the information that will be printed on the sign.

Your Turn

1. Open the file **3-4 Project 1**, and save it as *urs*Lostdog.

2. Keep the file open for Project 1.

Lost Dog

Reward!
$50.00

Yellow Lab
About 70 lbs.
4 yrs. old
Purple collar with name tag
Male

His name is Ringo.

Ashton Woods
Subdivision

Contact:
555-5555

Create a Table and Enter Data

When we look up a friend's phone number in the school directory, search for something on the Internet, or look up a topic in an encyclopedia, we are finding and using information. A **database** is an organized collection of information on a given subject or topic. Databases allow you to store and manage a collection of information.

Your Turn

1. **Open a new database.** Name the database *urs*Friends.

2. **Create a database table.**

Field Name	Data Type
First Name	Text
Last Name	Text
City	Text
State	Text
E-Mail	Text
Phone	Text

3. **Name the fields** as follows: First Name, Last Name, City, State, E-Mail, and Phone .

4. **Set the field type** for each of the fields to "Text." It is important to note that while a text field can hold a number (or a combination of letters and numbers), a number or integer field can hold **only** numbers (no letters!). Check the field names and types with the illustration at left.

5. Save the table, naming it "Friends." If prompted about the lack of a "Primary Key," choose the option that will prevent one from being created (most often "No" or "Ignore").

Continued on next page

Formatting Fonts

A **font** is the general shape and style of the characters in your document. After you select a font, you can change the font size and add emphasis by applying bold, italic, or underline formats.

When you have finished formatting the document, you will want to preview the document before you print it. When you preview your document, you have a chance to see what it will look like before you print. If necessary, you can make changes before you print your document.

Your Turn

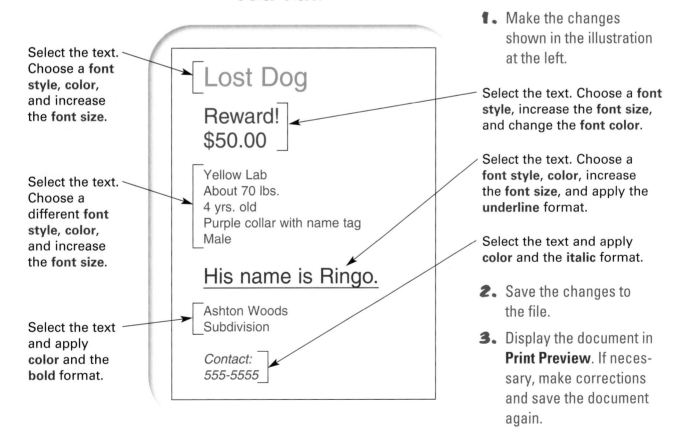

Select the text. Choose a **font style, color,** and increase the **font size.**

Select the text. Choose a different **font style, color,** and increase the **font size.**

Select the text and apply **color** and the **bold** format.

Lost Dog

Reward!
$50.00

Yellow Lab
About 70 lbs.
4 yrs. old
Purple collar with name tag
Male

His name is Ringo.

Ashton Woods
Subdivision

Contact:
555-5555

1. Make the changes shown in the illustration at the left.

Select the text. Choose a **font style,** increase the **font size,** and change the **font color.**

Select the text. Choose a **font style, color,** increase the **font size,** and apply the **underline** format.

Select the text and apply **color** and the **italic** format.

2. Save the changes to the file.

3. Display the document in **Print Preview**. If necessary, make corrections and save the document again.

4. Keep the file open for Project 2.

Create Database Tables and Enter Data

GOALS: Demonstrate the ability to:

- ▶ Create a table.
- ▶ Identify database parts.
- ▶ Define fields.
- ▶ Enter data into a table.

PROOFREADING WARMUP

In a word processing document, key each line 3 times. Proofread your work.

We have to learn to make introductions with poise and ease.
Mo brought back five or six dozen pieces of quaint jewelry.
The trip to Grandma's house was farther than they expected.

Making the Connection

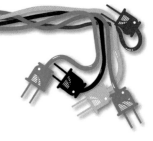

What types of information would you keep about your friends in a telephone book? Some categories might include name, address, and telephone number. The information you collect can be organized so it is easy to find and use.

Your Turn

1. On a sheet of paper, make six columns as shown with the following headings: first name, last name, city, state, e-mail address, and phone number.

First Name	Last Name	City	State	E-Mail	Phone
1					
2					
3					
4					
5					

2. Fill each column with information about five friends.

3. Save your information for Project 1.

Practice

Aligning Text and Printing Documents

You can also enhance the appearance of your document by changing the alignment of the text. **Alignment** is how text is positioned between the left and right margins. When you choose center alignment, your text is positioned at the center of the page between the left and right margins. Similarly, left alignment positions the text at the left margin, and right alignment positions the text at the right margin.

Your Turn

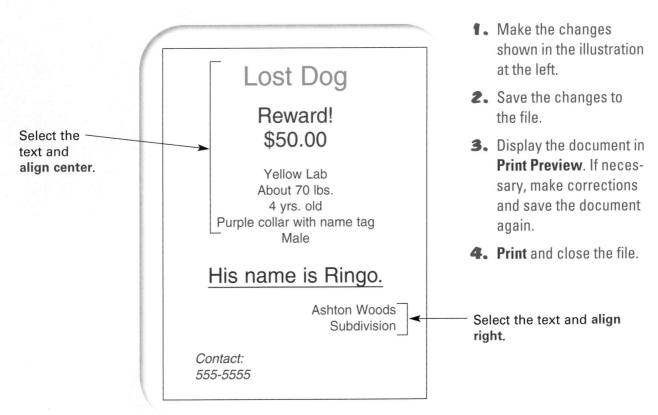

Select the text and **align center.**

Lost Dog

Reward!
$50.00

Yellow Lab
About 70 lbs.
4 yrs. old
Purple collar with name tag
Male

His name is Ringo.

Ashton Woods
Subdivision

Select the text and **align right.**

Contact:
555-5555

1. Make the changes shown in the illustration at the left.

2. Save the changes to the file.

3. Display the document in **Print Preview**. If necessary, make corrections and save the document again.

4. **Print** and close the file.

Good Keyboarding Habits

Focus on your feet.
To keep your body positioned properly
while at the keyboard—place your feet:

- **Apart, with 6 or 7 inches between the ankles.**

- **In front of the chair.**

- **One foot a little ahead of the other.**

- **Flat on the floor.**

Practice

Using Proofing Tools

The **Spelling** feature of your word processor can be used as an online dictionary to check your document for spelling errors. The **Grammar** feature will check for errors, such as punctuation and capitalization, in your writing.

Your Turn

1. Open the file **3-4 Project 3**, and save it as *urs*Spelling.

2. Check to see if errors have been flagged by the Spelling and Grammar checker. The errors are circled in the illustration.

1. frank, please move to to the end of the line.

2. The deed was takn to The bank deposit box.

3. my cousin's home in Lattasburg is on a farm.

4. john Coista received the london Service Award.

5. Susan, are you going with the team to Charlotte, north carolina next month?

6. Ms. Mar, did the romans have a large merchant flet?

7. The bus tripp began on July 5, 1996, and lasted three weks.

8. People travelled frm Buffalo, New York, to join with the tour.

9. carol Warren, M.D., studied the efects of motion sicknes

10. Cassandra and and Mark enjoyd the comedy show.

3. Use the **Spelling and Grammar** feature to identify and correct the errors.

4. Save the changes, **print**, and close the file.

UNIT 8

Database

GOALS:

▶ Demonstrate how to create a database table and enter data.

▶ Demonstrate how to add database fields and records.

▶ Demonstrate how to delete database records.

▶ Demonstrate how to edit database records.

▶ Demonstrate how to sort a database.

Reinforce

Basic Formatting Skills

Your Turn

1. Open the file **3-4 Project 4**, and save it as *urs*Columbus.

2. Use the **Spelling and Grammar** feature to identify and correct the errors.

3. Make the changes indicated in the illustration.

Select all the text. Choose a different **font style**, increase the **font size**, and **align center**.

Columbus's First Voyage

Use **italic** for the names of the three ships.

On August 3, 1492, Columbus set out from Palos, Spain. He had two smal ships, the Nina and the Pinta, and larger one, the Santa Maria, carrying a total of about 90 sailors. The smal fleet stopped at the canary islands for repairs and suplies, then it sailed westward into the unknown.

the ships had good winds, but after a month at sea the sailors began to wory. Provisions were runing low, and they had not sihgted any land. columbus wrote that he was "having trouble with the crew…I am told that if I persit in going onward, the best corse of action will be to throw me into the sea."

4. Save the changes.

5. **Print Preview** the file.

6. **Print** and close the file.

ENRICH

Curriculum Portfolio

LANGUAGE ARTS:

Create a reading minutes spreadsheet.

Create a spreadsheet to keep track of how many minutes you read each day of the week for a one-month period. Calculate the average number of minutes you read each week. Then create a line chart comparing the number of weekly minutes read.

MATH:

Create a budget spreadsheet.

Create a spreadsheet to keep track of how you spend your money for a six-month period. Calculate how much money you have left at the end of each month. Then create a bar chart comparing your monthly expenses.

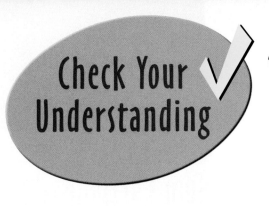

Check Your Understanding

1. Did you make the following corrections in the Spelling document?
    Sentence 1: Frank, delete the "to"
    Sentence 2: taken, the
    Sentence 3: My, no correction necessary
        for Lattasburg
    Sentence 4: John, no correction necessary
        for Coista, London
    Sentence 5: North Carolina
    Sentence 6: Romans, fleet
    Sentence 7: trip, weeks
    Sentence 8: traveled, from
    Sentence 9: Carol, effects, sickness
    Sentence 10: delete "and," enjoyed

2. Did you make the following corrections in the Columbus document?
    a. small
    b. *Nina, Pinta, Santa Maria*
    c. small, Canary Islands, supplies
    d. The, worry
    e. running, sighted, Columbus
    f. persist
    g. course

COMPLETING UNIT 7

=SUM(B2:B10)

ENRiCh

Curriculum Portfolio

Use the spreadsheet skills you have learned to create your curriculum portfolio project. Choose from one of the following topics:

SCIENCE:

Create a temperature spreadsheet.

Create a spreadsheet to keep track of the daily temperature for a one-week period. Calculate the average, high, and low temperatures for the week. Then create a line chart comparing the daily temperatures for the week.

SOCIAL STUDIES:

Create a sales spreadsheet.

Create a spreadsheet to keep track of the weekly sales of a school fundraiser. Calculate the total weekly sales. Then create a bar chart comparing the sales for one week.

Continued on next page

SECTION 3.5

Internet Basics

GOALS: Demonstrate the ability to:
- ▶ Use Boolean search operators for the Internet.
- ▶ Use hyperlinks.
- ▶ Add bookmarks.

PROOFREADING WARMUP

In a word processing document, key each line 3 times.
Proofread your work.

```
I am quite sure that we have had rain every day this month.
Zanzibar, a part of Tanzania, exports cassava and coconuts.
Except for one, all students wanted to take a French class.
```

Making the Connection

What's the difference between surfing the Internet and searching the Web? There is no difference. Where do you start? To find your way through the mass of information on the Internet, you can use search tools and more effective search techniques.

Your Turn

1. Open your Internet browser. Key Leonardo da Vinci in your browser. Are your results similar to the illustration below?

    Results 1 - 10 of about 2,550,000

2. On a piece of paper, record the number of results from this search. You will need to refer to this information for Projects 1 and 2.

3. Keep your browser open for Project 1.

APPLY

Spreadsheet Review

8. Open a new spreadsheet file. Save as *urs*Animal Speeds.

9. Key the data as shown in the illustration below.

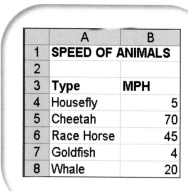

	A	B
1	SPEED OF ANIMALS	
2		
3	Type	MPH
4	Housefly	5
5	Cheetah	70
6	Race Horse	45
7	Goldfish	4
8	Whale	20

10. Create a pie chart from the data.

11. Show the percentage labels for each animal type.

12. Save the changes.

13. Print the spreadsheet and the pie chart. Keep the spreadsheet open.

14. Change the pie chart to a column bar chart by selecting the appropriate data.

15. Save the changes.

16. Print the spreadsheet and the bar chart. Keep the spreadsheet open.

17. Change the bar chart to a line chart by selecting the appropriate data.

18. Include the data labels.

19. Save the changes. Print the spreadsheet and the line chart. Close the file.

Practice

Using Search Engines

Keywords

Search
Leonardo da Vinci
Search Tips

Your Internet browser uses keywords to search for information. **Keywords** can be one or more words that help the search engine find the most appropriate matches. **Boolean operators** are keywords or symbols that refine your search.

Your Turn

1. Enter one of the keywords and operators in the search box of your search engine.

BOOLEAN OPERATORS AND OTHER RESTRICTIONS		
Operator	**Keywords**	**Results**
AND	Leonardo da Vinci **AND** science	Finds Web pages with both words.
OR	Leonardo da Vinci **OR** science	Finds Web pages with either word.
NOT	Leonardo da Vinci **NOT** science	Finds Web pages about Leonardo da Vinci and not science.
Quotes " "	"Leonardo da Vinci"	Finds Web pages with only the exact phrase.
Title:	**Title:** Leonardo da Vinci	Finds Web pages with the keywords in the title.

2. Record the number of results of your new searches.

3. Compare the number of results using Boolean operators with your original search. Did using the Boolean operator technique reduce the number?

Spreadsheet Review

6. Key the formula shown.

To figure the speed of each runner, divide the meters by the seconds. Use the Fill Down command to copy the formula to the rest of the cells.

	A	B	C	D	E
1	**WORLD TRACK RECORDS**				
2					
3	**Holder**	**Country**	**Speed**	**Distance**	**Record**
4			(Meter/Second)	(Meters)	(Seconds)
5					
6	Deratu Tulu	Ethiopia	=D6/E6	10,000	1,800.17
7	Cathy Freeman	Australia		400	49.11
8	Donovan Bailey	USA		100	9.84
9	Florence Griffith-Joyner	USA		100	10.49
10	Florence Griffith-Joyner	USA		200	21.34
11	Gabriela Szabo	Romania		5,000	840.41
12	Marie-Jose Perec	France		400	48.25
13	Michael Johnson	USA		200	19.32
14	Michael Johnson	USA		400	43.49
15	Noah Ngeny	Kenya		1,500	180.32
16					
17	Highest Speed				
18	Lowest Speed				

Use the Max and Min function formulas to find the highest and lowest speeds.

Format the Speed column to 2 decimal places.

7. Save the changes. Print and close the file.

Continued on next page

Practice

Effective Searches

In this project, you will refine your Web searches.

Your Turn

1. Read steps 1–3 in "Steps for Effective Searches" shown below.

STEPS FOR EFFECTIVE SEARCHES

1. **Identify a topic.**
   Example: Leonardo da Vinci

2. **State your topic as a problem or question.**
   Example: How did Leonardo da Vinci influence the field of science?

3. **Make a list of keywords that might help you find more information.**
   Example: Leonardo da Vinci, science, invention, engineering, experiment

---

2. Conduct a search by following the steps in the figure below.

---

4. **Enter your keywords in the search box in a form a search engine will understand.**
   Example 1: "Leonardo da Vinci" AND science

   Example 2: "da Vinci" AND science NOT painting

5. **Press ENTER to begin the search.**

---

3. Record and compare your search results. Did you reduce the number of results?

When a Web page interests you, you can create an electronic bookmark by clicking the **Bookmark** or **Favorite** command. The **bookmark** makes it easy to quickly return to a Web page in the future.

4. Keep your Web browser open.

1 - 20 of 11,300,000 | Next 20

You can click on a **hyperlink** to jump or link to information on another page.

Spreadsheet Review

5. Edit the spreadsheet as shown.

Insert a column before column "Distance." Format the title "Speed." Add the subheading (Meter/Second).

	A	B	C	D	F
1	**WORLD TRACK RECORDS**				
2					
3	**Holder**	**Country**	**Speed**	**Distance**	**Record**
4			(Meter/Second)	(Meters)	(Seconds)
5					
6	Deratu Tulu	Ethiopia		10,000	1,800.17
7	Cathy Freeman	Australia		400	49.11
8	Donovan Bailey	USA		100	9.84
9	Florence Griffith-Joyner	USA		100	10.49
10	Florence Griffith-Joyner	USA		200	21.34
11	Gabriela Szabo	Romania		5,000	840.41
12	Marie-Jose Perec	France		400	48.25
13	Michael Johnson	USA		200	19.32
14	Michael Johnson	USA		400	43.49
15	Noah Ngeny	Kenya		1,500	180.32
16					
17	Highest Speed				
18	Lowest Speed				

Add the two rows shown.

Continued on next page

Reinforce

Internet Search Results

Your Turn

1. Open **3-5 Project 3**, and print one copy. This file contains a form that will help you prepare for an effective Internet search.

2. Complete the form as indicated below.

This column identifies the topic.

State your topic as a problem or question.

Identify the keywords you will use in your search.

Use Boolean operators and other restrictions.

Record the number of results from your search.

Topic	Problem or Question	Keywords	Keyword Combinations	Results
Compare the populations of Boston, Chicago, Houston, and San Francisco.				
Compare length of time to travel to each planet in the solar system.				
Compare men's and women's world track records.				
Compare the height of geysers found in Yellowstone National Park.				

3. Keep your Web browser open.

APPLY

Spreadsheet Review

Insert a column before column B "Distance."

3. Edit the spreadsheet as indicated.

	A	B	C
1	**WORLD TRACK RECORDS**		
2			
3	**Holder**	**Distance**	**Record**
4		(Meters)	(Seconds)
5			
6	Deratu Tulu	10,000	1,800.17
7	Gabriela Szabo	5,000	840.41
8	Carl Lewis	100	9.86
9	Cathy Freeman	400	49.11
10	Florence Griffith-Joyner	100	10.49
11	Florence Griffith-Joyner	200	21.34
12	Donovan Bailey	100	9.84
13	Michael Johnson	200	19.32
14	Noah Ngeny	1,500	180.32
15	Marie-Jose Perec	400	48.25

Delete row 8 containing information about Carl Lewis.

Insert one row under the row containing information about Michael Johnson.

4. Add the data as indicated.

	A	B	C	D
1	**WORLD TRACK RECORDS**			
2				
3	**Holder**	**Country**	**Distance**	**Record**
4			(Meters)	(Seconds)
5				
6	Deratu Tulu	Ethiopia	10,000	1,800.17
7	Gabriela Szabo	Romania	5,000	840.41
8	Cathy Freeman	Australia	400	49.11
9	Florence Griffith-Joyner	USA	100	10.49
10	Florence Griffith-Joyner	USA	200	21.34
11	Donovan Bailey	USA	100	9.84
12	Michael Johnson	USA	200	19.32
13	Michael Johnson	USA	400	43.49
14	Noah Ngeny	Kenya	1,500	180.32
15	Marie-Jose Perec	France	400	48.25

Key the title "Country." Format bold. Change the font size to 12 pt. Align center the title. Key the data shown.

Key in the additional information about Michael Johnson.

Continued on next page

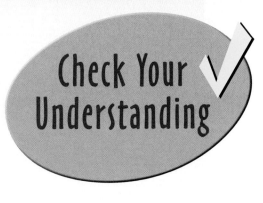

Check Your Understanding

1. Open a new word processing document.
2. Key your responses to the following questions:
   a. If you key Mohs Mineral Scale in the search box, what results would you expect to get?
   b. If you key Mohs NOT Scale, how would the Boolean operator affect the results?
   c. If you key "Mohs Mineral Scale" in quotations, how would the results be affected?
3. Save the document as *urs*Mohs.
4. Print the document.
5. Close the file.
6. Go to your Web browser and locate and use the bookmark you created for the Leonardo da Vinci Web page. Did the bookmark take you back to the correct page?

_inter_NET CONNECTION

In this section, you learned how to perform effective Web searches. Search engines also provide more information about how to define your search criteria in very specific ways.

1. Open your Web browser.
2. Locate the Help feature related to a search engine of your choice.
3. Look for information and/or tips for using that particular search engine. Did you find similar or additional information about search techniques?
4. Open a new word processing document, and compose a paragraph about your findings. Save as *urs*Search Help.

Apply

Spreadsheet Review

In this review project you will apply the skills you have learned to create and edit a spreadsheet. You will also calculate with simple and function formulas, then create a chart. Refer to previous projects as needed.

Your Turn

1. Open a new spreadsheet file, and save as *urs*Track Records.

2. Key and format the information shown.

Format the title bold and change the font size to 12 pt.

Center align the headings and format bold.

	A	B	C
1	**WORLD TRACK RECORDS**		
2			
3	**Holder**	**Distance**	**Record**
4		(Meters)	(Seconds)
5			
6	Deratu Tulu	10,000	1,800.17
7	Gabriela Szabo	5,000	840.41
8	Carl Lewis	100	9.86
9	Cathy Freeman	400	49.11
10	Florence Griffith-Joyner	100	10.49
11	Florence Griffith-Joyner	200	21.34
12	Donovan Bailey	100	9.84
13	Michael Johnson	200	19.32
14	Noah Ngeny	1,500	180.32
15	Marie-Jose Perec	400	48.25

Change the column width so the cell with the most data fits.

Format the numbers to separate the thousands with a comma.

Continued on next page

SECTION 3.6

Data Collection

GOALS: Demonstrate the ability to:

▶ Switch windows between applications.

▶ Copy and paste information, an image, and a URL from a Web page to a document.

▶ Develop a basic understanding of citing Web sources.

PROOFREADING WARMUP

In a word processing document, key and complete the paragraph starter. Proofread your work.

```
If I could spend one hour with the President of
the United States, I would ask the following
five questons:
```

Making the Connection

If you have ever searched the Web to find information for a report, copy a picture, download music, or gather any type of data, you have used information that was owned by someone.

When you gather information from the Web, give credit to the owner of the material and cite the source.

Your Turn

1. Open a new word processing document.

2. Key the title Citing Internet Sources; then center the title. Press ENTER 2 times. Save the document as *urs*Citing. Keep the document open for Project 1.

Reinforce

Create a Chart

In this project you will reinforce what you have learned by creating a chart.

Your Turn

1. Open a new spreadsheet file, and save as *urs*Zoo Animals.

	A	B
1	**ANIMALS IN THE ZOO**	
2		
3	**Type**	**Number**
4	Birds	125
5	Reptiles	56
6	Amphibians	145
7	Herd Animals	91
8	Predators	43

2. Key the data as shown in the illustration at left.

3. **Create a pie** chart from the data.

4. **Show the percentage labels** for each animal type.

5. Save the changes to the spreadsheet.

6. Print the spreadsheet and the pie chart. Keep the spreadsheet open.

7. Change the pie chart to a **column bar chart** by selecting the appropriate data.

8. Save the changes to the spreadsheet.

9. Print the spreadsheet and the bar chart. Keep the spreadsheet open.

10. Change the bar chart to a **line chart** by selecting the appropriate data.

11. Include the **data labels**.

12. Save the changes to the spreadsheet.

13. Print the spreadsheet and the line chart. Close the file.

Practice

Collect Data From the Internet

Citing where you found information from the Web is very similar to citing information from a book, journal, or periodical. Cite the author or owner of the information to describe where you got the material.

Your Turn

1. Open your Web browser. Go to <**www.whitehouse.gov**> to find the home page of the White House. Find the history of U.S. presidents and the biography of George Washington. Refer to the illustration.

Biography of George Washington

Continued on next page

Create a Pie Chart

2. Open the file **10-5 Project 3**, and save it as *urs*Rainfall Season.

3. **Create a pie chart** from the spreadsheet data shown.

	A	B
1	RAINFALL BY SEASON	
2		
3		Inches
4	Winter	10
5	Spring	15
6	Summer	6
7	Fall	8
8	Total	39

Include cells A4 through B7 in the range selected for the chart.

4. Key RAINFALL BY SEASON for the chart title.

5. Include the **show percentage labels**.

6. If your chart appears on the same page with the spreadsheet, position the chart under the spreadsheet data. Resize the chart as needed so that all the information displays clearly.

7. Save the changes to the spreadsheet.

8. Print the spreadsheet and the pie chart. Close the file.

Practice

Collect Data From the Internet

George Washington

On April 30, 1789, George Washington, standing on the balcony of Federal Hall on Wall Street in New York, took his oath of office as the first President of the United States. "As the first of every

2. Select and copy a few sentences of text about George Washington as shown at the left.

3. Switch to your word processing document, and paste the text as shown below.

Citing Internet Sources

Paste the text. ──────▶ On April 30, 1789, George Washington, standing on the balcony of Federal Hall on Wall Street in New York, took his oath of office as the first President of the United States.

4. Switch to the Web page, and copy the Web site URL as shown.

Address 🔘 http://www.whitehouse.gov/history/presidents/gw1.html

5. Switch to the word processing document, and paste the URL as shown.

Citing Internet Sources

On April 30, 1789, George Washington, standing on the balcony of Federal Hall on Wall Street in New York, took his oath of office as the first President of the United States.

Copy and paste ──────▶ http://www.whitehouse.gov/history/presidents/gw1.html
the URL.

6. Save the changes to the document. Keep the file and Web page open for Project 2.

Create a Pie Chart

A **pie chart** uses a circle divided into pieces or slices to graphically show the relationship among values in a spreadsheet. All the values make up the entire circle or "pie."

Your Turn

1. Use the illustration to help you identify the parts of the pie chart.

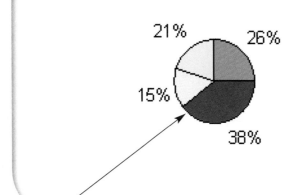

RAINFALL BY SEASON

21%   26%

15%

38%

■ Winter
■ Spring
□ Summer
□ Fall

Each piece of the pie represents one of the values in the spreadsheet.

Continued on next page

Complete the Source Citation

Now you will complete the citation for the information about George Washington that you copied from the Web.

Your Turn

1. Use the Internet text citation illustration below to help you complete your citation. Pay attention to each part of the citation.

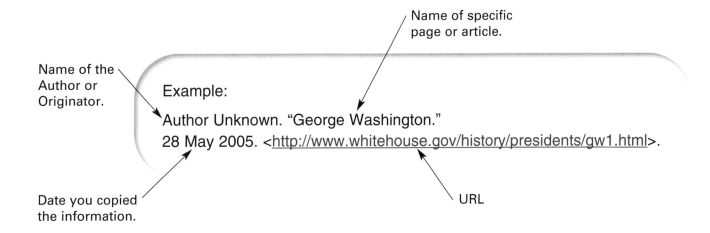

Name of specific
page or article.

Name of the
Author or
Originator.

Example:

Author Unknown. "George Washington."
28 May 2005. <http://www.whitehouse.gov/history/presidents/gw1.html>.

Date you copied
the information.

URL

Continued on next page

Practice

Create a Line Chart

2. Open the data file **10-5 Project 2**, and save it as *urs*Temperatures.

3. Create a line chart from the spreadsheet data shown.

	A	B	C
1	**AVERAGE TEMPERATURES**		
2			
3	**Month**	**Degree**	
4	January	32	
5	February	38	
6	March	54	
7	April	65	
8	May	78	

Include cells A3 through B8 in the range selected for the chart.

4. Key AVERAGE TEMPERATURES for the chart title.

5. Include the **data labels**.

6. If your chart appears on the same page with the spreadsheet, position the chart under the spreadsheet data. Resize the chart as needed so that all the information displays clearly.

7. Save the changes to the spreadsheet.

8. Print the spreadsheet and the line chart. Close the file.

Complete the Source Citation

URL ————————

Name of specific ————
page or article.

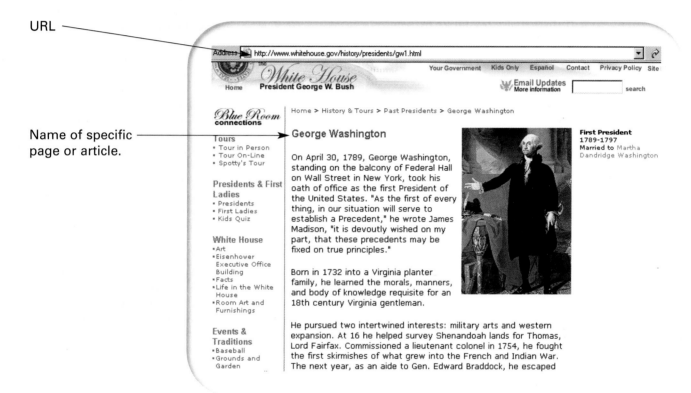

Citing Internet Sources

On April 30, 1789, George Washington, standing on the balcony of Federal Hall on Wall Street in New York, took his oath of office as the first President of the United States.

http://www.whitehouse.gov/history/presidents/gw1.html

2. Find the necessary information on the Web page. Then **switch** to the word processing document, and key the rest of the citation. You will probably need to switch between the document and the Web page several times to complete the process.

3. Save the changes to the document. Keep the file and Web page open for Project 3.

Practice

Create a Line Chart

A **line chart** uses points on a grid connected by lines to represent the spreadsheet values. A line chart is often the best choice for showing trends or changes in values over time.

Your Turn

1. Use the illustration to help you identify the parts of the line chart.

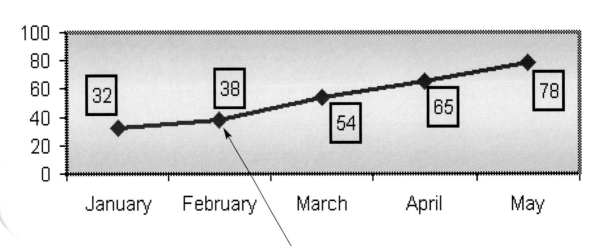

AVERAGE TEMPERATURES

The chart values are represented by points on the grid. Lines connect the points.

Continued on next page

Practice

Copy Images From the Web and Cite the Source

Press and choose Copy with the right mouse button.

Right-click to view the word processing options.

Your Turn

1. Return to the Web page on which you found the photo, or image, of George Washington. Position the mouse pointer over the photo of George Washington and click the right button of your mouse to copy the image.

2. **Switch** to your word processing document, and paste the image below the text citation as shown.

Citing Internet Sources

On April 30, 1789, George Washington, standing on the balcony of Federal Hall on Wall Street in New York, took his oath of office as the first President of the United States.

http://www.whitehouse.gov/history/presidents/gw1.html

Paste image.

Continued on next page

Practice

Create a Bar Chart

2. **Create a column bar chart** from the spreadsheet data shown.

	A	B	C	D	E
1	STUDENT COUNCIL ELECTION				
2	Votes Received				
3					
4		Grade 6	Grade 7	Grade 8	Total Votes
5	Janis Roberts	20	12	10	42
6	Tomas Perez	12	24	31	67
7	Kim Yung	18	23	15	56

Include cells A4 through E7 in the range selected for the chart.

3. Key STUDENT COUNCIL ELECTION for the chart title.

4. If your chart appears on the same page with the spreadsheet, position the chart under the spreadsheet data. Resize the chart as needed so that all the information displays clearly.

5. Save the changes to the spreadsheet.

6. Print the spreadsheet and the bar chart. Close the file.

Copy Images From the Web and Cite the Source

3. Follow the illustration below to help you cite the source for the photo/image.

Description or title of the photo/image.

Name of the Author or Originator.

Example:

Author Unknown. "Photo: George Washington."
28 May 2005. <http://www.whitehouse.gov/history/presidents/gw1.html>.

The date you copied the information.

URL

4. Create the citation below the photo.

Copy and paste the URL to include in the citation.

Author unknown. "Photo: George Washington."
28 May 2005. <http://www.whitehouse.gov/history/presidents/gw1.html>

Add angle brackets after you copy your citation < >.

5. Save the changes to the document. Print and close the file.

Create a Bar Chart

Spreadsheet programs allow you to create charts from data in a spreadsheet. Spreadsheets provide many different chart types, such as bar, line, and pie charts. A **bar chart** has vertical or horizontal bars representing spreadsheet values.

Your Turn

1. Use the illustration to help you identify the parts of the bar chart.

The **title** describes the subject of the chart.

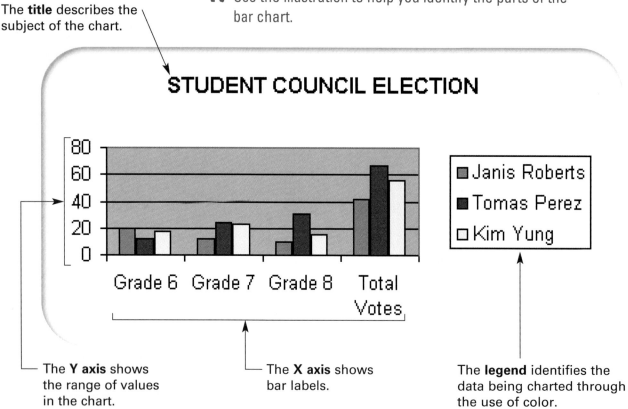

The **Y axis** shows the range of values in the chart.

The **X axis** shows bar labels.

The **legend** identifies the data being charted through the use of color.

Continued on next page

Citing Internet Data

Your Turn

1. Open a new word processing document, and save it as *urs*Internet Data.

2. Search for text and photos/images about one of the following topics:

   a. Your favorite athlete.

   b. Your favorite pet.

   c. A president of the United States.

3. Copy the text and images from the Web, and paste them into the word processing document.

4. Create the proper citations for each item you copy and paste into your document.

5. Save the changes. Print and close the file.

Create Charts

GOALS: Demonstrate the ability to:

▶ Understand the parts of a chart.
▶ Create a bar chart.

▶ Create a line chart.
▶ Create a pie chart.

PROOFREADING WARMUP

In a word processing document, key each line 3 times.
Proofread your work.

Some people seem to have more hours in the day than others.
Jeff quietly moved a dozen boxes last night by power truck.
First we washed our hands, then it was time to enjoy lunch.

Making the Connection

You can create a chart to graphically display your spreadsheet data. Charts allow you to easily compare data.

Your Turn

1. Open the file **10-5 Project 1**, and save it as *urs*Student Council.

2. Keep the spreadsheet open for Project 1.

Student Council Election
Votes Received

	Grade 6	Grade 7	Grade 8	Total Votes
Janis Roberts	20	12	10	42
Tomas Perez	12	24	31	67
Kim Yung	18	23	15	56

Check Your Understanding

1. Open a new word processing document.
2. Describe where you usually find the author of the information you found at the Web site.
3. Describe where you usually find the title at the Web site.
4. Describe how you switch between the Web page and the word processing document.
5. Describe how you copy a photo or image from a Web page.
6. Describe the differences between a text citation and a photo or image citation.
7. Save the document as *urs*Citing Questions. Print and close the file.

*inter***NET**
CONNECTION

In this section you learned how to cite Internet sources for text and photos/images. How would you cite sources for video clips or sound clips?

1. Open your Web browser, and search for sites that provide examples for citing Internet sources.
2. Open a new word processing document. Provide an example of a citation for a video clip and a citation for a sound clip.
3. Save the document as *urs*Sources.
4. Print and close the file.

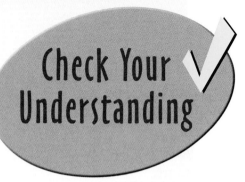

Check Your Understanding

1. Open a new word processing document, and save it as *urs*Function Formulas.
2. Explain how the function formula can save you time.
3. Discuss how the Sum function adds numbers.
4. Discuss how the Average function averages numbers.
5. Discuss how the Fill Down and Fill Right commands can save you time.

	A	B	C	D	E	F	G
1							Student
2	**Name**	**Test 1**	**Test 2**	**Test 3**	**Test 4**	**Test 5**	**Average**
3	Janet	95	85	100	92	88	92.0
4	Ramon	96	90	95	83	91	91.0
5	Sam	84	88	94	81	93	88.0
6	Laura	74	88	90	78	85	83.0
7	Irma	89	93	87	88	92	89.8
8	Dan	88	84	92	80	91	87.0
9	Jacob	80	88	91	93	84	87.2
10	Ali	93	87	90	98	92	92.0
11	Nora	96	93	90	93	100	94.4
12							
13	**Test Average**	88.3	88.4	92.1	87.3	90.7	
14	**Lowest Grade**	74.0	84.0	87.0	78.0	84.0	
15	**Highest Grade**	96.0	93.0	100.0	98.0	100.0	

Compare ursGrades with the illustration.

APPLY

Computer Basics

In this project, you will apply the basic editing skills you have learned to format a poem. You will also use your Internet search skills to find and collect information.

Your Turn

1. Open the file **3-Review**, and save it as *urs***Colossus**.

2. Edit the poem as shown in the illustration.

Align center all three lines.

THE NEW COLOSSUS

By ∧Emma Lazarus

Written in 1883

Format the title with an appropriate **font style**, **font color**, and **font size**.

"keep, ancient lands, your storied pomp!" cries she
With silent lips. "give me your tired, your poor,
Your huddled masses yearning to breathe free,
The wretched with refuse of your teeming shore.
Send these, the homeless, tempest-tossed to me,
I lift my lamp beside the golden door."

move

Not like the brazen giant of greek fame,
With conquering limbs astride from land to land;
Here at our sea-washed, sunset gates shall stand
A woman mighty with a torch, whose flame
Is the imprisoned lightning and her name
mother of exiles. From her beacon-hand
Glows world-wide welcome; her mild eyes command
The air-bridged harbor that Twin Cities frame.

3. Save the changes. Print and close the file.

Continued on next page

Reinforce

Calculate Formulas

In this project you will reinforce what you have learned by entering simple function formulas to calculate student averages.

Find the test average with the **Average function formula**. Use the **Min function formula** to find the lowest grade. Use the **Max function formula** to find the highest grade.

Your Turn

1. Open the file **10-4 Project 5**, and save it as *urs*Grades.

2. Enter **function formulas** to complete the student averages shown below.

Find the student average with the **Average function formula**.

	A	B	C	D	E	F	G
1							**Student**
2	**Name**	Test 1	Test 2	Test 3	Test 4	Test 5	**Average**
3	Janet	95	85	100	92	88	
4	Ramon	96	90	95	83	91	
5	Sam	84	88	94	81	93	
6	Laura	74	88	90	78	85	
7	Irma	89	93	87	88	92	
8	Dan	88	84	92	80	91	
9	Jacob	80	88	91	93	84	
10	Ali	93	87	90	98	92	
11	Nora	96	93	90	93	100	
12							
13	**Test Average**						
14	**Lowest Grade**						
15	**Highest Grade**						

Use the **Fill Down command** to copy the formulas to the rest of the cells.

Use the **Fill Right command** to copy the formulas to the rest of the cells.

3. **Format** the average **numbers** to one decimal place.

4. **Format** the lowest- and highest-grade **numbers** to one decimal place.

5. Save the changes. Print and close the file.

Computer Basics

4. Open a new document, and save it as *urs*History.

5. Key the copy shown in the illustration below. Make the changes indicated.

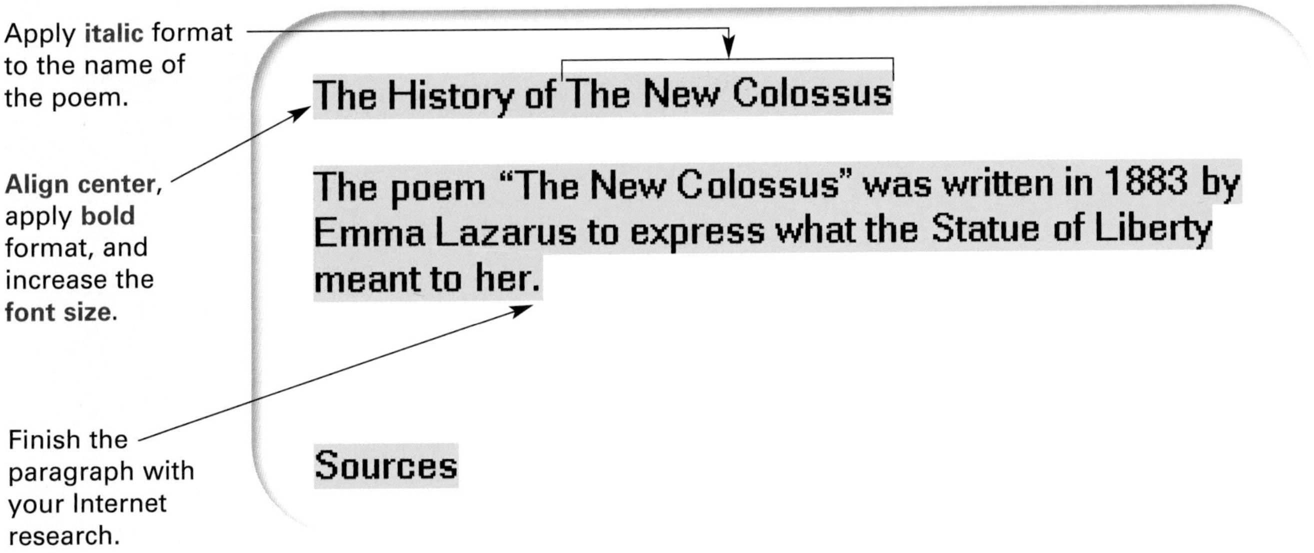

Apply **italic** format to the name of the poem.

The History of The New Colossus

Align center, apply **bold** format, and increase the **font size.**

The poem "The New Colossus" was written in 1883 by Emma Lazarus to express what the Statue of Liberty meant to her.

Finish the paragraph with your Internet research.

Sources

6. Use a search engine to find information to answer the following questions. Then summarize your findings by adding the information to the last paragraph in the document. Be sure to cite your source(s).

a. What is a colossus?

b. Who is the "mighty woman with a torch"?

c. What do you think the author is trying to say in the second paragraph that begins, "Keep, ancient lands, . . ."?

7. Use a search engine to find a photo or clip art image related to the poem. Copy and paste the image to the document; then position it appropriately on the page. Be sure to cite the URL of your source at the end of the document.

8. Check your spelling and grammar.

9. Save the changes. Print and close the file.

Practice

Using the Fill Right and Fill Down Command

4. Use the **Fill Down command** to copy the total formula in cell F2 to cells F3 through F10. The answers appear as shown in the illustration below.

	A	B	C	D	E	F
1	**Name**	**Week 1**	**Week 2**	**Week 3**	**Week 4**	**Total Sales**
2	Ben	$21.65	$43.00	$22.73	$19.84	$107.22
3	Haris	$25.89	$28.86	$18.15	$35.23	$108.13
4	Leticia	$18.00	$29.19	$27.65	$31.00	$105.84
5	Erin	$11.87	$29.76	$41.00	$16.50	$99.13
6	Diana	$23.87	$17.44	$20.65	$22.00	$83.96
7	Trang	$33.45	$24.86	$29.65	$25.83	$113.79
8	Katie	$13.75	$21.00	$26.75	$28.24	$89.74
9	Clay	$22.55	$14.89	$24.75	$18.65	$80.84
10	Scott	$16.50	$38.73	$23.45	$20.25	$98.93

5. Click in cell F3, and notice the formula. The cells that are referenced have changed. Now the formula reads =SUM(B3:E3). **Cell references** identify a cell in a spreadsheet, such as A1, A2, etc.

6. Click in cell B17, and key the number 9.

7. Hold down the SHIFT key, and click in cell E17. The row is highlighted as shown in the illustration below.

17	**Enrollment**	9			

8. Use the **Fill Right command** to copy the number in cell B17 to cells C17, D17, and E17. The numbers appear as shown in the illustration below.

17	**Enrollment**	9	9	9	9

9. Click in cell C17, and notice the cell reference changes.

10. Save the changes. Print and close the file.

COMPLETING UNIT 3

ENRICH

Curriculum Portfolio

Use the word processing skills you have learned to help you create your curriculum portfolio project. Choose from one of the following topics.

SCIENCE:

Compose a paragraph describing fossils.

What are living fossils? Use the Internet to find at least two examples. Compose a paragraph describing the fossils. Add a title. Be sure to cite your sources at the end of the paragraph.

SOCIAL STUDIES:

Compose two paragraphs about citizenship.

Persons born in the United States are citizens. Others, through naturalization, can become citizens and enjoy the same privileges and responsibilities. Use the Internet to find facts about the steps a person must take to success-fully emigrate to the United States. Be sure to answer the following questions.

1. Who is a citizen?
2. If a person is not born in the United States, how can he or she become a citizen?
3. How does a person become a citizen?
4. What are the rights and duties of a citizen?
5. How can a citizen lose his or her citizenship?

Add a title. Be sure to cite your sources at the end of the paragraphs.

Continued on next page

Practice

Using the Fill Right and Fill Down Command

You can reduce the number of keystrokes to produce a formula by using a fill command. The **Fill Down command** copies data or formulas in columns. The **Fill Right command** copies data or formulas in rows.

Your Turn

1. Click in cell F2, and key the Sum function formula =SUM(B2:E2). Compare your spreadsheet with the illustration shown below.

SUM	X ✓ =	=SUM(B2:E2)			
	A	B	C	D	E	F
1	**Name**	**Week 1**	**Week 2**	**Week 3**	**Week 4**	**Total Sales**
2	Ben	$21.65	$43.00	$22.73	$19.84	=SUM(B2:E2)
3	Haris	$25.89	$28.86	$18.15	$35.23	

2. Press ENTER. The answer $107.22 appears.

3. Hold down the SHIFT key and click in cell F10. The column is highlighted as shown in the illustration at right.

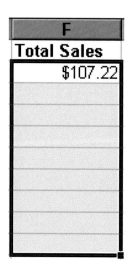

F
Total Sales
$107.22

Continued on next page

ENRICH

Curriculum Portfolio

LANGUAGE ARTS:

Compose two paragraphs about family traditions.

Does your family have a special celebration? Talk to your parents, grandparents, and other family members about a celebration that has become a tradition in your family. Add a title.

MATH:

Compose two paragraphs about George Boole.

George Boole was a self-taught mathematician. Use the Internet to research how Boole contributed to the creation of the Internet and the Information Age. Add a title. Be sure to cite your sources at the end of the paragraphs.

Practice

Enter the MINIMUM and MAXIMUM Function Formulas

4. Click in cell B15, and key the Maximum function formula =MAX(B2:B10). Compare your spreadsheet with the illustration shown below.

	MAX	▼ ✗ ✓ =	=MAX(B2:B10)	
	A	B	C	D	E
1	**Name**	**Week 1**	**Week 2**	**Week 3**	**Week 4**
2	Ben	$21.65	$43.00	$22.73	$19.84
3	Haris	$25.89	$28.86	$18.15	$35.23
4	Leticia	$18.00	$29.19	$27.65	$31.00
5	Erin	$11.87	$29.76	$41.00	$16.50
6	Diana	$23.87	$17.44	$20.65	$22.00
7	Trang	$33.45	$24.86	$29.65	$25.83
8	Katie	$13.75	$21.00	$26.75	$28.24
9	Clay	$22.55	$14.89	$24.75	$18.65
10	Scott	$16.50	$38.73	$23.45	$20.25
11					
12	**Total Sales**	$187.53	$247.73	$234.78	$217.54
13	**Average Sales**	$20.84	$27.53	$26.09	$24.17
14	**Lowest Sales**	$11.87	$14.89	$18.15	$16.50
15	**Highest Sales**	=MAX(B2:B10)			

The Maximum function formula =MAX(B2:B10) finds the largest number in cells B2, B3, B4, B5, B6, B7, B8, B9, and B10.

5. Press ENTER. The answer $33.45 appears.

6. Enter a **Maximum function formula** to find the highest total sales for Week 2, Week 3, and Week 4.

7. Save the changes. Keep the spreadsheet open for Project 4.

Word Processing

GOALS:

- ▶ Demonstrate how to format and edit text.
- ▶ Demonstrate how to proofread and correct errors.
- ▶ Demonstrate how to create tables.
- ▶ Demonstrate how to format personal and business letters and envelopes.
- ▶ Demonstrate how to format reports, outlines, and title pages.
- ▶ Demonstrate how to format bibliography, reference, and works cited pages.

Practice

Enter the MINIMUM and MAXIMUM Function Formulas

The **MINIMUM and MAXIMUM functions** find the largest or smallest number in a range of cells.

Your Turn

1. Click in cell B14, and key the Minimum function formula =MIN(B2:B10). Compare your spreadsheet with the illustration shown below.

2. Press ENTER. The answer $11.87 appears.

3. Enter a **Minimum function formula** to find the lowest total sales for Week 2, Week 3, and Week 4.

MIN	▾ X ✓ =	=MIN(B2:B10)		
	A	B	C	D	E
1	**Name**	**Week 1**	**Week 2**	**Week 3**	**Week 4**
2	Ben	$21.65	$43.00	$22.73	$19.84
3	Haris	$25.89	$28.86	$18.15	$35.23
4	Leticia	$18.00	$29.19	$27.65	$31.00
5	Erin	$11.87	$29.76	$41.00	$16.50
6	Diana	$23.87	$17.44	$20.65	$22.00
7	Trang	$33.45	$24.86	$29.65	$25.83
8	Katie	$13.75	$21.00	$26.75	$28.24
9	Clay	$22.55	$14.89	$24.75	$18.65
10	Scott	$16.50	$38.73	$23.45	$20.25
11					
12	**Total Sales**	$187.53	$247.73	$234.78	$217.54
13	**Average Sales**	$20.84	$27.53	$26.09	$24.17
14	**Lowest Sales**	=MIN(B2:B10)			

The Minimum function formula =MIN(B2:B10) finds the smallest number in cells B2, B3, B4, B5, B6, B7, B8, B9, and B10.

Continued on next page

Good Keyboarding Habits

Focus on your head and neck.
To prevent neck strain:

- **Never lean your head back to view the monitor.**

- **Center your head and neck in the middle of your shoulders.**

- **Make sure the line of reading on the monitor is not above eye level.**

- **Relax your shoulders— never slump your shoulders.**

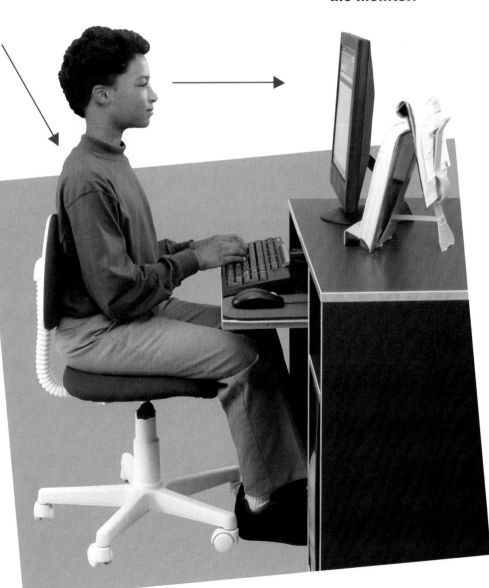

Enter the AVERAGE Function Formula

The **AVERAGE function** adds the values in a selected range of cells and divides the sum by the number of values in the range.

Your Turn

1. Click in cell B13, and key the Average function formula =AVERAGE(B2:B10). Compare your spreadsheet with the illustration shown below.

AVERAGE			=AVERAGE(B2:B10)	
	A	**B**	**C**	**D**	**E**
1	**Name**	**Week 1**	**Week 2**	**Week 3**	**Week 4**
2	Ben	$21.65	$43.00	$22.73	$19.84
3	Haris	$25.89	$28.86	$18.15	$35.23
4	Leticia	$18.00	$29.19	$27.65	$31.00
5	Erin	$11.87	$29.76	$41.00	$16.50
6	Diana	$23.87	$17.44	$20.65	$22.00
7	Trang	$33.45	$24.86	$29.65	$25.83
8	Katie	$13.75	$21.00	$26.75	$28.24
9	Clay	$22.55	$14.89	$24.75	$18.65
10	Scott	$16.50	$38.73	$23.45	$20.25
11					
12	**Total Sales**	$187.53	$247.73	$234.78	$217.54
13	**Average Sales**	=AVERAGE(B2:B10)			

The Average function formula =AVERAGE(B2:B10) adds the values in cells B2, B3, B4, B5, B6, B7, B8, B9, and B10, then divides the sum by 9.

2. Press ENTER. The answer $20.84 appears.

3. Enter an **Average function formula** to average the total sales for Week 2, Week 3, and Week 4.

4. Save the changes. Keep the spreadsheet open for Project 3.

Edit and Format Short Stories

GOALS: Demonstrate the ability to:

▶ Format line spacing.

▶ Work from rough-draft material.

▶ Proofread, use proofreaders' marks, and correct errors.

▶ Use command and function keys.

PROOFREADING WARMUP

In a word processing document, key and complete the paragraph starter. Proofread your work.

```
Let me tell you about the person
I most admire.
```

Making the Connection

Practice reading a short story and correcting the errors in the story by using the proofreaders' marks.

Your Turn

1. Open the file **4-1 Project 1**, and then save the document as *urs*Admire.

2. Keep the file open for Project 1.

The Person I Most Admire

The person I most admire is Shawn. He is 19 years old, and I admire him because

Enter the SUM Function Formula

The **SUM function** allows you to add an entire row or column instantly. Functions are convenient to use because they reduce keystrokes. **Functions** are built-in formulas that the spreadsheet provides.

Your Turn

1. Click in cell B12, and key the Sum function formula =SUM(B2:B10). A colon (:) in a formula represents a range of cells. Compare your spreadsheet with the illustration shown below.

SUM	▼	✗ ✓ =	=SUM(B2:B10)		
	A	**B**	**C**	**D**	**E**
1	**Name**	**Week 1**	**Week 2**	**Week 3**	**Week 4**
2	Ben	$21.65	$43.00	$22.73	$19.84
3	Haris	$25.89	$28.86	$18.15	$35.23
4	Leticia	$18.00	$29.19	$27.65	$31.00
5	Erin	$11.87	$29.76	$41.00	$16.50
6	Diana	$23.87	$17.44	$20.65	$22.00
7	Trang	$33.45	$24.86	$29.65	$25.83
8	Katie	$13.75	$21.00	$26.75	$28.24
9	Clay	$22.55	$14.89	$24.75	$18.65
10	Scott	$16.50	$38.73	$23.45	$20.25
11					
12	**Total Sales**	=SUM(B2:B10)			

The Sum function formula =SUM(B2:B10) adds the values in cells B2, B3, B4, B5, B6, B7, B8, B9, and B10.

2. Press ENTER. The answer $187.53 appears.

3. Enter a **Sum function formula** to sum the total sales for Week 2, Week 3, and Week 4.

4. Save the changes. Keep the spreadsheet open for Project 2.

Practice

Edit Short Stories

Notice the **proofreaders' marks** below. You will want to learn what each mark means. Use proofreaders' marks and a red ink pen or pencil to proofread and correct errors.

Proofreading includes checking for formatting and line spacing. Double-space means that there is 1 blank line between each line of text. **Line spacing** is the amount of space between lines of text.

Symbols			
≡	capital letter	⊙	add period
∧	insert	⸜⹁	insert comma
ℛ	delete	/	lowercase
∩	transpose	#	add space
⁋	new paragraph	DS	double-space

To use keyboard commands (CTRL + B).

Your Turn

1. To bold the title: select the title.

2. Press and hold down the CTRL key.

3. Then press the B key.

4. Then release both keys at the same time.

Continued on next page

SECTION 10.4

Enter Functions

GOALS: Demonstrate the ability to:

▶ Use simple functions in formulas.
▶ Use the Fill Right Command.
▶ Use the Fill Down Command.

PROOFREADING WARMUP

*In a word processing document, key each line 3 times.
Proofread your work.*

We can all speak well if we think about what we are saying.
Because he was very lazy, Jake paid for six games and quit.
The chapter was much longer than she had expected it to be.

Making the Connection

How long would it take you to add a list of numbers?

Your Turn

1. Open the file **10-4 Project 1**, and save it as *urs*Fundraiser.

2. Keep the file open for Project 1.

Week 1
$21.65
$25.89
$18.00
$11.87
$23.87
$33.45
$13.75
$22.55
$16.50

PROJECT 1 Continued

Practice

Edit Short Stories

5. Make the corrections shown in the illustration below.

DS

The Person I Most Admire

The person I most admire is Shawn. He is 19 years old, and I admire him because he is like a brother to me. He makes me feel good when I don't. He takes me to get an ice cream cone when I wash his car. He taught me how to do a flip on a wakeboard. When I finally made a flip, this summer he was so happy for me.

Then one day Shawn was in a ~~really bad~~ car accident. They took him to the hospital. He had a spinal concussion, and he couldn't move from the waist down. I was scared that Shawn would never walk again. I did not know what to do if he was always going to be in a wheelchair. We wouldn't be able to go get ice cream. We wouldn't be able to go wakeboarding. ¶The next day Shawn was able to move. I was so happy. For two weeks he could not move very much, but he got better every day. Now Shawn is able to walk again, and he is living a good life. He is going to College and has many new friends. He still takes me for icecream, and he is teaching me more wakeboarding tricks.

Change the **line spacing** to **double** by selecting all the text and using CTRL + 2. The default line spacing is single.

6. Save the changes. Close the file.

1. Open a new word processing document, and save it as *urs*Spreadsheet Formulas.

2. Discuss why formulas must begin with an equal sign (=).

3. Describe the four kinds of symbols used to create simple formulas.

4. Discuss why the cell location is used to create a formula.

5. Save the changes. Print and close the file.

	A	B	C	D
1	**Item**	**Quantity**	**Price**	**Amount**
2	pencils	5	$0.50	$2.50
3	pens	6	$1.45	$8.70
4	ruled paper	5	$0.95	$4.75
5	folders	6	$1.25	$7.50
6	spiral notebook	1	$8.50	$8.50
7	three-ring binders	5	$1.25	$6.25
8	**Total Amount Spent**			$38.20
9				
10	**Budgeted Amount**	$40.00		
11	**Difference from Budget**	$1.80		
12	**Percentage of Budget Spent**	95.50%		

Compare urs School Supplies with the illustration.

Reinforce

Proofread and Edit Documents

Your Turn

1. Open a new word processing document.

2. Key the story shown below. Make the corrections shown by the proofreaders' marks as you enter the text.

How Did Salt Get in the Ocean Water?

Have you ever wondered why ocean water is salty?
Well then, I shall tell you. The story I'm about to tell you has
been told for thousands of years. Once long ago, there was an
Old Man named Hazard. He was no ordinary old man because
he was over well sixty feet tall. Hazard said to the men and
women in the village, I shall fill all the oceans with salt. Hazard
found a mountain full of salt. He picked up the mountain and
carried it to the ocean. He turned the mountain upsidedown
and shook it like a salt shaker. The salt from the mountain
poured into the ocean and that is why ocean water is salty.

3. Save the document as *urs*Salt Water by using the F12 key.

4. Spell-check, proofread, and correct errors.

5. Print and close the file.

Reinforce

Create Formulas

In this project you will reinforce what you have learned by entering simple formulas in a spreadsheet to calculate the cost of school supplies.

Your Turn

1. Open the file **10-3 Project 5**, and save it as *urs***School Supplies**.

2. Create formulas to complete the budget shown below.

	A	B	C	D
1	**Item**	**Quantity**	**Price**	**Amount**
2	pencils	5	$0.50	
3	pens	6	$1.45	
4	ruled paper	3	$0.95	
5	folders	6	$1.25	
6	spiral notebook	1	$8.50	
7	three-ring binders	4	$1.25	
8	**Total Amount Spent**			
9				
10	**Budgeted Amount**	$40.00		
11	**Difference from Budget**			
12	**Percentage of Budget Spent**			
13				
14				

To figure the amount of each item, multiply the Quantity by the Price.

To figure the total amount spent on school supplies, add the prices in the Amount column.

To see if you spent within the budgeted amount, subtract the Total Amount Spent from the Budgeted Amount.

To see what percentage of the budget was spent, divide the Total Amount Spent by the Budgeted Amount.

3. You decided that you will need five, 3-ring binders and five packages of ruled paper. Change the quantity of each of those items to 5.

4. Save the changes. Print and close the file.

1. Open the file *urs*SaltWater.
2. Did you double-space the entire document?
3. Is the title of the story keyed in all-caps?
4. In the second sentence, did you insert a comma after the word "then"?
5. Did you make a new paragraph that begins with "Once long ago"?
6. Did you transpose the words "over" and "well"?
7. Check the third sentence in the second paragraph. It should read as follows:

   Hazard said to the people in the village, "I shall fill all the oceans with salt."

8. Did you insert a hyphen between "upside" and "down"?
9. Check the last sentence in the story. It should read as follows:

   That is why ocean water is salty.

10. Save any changes. Close the file.

*inter***NET**
CONNECTION

1. Open your Internet browser.
2. Type in the words **proofreaders' marks** in the Internet search box.
3. Locate a site that provides examples of proofreaders' marks.
4. Bookmark the site so you can easily return to this site in the future.

Enter a Division Formula

Another simple formula is dividing a cell value by another cell value. The symbol for division is the forward slash (/).

Your Turn

1. Open the file **10-3 Project 4**, and save it as *urs*Baseball.

2. Click in cell E2, and key the **formula** =c2/b2. Compare your spreadsheet with the illustration shown below.

SUM	▾	✕ ✓ =	=c2/b2

	A	B	C	D
1	**Player**	**At Bat**	**Hits**	**Batting Average**
2	Trammell	154	74	=c2/b2
3	Clark	220	182	
4	Abbott	176	115	
5	Gonzales	192	68	
6	Nguyen	238	169	

The formula =c2/b2 divides the value 74 in cell c2 by the value 154 in cell b2.

3. Press ENTER. The answer 0.481 appears. This means a player earned a hit 48% of the times he came to bat.

4. **Create formulas** to calculate the rest of the batting averages.

5. Save the changes. Print and close the file.

SECTION 4.2

Format and Edit Poems

GOALS: Demonstrate the ability to:

▶ Format paragraph alignment and fonts. ▶ Work from handwritten material.
▶ Use the thesaurus feature.

PROOFREADING WARMUP

In a word processing document, key each line 3 times.
Proofread your work.

```
It will help to put away worry and doubt about your skills.
The dozen extra blue jugs were quickly moved from the pool.
The number of items to remember to pick up is overwhelming.
```

Making the Connection

Practice formatting poetry by keying in the poem at right.

Your Turn

1. Open a new word processing document.

2. Key the poem *Dust of Snow* by Robert Frost.

3. Save the document as *urs*DustofSnow. Keep the file open for Project 1.

Dust of Snow
by Robert Frost

The way a crow
Shook down on me
The dust of snow
From a hemlock tree

Has given my heart
A change of mood
And saved some part
Of a day I had rued.

Double space

Single space

Format and Edit Poems ■ *Section 4.2* **64**

Practice

Enter a Multiplication Formula

5. Click in cell E2, and key the **formula** =b2−d2. Compare your spreadsheet with the illustration shown below.

	A	B	C	D	E
SUM		X ✓ =	=b2-d2		
1	Item	Price	% of Discount	$ of Discount	Sale Price
2	Shirt	$25.00	20%	$5.00	=b2-d2
3	Shorts	$32.00	15%		
4	Pants	$38.00	25%		
5	Shoes	$45.00	10%		

The formula =b2−d2 subtracts the value $5.00 in cell d2 from the value $25.00 in cell b2.

6. Press ENTER. The answer $20.00 appears.

7. **Create formulas** to calculate the rest of the Sale Price column.

8. Save the changes. Print and close the file.

Format Poems

You can change the font and alignment to make the poem more attractive. If you need additional help, use Function Key F1, the Help feature.

Your Turn

1. Format the poem as indicated.

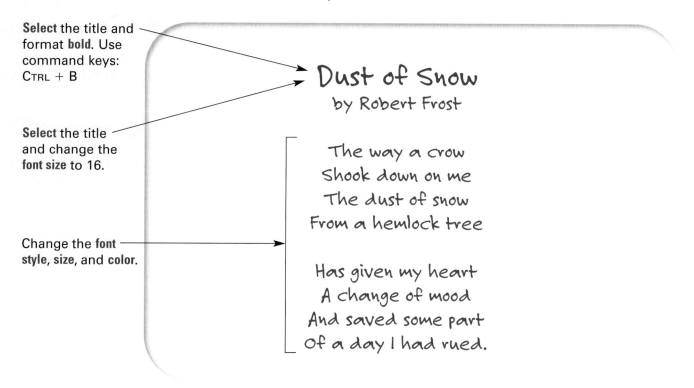

Select the title and format **bold**. Use command keys: CTRL + B

Select the title and change the **font size** to 16.

Change the **font style, size,** and **color**.

Dust of Snow
by Robert Frost

The way a crow
Shook down on me
The dust of snow
From a hemlock tree

Has given my heart
A change of mood
And saved some part
Of a day I had rued.

2. **Select** all the paragraphs. Apply **Center Alignment**.

3. Save the changes. Print and close the file.

Practice

Enter a Multiplication Formula

Another simple formula is multiplication of a cell value by another value. The mathematical sign for multiplication is the asterisk symbol (*).

Your Turn

1. Open the file **10-3 Project 3**, and save it as *urs*Sale.

2. Click in cell D2, and key the **formula** =b2*c2. Compare your spreadsheet with the illustration shown below.

SUM	▼	X	✓	=	=b2*c2		
	A	B	C		D		E
1	**Item**	**Price**	**% of Discount**		**$ of Discount**		**Sale Price**
2	Shirt	$25.00		20%	=b2*c2		
3	Shorts	$32.00		15%			
4	Pants	$38.00		25%			
5	Shoes	$45.00		10%			

The formula =b2*c2 multiplies the value $25.00 in cell b2 by the value 20% in cell c2.

3. Press ENTER. The answer $5.00 appears.

4. **Create formulas** to calculate the rest of the "$ of Discount" column.

Continued on next page

Practice

Use the Thesaurus

The thesaurus can be very helpful when writing poetry. The **thesaurus** is a word list stored in the software. You can use the thesaurus to find suggestions for synonyms.

Your Turn

1. Open a new word processing document.

2. Key the cinquain poem shown below.

> Puppy
> Frisky, cuddly
> Barking, running, sleeping
> She likes to chew my dad's slippers.
> Heidi

3. Apply **center alignment**. Select all lines and use command keys: CTRL + E.

4. Save the document as *urs*Puppy.

5. Use SHIFT + F7 to access the **thesaurus** feature to replace the word "frisky" with a synonym.

6. Save the changes. Print and close the file.

Practice

Enter a Subtraction Formula

Another simple formula is subtracting one cell value from another. The mathematical sign for subtraction is the minus sign ($-$).

	A	B
1		**Week 1**
2	**Income**	
3	mowed lawn	$15.00
4	baby-sat	$10.00
5	**Total**	$25.00
6		
7	**Expenses**	
8	movie rental	$4.00
9	game rental	$3.00
10	snacks	$1.50
11	**Total**	$8.50
12		
13	**Amount Left**	=b5-b11

Your Turn

1. Click in cell A13 and key Amount Left.

2. Click in cell B13 and key the **formula** =b5-b11. Compare your spreadsheet with the illustration shown at the left.

3. Press ENTER. The answer $16.50 appears.

4. Compare your paper calculation with the spreadsheet answer.

The formula =b5-b11 subtracts the value $8.50 in cell b11 from the value $25.00 in cell b5.

5. **Create a formula** to calculate the Amount Left for Weeks 2, 3, and 4 as shown below.

Subtract Expense Total from Income Total.

12		
13	**Amount Left**	$16.50

6. Oops! You just realized that you have a mistake. The cost of the game rental for Week 3 was $3.00 instead of $2.50. Change the amount in cell D9 to $3.00. Notice the Total Expenses and the Amount Left for Week 3 change.

7. Save the changes. Print and close the file.

Reinforce

Format Poems

Reinforce what you have learned about formatting poems and using the thesaurus feature.

Your Turn

1. Open the file **4-2 Project 3**, and format the poem as indicated.

Format all paragraphs with center alignment.

Copy and **Paste** the title below each verse. To copy use CTRL + C. To paste use CTRL + V.

What a Day! What a Day!

My cat Felix ran away,
And my dog Spot wouldn't obey.
And then much to my dismay,
My wave runner sunk in the bay.
What a Day! What a Day!

It seemed like things were not going my way.
So I decided to go to the park to play.
When I got to the park, the sky turned gray,
A tornado blew in and I ran home that day.
What a Day! What a Day!

Replace the words "tornado" and "friend" with synonyms.

Then just when I thought things were okay,
I talked to my best friend José.
We went to buy candy and he said I should pay.
What else could I say?
What a Day! What a Day!

Right align the author's name.

By Maria

2. Save the document as *urs*What a Day.

3. If desired, change the font style, font size, and/or font color.

4. Save the changes. Print and close the file.

Practice

Introduction to Formulas

5. Create a formula to add the rest of the Income and Expenses Totals for each week.

Format cells B3 through F11 with currency format.

	B5	▼	fx =B3+B4		
	A	B	C	D	E	F
1		Week 1	Week 2	Week 3	Week 4	Total
2	Income					
3	mowed lawn	$15.00	$15.00	$15.00	$15.00	
4	baby-sat	$10.00	$12.00	$8.00	$10.00	
5	Total	$25.00				
6						
7	Expenses					
8	movie rental	$4.00	$1.99	$4.00	$4.00	
9	game rental	$3.00	$3.00	$2.50	$3.00	
10	snacks	$1.50	$1.00	$2.35	$3.25	
11	Total					
12						

Add total amount for each week.

Add total amount for all four weeks.

6. Save the changes. Keep the spreadsheet open for Project 2.

Check Your Understanding

1. Open a new word processing document.
2. Key the following sentence: Alex was thankful that I helped format the poem.
3. Use the thesaurus feature to replace the word "poem."
4. Use the thesaurus feature to replace the word "thankful."
5. Describe how you would center all the paragraphs in a document at the same time.
6. Save the document as *urs*Poemcheck. Print and close the file.

*inter*NET
CONNECTION

1. Open your Web browser.
2. Key "cinquain" and use Google to locate a site that explains cinquain poems.
3. Bookmark the site so you can easily return to this site in the future.

Practice

Introduction to Formulas

To add, subtract, multiply, and divide, create a spreadsheet **formula**, which is a mathematical equation. All formulas must begin with an equal sign (=).

Your Turn

1. Open the file **10-3 Project 1**, and save it as *urs*Budget.

2. Click in cell B5, and key the formula =b3+b4. Compare your spreadsheet with the illustration shown below.

The **formula bar** displays the formula for the cell.

SUM	▾ ✕ ✓ *fx* =b3+b4				
	A	B	C	D	E	F
1		**Week 1**	**Week 2**	**Week 3**	**Week 4**	**Total**
2	**Income**					
3	mowed lawn	$15.00	$15.00	$15.00	$15.00	
4	baby-sat	$10.00	$12.00	$8.00	$10.00	
5	**Total**	=b3+b4				
6						

The formula =b3+b4 adds the value $15.00 in cell b3 and the value $10.00 in cell b4.

3. Press ENTER. The answer $25.00 appears.

4. Compare your paper calculation with the spreadsheet answer.

Continued on next page

Format a Journal Entry and Proof Text

GOALS: Demonstrate the ability to:

▶ Format a journal entry.
▶ Use the grammar check feature.

▶ Proofread text and correct errors.
▶ Compose at the keyboard.

PROOFREADING WARMUP

In a word processing document, key and complete the paragraph starter. Proofread your work.

```
When I am with my friends, I love to laugh. The things
that make me laugh are...
```

Making the Connection

A journal is a record of day-to-day activities. People write journal entries about their experiences, their ideas, and their feelings. You may have a special book where you write journal entries. Have you ever thought about using your word processor to create an electronic journal?

Your Turn

1. Open a new word processing document.

2. Key today's date at the top of the document. Press ENTER 2 times.

3. Key the paragraph to the right exactly as shown. Be sure to press TAB to indent the first line of text.

4. Save the document as *urs*Camp. Keep the file open for Project 1.

(Today's Date)
    Tomorrow I leave for camp. I am so excited, I had so much fun last year. I met a new friend Jesse. I hope Jesse will be their again this year.

Use Simple Formulas

GOALS: Demonstrate the ability to:

▶ Enter a simple formula to add.
▶ Enter a simple formula to subtract.

▶ Enter a simple formula to multiply.
▶ Enter a simple formula to divide.

PROOFREADING WARMUP

In a word processing document, key and complete the paragraph starter. Proofread your work.

```
If I won one million dollars, I would...
```

Making the Connection

Peter has been keeping a monthly budget plan on paper. When he needs to keep track of his money, he uses pencil, paper, and a calculator to figure it out.

Your Turn

1. Use a sheet of paper to calculate the amount of money Peter has left over each week.

Add total amount for each week. →

Subtract Expenses Total from Income Total.

	Week 1	Week 2	Week 3	Week 4	Total
Income					
mowed lawn	$15.00	$15.00	$15.00	$15.00	
baby-sat	$10.00	$12.00	$8.00	$10.00	
Total					
Expenses					
movie rental	$4.00	$1.99	$4.00	$4.00	
game rental	$3.00	$3.00	$2.50	$3.00	
snacks	$1.50	$1.00	$2.35	$3.25	
Total					
Amount left					

← Add total amount for all four weeks.

Practice

Format a Journal Entry and Proof Text

Typical errors in grammar include the following:

- Punctuation errors
- Misused words
- Sentence fragments
- Subject and verb agreement
- Capitalization errors

The journal entry you just keyed for document **ursCamp** contains three grammatical errors. Can you find the errors?

If your software has a **grammar check feature**, possible errors may be identified with a wavy line as shown in the illustration below. However, you should always proofread your work carefully. The grammar check feature isn't always correct.

Instead of a comma, the correct punctuation should be a period or a semicolon.

Tomorrow I leave for camp. I am so excited, I had so much fun last year. I met a new friend Jesse. I hope Jesse will be their again this year.

Insert a comma after friend.

The word "there" should be used instead of "their."

Your Turn

1. Make the corrections identified in the illustration above. If you see a wavy line, right-click the text and choose a suggested correction from the shortcut menu.

2. Save the changes. Print and close the file.

Check Your Understanding

1. Open a new word processing document, and save it as *urs*Spreadsheet Editing.
2. Describe when it would be necessary to change a column width.
3. Describe why ### symbols sometimes appear in a column.
4. Describe how to insert a column or row.
5. Describe how to delete a column or row.
6. Describe how to organize information alphabetically.
7. Save the changes. Print and close the file.

	A	B	C
1	**COUNTRY INFORMATION**		
2			
3	**Country**	**Capital**	**Population**
4			
5	Brazil	Brasilia	176,029,560
6	China	Beijing	1,284,303,705
7	Germany	Berlin	83,251,887
8	South Korea	Seoul	10,432,774
9	United States	Washington, D.C.	278,058,881
10	Vietnam	Hanoi	81,098,416

Compare urs*Country with the illustration.*

Reinforce

Format a Journal Entry

Reinforce what you have learned about formatting journal entries and proofreading text.

Your Turn

1. Open a new word processing document.

2. Key the journal entry exactly as shown below.

Today's Date

We one our basball game today. The score was 6 to 1.
I struck out in the first inning. I was so embarrassed! I did
better in the third inning. I got an hit and scored a run.
I was happy because Coach Ruez told me I did a good job.

---

3. The journal entry contains two grammatical errors. Proofread carefully and correct the errors. Use F7 to quickly access the spelling and grammar feature.

4. Save the document as *urs*Baseball. Print and close the file.

Create a Spreadsheet

5. Edit the spreadsheet as shown.

Insert 2 rows above "Country." Key the title shown. Format bold. Change the font size to 12 pt.

	A	B	C	D
1	**COUNTRY INFORMATION**			
2				
3	**Country**	**Area (sq. mi.)**	**Capital**	**Population**
4				
5	China	3,705,386	Beijing	1,284,303,705
6	Brazil	3,286,470	Brasilia	176,029,560
7	South Korea	38,450	Seoul	10,432,774
8	Germany	137,823	Berlin	83,251,887
9	United States	3,679,192	Washington, D.C.	278,058,881
10	Vietnam	127,243	Hanoi	81,098,416

Delete the column named "Area (sq. mi.)."

6. Use the sort feature to alphabetize the "Country" column as shown.

	A	B	C	D
1	**COUNTRY INFORMATION**			
2				
3	**Country**	**Capital**	**Population**	
4				
5	China	Beijing	1,284,303,705	
6	Brazil	Brasilia	176,029,560	
7	South Korea	Seoul	10,432,774	
8	Germany	Berlin	83,251,887	
9	United States	Washington, D.C.	278,058,881	
10	Vietnam	Hanoi	81,098,416	
11				

Sort the list in ascending order.

7. Save the changes. Print and close the file.

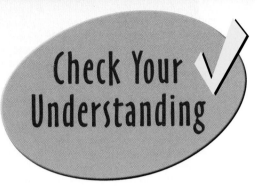

Check Your Understanding

1. Open a new word processing document.
2. Describe some of the errors that the grammar checker can find. Provide at least one example. Then describe some of the errors the grammar checker may not find. Provide at least one example.
3. Save your document as *urs*Grammar Check. Print and close the file.

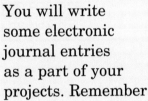

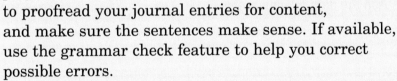

You will write some electronic journal entries as a part of your projects. Remember to proofread your journal entries for content, and make sure the sentences make sense. If available, use the grammar check feature to help you correct possible errors.

1. Open a new word processing document.
2. Key today's date.
3. Write a journal entry about your favorite movie. Explain why you like the movie. Provide some details.
4. Save the document as *urs*Journal.
5. Close the file.

Reinforce

Create a Spreadsheet

3. Edit the spreadsheet as shown in the illustration.

Insert one **row** above row 5 containing information about the country Germany.

Delete the row containing information about the country Czech Republic.

	A	B	C
1	**Country**	**Area (sq. mi.)**	**Population**
2			
3	China	3,705,386	1,284,303,705
4	Brazil	3,286,470	176,029,560
5	Germany	137,823	83,251,887
6	United States	3,679,192	278,058,881
7	Czech Republic	30,450	10,432,774

Insert a column before column C, "Population."

4. Add the data as indicated.

	A	B	C	D
1	**Country**	**Area (sq. mi.)**	**Capital**	**Population**
2				
3	China	3,705,386	Beijing	1,284,303,705
4	Brazil	3,286,470	Brasilia	176,029,560
5	South Korea	38,450	Seoul	10,432,774
6	Germany	137,823	Berlin	83,251,887
7	United States	3,679,192	Washington, D.C.	278,058,881
8	Vietnam	127,243	Hanoi	81,098,416

Key the information about South Korea and Vietnam.

Key the title "Capital." Format bold. Change the font size to 12 pt. Align center the title. Key the remaining data as shown.

Continued on next page

SECTION 4.4

Create and Format Tables

GOALS: Demonstrate the ability to:
- ▶ Create a new table.
- ▶ Add a new row at the end of a table.
- ▶ Format cell contents.
- ▶ Align cell contents.
- ▶ Work from handwritten material.
- ▶ Proofread and make corrections to documents.

PROOFREADING WARMUP

In a word processing document, key each line 3 times.
Proofread your work.

```
You can learn to type at a fast speed if you will practice.
Olmec, Zapotec, Mixtec, and Aztec were early civilizations.
The homework for math class was problems 45-49 on page 549.
```

Making the Connection

An effective way to organize data is to use a table. You will learn how to create and format a table.

Your Turn

1. Open a new word processing document.

2. Key and center the title Effects on Litmus Paper.

3. Press ENTER 2 times. Press CTRL + L to left align.

4. Save the document as *urs*Acid or Base.

5. Keep the file open for Project 1.

Effects on Litmus Paper

R**e**inf**o**r**c**e

Create a Spreadsheet

In this project you will reinforce what you have learned by creating and editing a spreadsheet about the area, population, and capital cities of several countries.

Your Turn

1. Open a **new** spreadsheet **file**, and save as *urs*Country.

2. Key and format the information shown.

Click and drag the column boundaries to **change** the **column width** so the cell with the most data fits.

Align center the headings, format bold, and change the font size to 12 pt.

	A	B	C
1	Country	Area (sq. mi.)	Population
2			
3	China	3,705,386	1,284,303,705
4	Brazil	3,286,470	176,029,560
5	Germany	137,823	83,251,887
6	United States	3,679,192	278,058,881
7	Czech Republic	30,450	10,432,774

Format the numbers to separate the thousands with a comma.

Continued on next page

Practice

Create a Table

The table feature makes creating a table quick and easy. A **table** contains rows and columns. The intersection of each column and row creates a **cell**. You enter data within the cells.

Row→   Column   Cell

Your Turn

1. Make sure your document is open from Making the Connection. Position the insertion point below the title.

2. **Create a table** with 4 columns and 6 rows.

3. The insertion point should be positioned in the first cell. Key the data shown below. Press TAB to move from cell to cell.

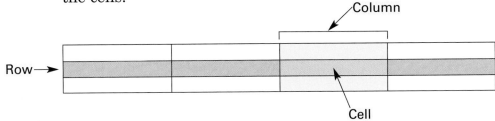

Substance Tested	Blue	Red	No Change
Lemon juice		X	
Ammonia	X		
Baking soda	X		
Vinegar		X	
Table salt			X

← Press TAB to create a new row.

4. You need to add one more row of data. Position the insertion point in the last cell in the last row and press TAB. Key **Cola** in the first cell and then key an X in the Red column.

5. Save the changes. Print and close the file.

Sort a List of Data

You can **sort** your data in a spreadsheet either alphabetically or numerically. This is helpful when you want to organize your information.

Your Turn

1. Select cells A4 through B13 as shown.

2. Sort in ascending order the "Length of Life" column.

Sort the list in ascending order. →

	A	B
1	**My Research**	
2		
3	**Length of Life**	**Years**
4	Blue jay	4
5	Canada goose	32
6	Penguin	26
7	Raven	25
8	Ostrich	50
9	Whale	20
10	Alligator	56
11	Crocodile	13
12	Bullfrog	15
13	Rattlesnake	18

3. Save the changes. Print and close the file.

Practice

Format a Table

You can format text in a table just as you would format any other text in your document. Your word processor may have a feature that enables you to automatically adjust the column widths. If you do not want the table cell borders to show, you can remove them.

Your Turn

1. Open a new word processing document.

2. Key the title OCEAN DATA. (Leave the title formatted for left alignment.)

3. Press ENTER 2 times.

4. Create the table with 3 columns and 6 rows. Apply the formats indicated.

Bold the column headings.

Leave this row blank.

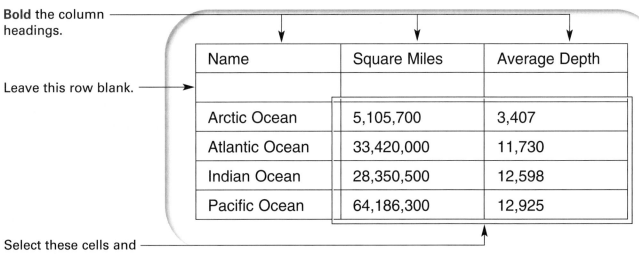

Name	Square Miles	Average Depth
Arctic Ocean	5,105,700	3,407
Atlantic Ocean	33,420,000	11,730
Indian Ocean	28,350,500	12,598
Pacific Ocean	64,186,300	12,925

Select these cells and format **right alignment** by using CTRL + R.

5. Save the document as *urs*Ocean Data.

6. **Fit** the table to adjust for the contents in the table.

7. **Remove** the **table borders** so that the borders do not show.

8. Save the changes. Print and close the file.

Insert and Delete Columns and Rows

3. Add the data as indicated.

	A	B	C
1	**Length of Life**	**Years**	**Months**
2	Blue jay	4	48
3	Canada goose	32	384
4	Penguin	26	312
5	Raven	25	300
6	Ostrich	50	600
7	Whale	20	240
8	Alligator	56	672
9	Crocodile	13	156
10	Bullfrog	15	180
11	Rattlesnake	18	216

Key the title "Years." Format bold. Change the font size to 12 pt., and align center. Enter the data shown.

Key the information about the ostrich.

4. Edit the spreadsheet as shown.

	A	B	C
1	**My Research**		
2			
3	**Length of Life**	**Years**	**Months**
4	Blue jay	4	48
5	Canada goose	32	384
6	Penguin	26	312
7	Raven	25	300
8	Ostrich	50	600
9	Whale	20	240
10	Alligator	56	672
11	Crocodile	13	156
12	Bullfrog	15	180
13	Rattlesnake	18	216

Insert 2 rows above "Length of Life." Key the title shown. Format bold. Change the font size to 12 pt.

Delete the column named "Months."

5. Save the changes. Keep the file open for Project 3.

Create Tables

Reinforce what you have learned about creating and formatting tables. Suppose your club is selling concessions at the game tonight and you have volunteered to create a price list for the items you will sell.

Your Turn

1. Open a new word processing document.

2. Create and format the table shown below.

Select all the table cells. Change the **font style** and **font size** to make the text as large as possible—and still fit all the text on one page.

Format **bold** and **center align** the column headings. To center align select column headings and press CTRL + E.

Item	Price
Popcorn	$1.50
Hot dogs	$1.50
Nachos	$1.50
Giant pretzels	$2.00
Fruit	$.75
Small drink	$1.25
Large drink	$2.00
Bottled water	$1.50
Candy bars	$.75
Ice cream	$1.25

Right align the *Price* column.

Remove the **table borders.**

3. Save the document as *urs*Concessions.

4. Print and close the file.

Practice

Insert and Delete Columns and Rows

You can delete a row or column to remove data you no longer want in your spreadsheet. You can also add a row or column to insert additional data.

Your Turn

1. Open the file **10-2 Project 2**, and save it as *urs*Animals.

2. Edit the spreadsheet as indicated.

Insert a column before column B "Months."

Insert one row above row 6 about the whale.

Delete the row containing information about the gila monster.

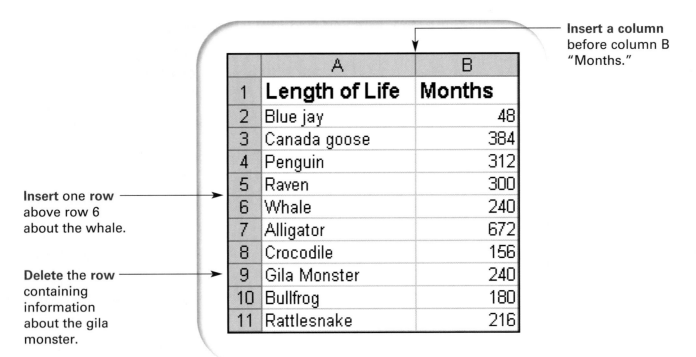

	A	B
1	**Length of Life**	**Months**
2	Blue jay	48
3	Canada goose	384
4	Penguin	312
5	Raven	300
6	Whale	240
7	Alligator	672
8	Crocodile	156
9	Gila Monster	240
10	Bullfrog	180
11	Rattlesnake	216

Continued on next page

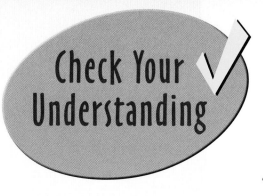

1. In Project 1, did you key each X in the correct column? Each X indicates the results of your lab activity. Compare your word processing document with the notes page shown in Project 1 to check for accuracy. If necessary, open Project 1 to make corrections. Save the changes.

2. In Project 2, did you key the values for square miles and average depth? It is easy to make mistakes when keying numbers. Have a partner help you check for accuracy. One partner reads the number while the other partner checks the document. If necessary, open Project 2 to make any corrections. Save the changes.

3. In Project 3, did you enter the correct price for each item? Use a ruler or something with a straight edge to help guide your eyes; then compare each line in the document with the handwritten copy. If necessary, open Project 3 to make any corrections. Save the changes.

inter**NET** CONNECTION

You will find the table feature useful when you are researching and gathering data from the Internet. You can create a table quickly, and the table format will help you organize the information.

1. Open a new word processing document and create the table shown below.

Which time zone is:	Name the time zone
Boston, MA	
Pittsburgh, PA	
Atlanta, GA	
Cincinnati, OH	
San Diego, CA	

2. Save the document as *urs*TimeZone.

3. Open your Web browser and log onto http://www.time.gov where you can obtain information about times for cities in the United States.

4. Enter the data in the table.

5. Notice the clock on your computer screen. Is it accurate?

6. Save the changes. Print and close the file.

Continued on next page

Create a New Spreadsheet and Change Column Width

	A	B	C
1	Region	Population	
2			
3	Asia	3674863000	
4	Africa	778997999	
5	Europe	732855000	
6	North America	483211000	
7	South America	342841000	
8	Australia/Oceania	31643000	
9	Antarctica	0	
10			

4. Enter the Population data. Make the changes indicated.

Align center the headings, format bold, and change the font size to 12 pt.

Format the numbers to separate the thousands with a comma.

	A	B	C
1	**Region**	**Population**	
2			
3	Asia	############	
4	Africa	778,997,999	
5	Europe	732,855,000	
6	North America	483,211,000	
7	South America	342,841,000	
8	Australia/Oceania	31,643,000	
9	Antarctica	0	
10			

5. If necessary, widen the column borders as shown.

Change the **column width** to remove the number symbols and display the data.

6. Save the changes. Print and close the file.

4. Check Projects 2 and 3 to make sure you applied the text formats and alignments that are indicated in the directions. Save the changes. Reprint, if necessary. Close all files.

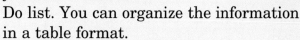

Write On!

The table feature can be useful for recording your journal entries. For example, suppose you want to create a To Do list. You can organize the information in a table format.

1. Open *urs*Journal, and position the insertion point at the end of the document. Key today's date, and press ENTER to create a new journal entry.

2. Write an opening sentence about things you need to get done.

3. Create a two-column table. In the first column, list the things you need to do, such as homework or study for a test.

4. In the second column of the table, list the due dates for each item.

5. Save the changes to your journal. Close the file.

Practice

Create a New Spreadsheet and Change Column Width

Create a new spreadsheet to enter data. You can easily adjust column widths to display the data.

Your Turn

1. Open a **new** spreadsheet **file**, and save as *urs*Population.

2. Key the column headings as shown.

	A	B	C
1	Region	Population	
2			
3			

3. Enter each Region, and change the column border as shown.

	A	B	C
1	Region	Population	
2			
3	Asia		
4	Africa		
5	Europe		
6	North America		
7	South America		
8	Australia/Oceania		
9	Antarctica		
10			

Click and drag the column boundary to **change** the **column width** so the cell with the most data fits.

Continued on next page

Format Outlines

GOALS: Demonstrate the ability to:

▶ Identify the parts of an outline.

▶ Key an outline from handwritten, unarranged copy.

▶ Use the alignment and outline features.

▶ Create an outline.

PROOFREADING WARMUP

In a word processing document, key and complete the paragraph starter. Proofread your work.

```
By the time I am 30 years old, I want to
accomplish 5 things:
```

Making the Connection

An outline is a list of main topics (major points) and subtopics (minor points) for a given subject. Indenting the points that are less important makes an outline clear and easy to follow.

Your Turn

1. Open a new word processing document.

2. Key the title (first line) and the list of topics exactly as shown on the right, including capitalization.

3. Save the Document as *ursOcean Water*. Keep the file open for Project 1.

OCEAN WATER AND LIFE

WAVES AND TIDES
Waves
How waves move
How waves form
Tides
The gravitational pull of the moon
Spring and neap tides
Life in the intertidal zone
OCEAN CURRENTS
Definition of currents
Upwellings

SECTION 10.2

Create and Edit a Spreadsheet

GOALS: Demonstrate the ability to:

▶ Create a new spreadsheet.
▶ Change column widths.
▶ Insert rows and columns.
▶ Delete rows and columns.
▶ Sort data.

PROOFREADING WARMUP

In a word processing document, key each line 3 times.
Proofread your work.

Elaine invited several of her friends over for the evening.
Why would quick brown foxes want to jump over any lazy dog?
Rather than go any farther, they stopped to get directions.

Making the Connection

Ingrid would like to create an attractive spreadsheet to display her research about world populations.

Your Turn

1. Think of some ways Ingrid might organize the data in a spreadsheet.
2. Share your answers with a partner.
3. Launch your spreadsheet software for Project 1.

Region	Population
Asia	3,674,863,000
Africa	778,997,999
Europe	732,855,000
North America	438,211,000
South America	342,841,000
Australia/Oceania	31,643,000
Antarctica	0

Format Outlines

An **outline** begins with a title describing the subject of the outline. The main topics are the major points of the outline, and the subtopics are the minor points. You will continue creating the outline you began in Making the Connection, using the file ***urs*Ocean Water**.

Your Turn

1. Indent and edit the list of topics as shown below.

Center the title, change the **font size** to 20 pt. and apply the **bold** format.

Level One Heading

Level Two Heading
To indent, position the insertion point at the beginning of the line of text and press TAB 1 time.

Level Three Heading
To indent, position the insertion point at the beginning of the line of text and press TAB 2 times.

OCEAN WATER AND LIFE

WAVES AND TIDES
Waves
    How waves move
    How waves form
Tides
    The gravitational pull of the moon
    Spring and neap tides
Life in the intertidal zone
OCEAN CURRENTS
Definition of currents
Upwellings

Continued on next page

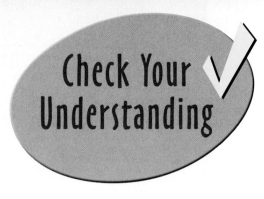

Check Your Understanding

1. Open a new word processing document, and save it as *urs*Spreadsheet Parts.
2. Describe the difference between a row and a column.
3. Describe what cell D4 stands for.
4. Describe ways you can move to each cell and enter data.
5. Discuss the benefits of formatting data with commas.
6. Save the changes. Print and close the file.

	A	B	C	D
1	**River**	**Continent**	**Miles (Approx.)**	**Kilometers (Approx.)**
2				
3	*Nile*	Africa	4,160	6,693
4	*Amazon*	South America	4,000	6,436
5	*Yangtze*	Asia	3,964	6,378
6	*Mississippi*	North America	3,740	6,017
7	*Yenisei-Angara*	Asia	2,543	4,091
8				

Compare urs*Rivers with the illustration.*

Format Outlines

2. Apply the **outline numbered list** feature. Choose an appropriate outline style. Your document should look similar to the one shown below, but your outline number style may differ.

OCEAN WATER AND LIFE

I. WAVES AND TIDES
   A. *Waves*
      1. How waves move
      2. How waves form
   B. *Tides*
      1. The gravitational pull of the moon
      2. Spring and neap tides
   C. *Life in the intertidal zone*
II. OCEAN CURRENTS
   A. *Definition of currents*
   B. *Surface currents*
   C. *Density currents*
   D. *Upwellings*

3. Add new topics to the outline:
   a. Position the insertion point at the end of the level two heading "Definition of currents."
   b. Press ENTER. A new paragraph formatted for a level two heading is inserted.
   c. Key **Surface currents** and press ENTER.
   d. Key **Density currents**.

4. Save the changes. Print and close the file.

Edit and Format Data

Select the column headings. **Align center** and format in **bold**. Change the **font size** to 12 pt.

3. Format the data as indicated so your spreadsheet will look like the one illustrated.

	A	B	C	D
1	**River**	**Continent**	**Miles (Approx.)**	**Kilometers (Approx.)**
2				
3	*Nile*	Africa	4,145	6,669
4	*Amazon*	South America	4,000	6,436
5	*Yangtze*	Asia	3,964	6,378
6	*Mississippi*	North America	3,740	6,017
7	*Yenisei-Angara*	Asia	3,442	5,538
8				

Select the names of rivers. Format in **italic**. Change the **font size** to 11 pt.

Select all the **cells** containing numbers. Format the numbers to **separate the thousands with a comma.**

4. Edit the additional spreadsheet data as follows:
 a. Change cell C3 to **4160**.
 b. Change cell D3 to **6693**.
 c. Change cell C7 to **2543**.
 d. Change cell D7 to **4091**.

5. Save the changes. Print and close the file.

Create an Outline

Your Turn

1. Open a new word processing document.

2. Key the outline illustrated below.

THE HUMAN BODY

BLOOD: THE TRANSPORTER OF LIFE
    Blood
        Blood composition
        Movement of blood
        Plasma
    The Functions of Blood
    Plasma
    Constant Flow
        Red blood cells
BLOOD: THE BODY'S DEFENSE
    Sealing the Leaks
    Natural Defense
    Specific Defenses
        Active immunity
        Vaccines
        Passive immunity
    Communicable Diseases

3. Apply the outline numbered list feature. Choose an appropriate outline style.

4. Save the document as *urs*Human Body.

5. Position the insertion point after the level three heading "Red blood cells." Press ENTER and key the level three headings:

    Hemoglobin
    White blood cells
    Platelets

6. Save the changes. Print and close the file.

Edit and Format Data

In this project you will reinforce what you have learned by editing and formatting a spreadsheet.

Your Turn

1. Open the file **10-1 Project 3**, and save it as *urs*Rivers.

2. Use the TAB key or arrow keys to move to each cell, and enter the data shown.

	A	B	C	D
1	River	Continent	Miles (Approx.)	Kilometers (Approx.)
2				
3	Nile	Africa	4145	6669
4	Amazon	South America	4000	6436
5	Yangtze	Asia	3964	6378
6	Mississippi	North America	3740	6017
7	Yenisei-Angara	Asia	3442	5538
8				

Continued on next page

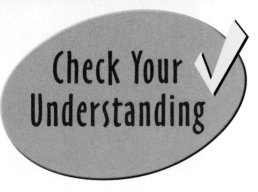

Check Your Understanding

1. Open a new word processing document.
2. In your own words, describe the steps for creating an outline numbered list. Be sure to include directions on how to distinguish the heading levels in the outline.
3. Save the document as *urs*Outlinecheck. Print and close the file.

◆ Contact Us!
◆ Home Page
◆ Products
  ❖ Orders
  ❖ Samples
◆ Service
  ❖ Customer Support
  ❖ Technical Support
  ❖ Downloads
  ❖ Frequently Asked Questions
◆ Awards

*inter*NET CONNECTION

Many Web sites include a link to a site map. Notice the topics in the site map listed.

In your Internet browser's address box, key the URL address: http://www.Learnthenet.com.

Are the Web site topics displayed in an outline format?

Practice

Edit and Format Data

You can change the way information is displayed in a cell by formatting the data. Information can be quickly and easily edited.

Select the column headings. **Align center** and format in **bold**. Change the **font size** to 12 pt.

Your Turn

1. Format the data as indicated so your spreadsheet will look like the one illustrated.

	A	B	C	D	E	F
1	**Country**	**East**	**Midwest**	**South**	**West**	
2						
3	*Argentina*	9,498	1,046	15,266	35,855	
4	*Honduras*	4,233	789	28,754	21,743	
5	*India*	15,940	5,821	8,474	12,840	
6	*Mexico*	14,833	52,830	229,731	718,992	
7	*Philippines*	10,583	3,581	1,947	16,884	
8						

Select the names of countries. Format in **italic**.

Select all the **cells** containing numbers. Format the numbers to **separate the thousands with a comma.**

2. **Select** cell B5, and key the new data 14,875.

3. Edit the additional spreadsheet data as follows:

a. Change cell D4 to **33,018**.

b. Change cell D7 to **2,196**.

c. Change cell C3 to **2,742**.

d. Change cell E6 to **802,451**.

4. Save the changes. Print and close the file.

APPLY

Review Word Processing

You will apply the skills you have learned to create and format a document about bike trails.

Your Turn

1. Use CTRL + O to open the file **Sec4Review**, and save it as *urs***Bike Trails**.

2. Edit and format the following document:

<u>**Bike Trails**</u>

We hope you enjoy the bike trails in our park ~~at any time.~~ All trails are open from ~~5~~ A.M. to 10 P.M. No *motorized* vehicles are permitted on the trails. For the safety of all, please obey the following rules.

Stay on the trail.
Keep to the right.
Wear protective head gear.

The park has bike trails for all ages and skill levels. The following information will help you choose a trail:

Create and format the table as shown. Remove the table borders.

Trail Name	Length of Trail	Trail Surface	Level of Difficulty
Cake Walk	6.2 miles	Paved	Easy
Mohican Trail	4.3 miles	Dirt	Easy
Tango	7.9 miles	Dirt	Moderate
Scorpion	12.8 miles	Paved	Moderate
Logger's Revenge	15.5 miles	Dirt	Challenging
Summit	7.6 miles	Dirt	Challenging

3. Spell-check, proofread, and correct errors.

4. Save the changes. Print and close the file.

Practice

Identify Spreadsheet Parts

3. Key the number **9498** in cell B3.

The number you enter in the cell appears in the bar.

B3	▼	f_x 9498		
	A	B	C	D	E
1	Country	East	Midwest	South	West
2					
3	Argentina	9498			
4	Honduras				
5	India				
6	Mexico				
7	Philippines				

4. Use the TAB key or arrow keys to move to each cell.

5. Enter the remaining data shown.

	A	B	C	D	E	F
1	Country	East	Midwest	South	West	
2						
3	Argentina	9498	1046	15266	35855	
4	Honduras	4233	789	28754	21743	
5	India	15940	5821	8474	12840	
6	Mexico	14833	52830	229731	718992	
7	Philippines	10583	3581	1947	16884	
8						

6. Save the changes. Keep the spreadsheet open for Project 2.

ENRiCh

Curriculum Portfolio

Use the word processing skills you have learned to create your curriculum portfolio project. Choose from creating an outline, creating a table, or writing a descriptive paragraph.

If you choose to create an outline, each list contains three outline levels. The lists contain outline subtopics and supporting details. The headings are in the correct sequence for an outline.

Note: The outlines have three outline levels, and the subject for each outline is indicated above the list. Do not include the subject in the outline level headings.

SOCIAL STUDIES:

Create a table about state facts.

Pick five states you would like to know more about. Look up the information about the state flag, bird, motto, song, tree, and flower. Create a table to organize the data. Format the text in the table with appropriate headings and borders.

Continued on next page

Practice

Identify Spreadsheet Parts

Software programs with **spreadsheets** help you manage and store numbers and text. Rows and columns are used to organize information. Each column is identified by a letter such as A, B, or C. Each row is identified by a number such as 1, 2, or 3. When a column and row form a rectangle, it is called a **cell**.

Your Turn

1. Use the illustration to help you identify the parts of the spreadsheet.

2. Click in cell B3 to **select** the **cell**.

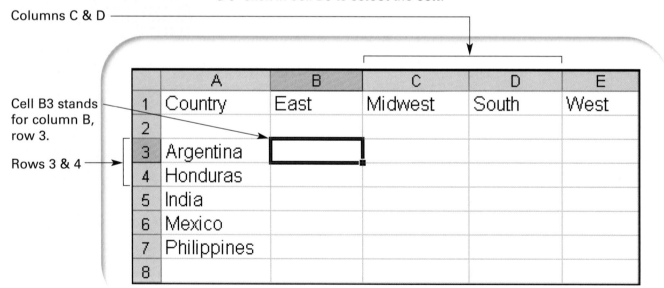

Columns C & D

Cell B3 stands for column B, row 3.

Rows 3 & 4

	A	B	C	D	E
1	Country	East	Midwest	South	West
2					
3	Argentina				
4	Honduras				
5	India				
6	Mexico				
7	Philippines				
8					

Continued on next page

ENRICH

Curriculum Portfolio

MATH:

Create an outline using the following title and list of topics:

COMMON WEIGHTS AND MEASURES

units of measure
weight and mass
pounds
ounces
grams
distance and length
miles
yards
feet
inches
time
days
hours
minutes
seconds
metric equivalents
meters
kilograms

LANGUAGE ARTS:

Write a descriptive paragraph.

You may have visited oceans, lakes, and rivers. Write a descriptive paragraph of your impressions of time spent by the water. Use a thesaurus to help you choose words that create a vivid picture.

SCIENCE:

Create an outline using the following title and list of topics:

ENVIRONMENT
water
sources
lakes
streams
oceans
uses
keeps living creatures
   alive
helps plants grow
produces energy
air
global warming
the ozone layer
air quality

Spreadsheet Basics

GOALS: Demonstrate the ability to:

- ▶ Identify spreadsheet parts.
- ▶ Enter data.
- ▶ Select cells.
- ▶ Format and edit data.

PROOFREADING WARMUP

In a word processing document, key each line 3 times. Proofread your work.

```
We are planning to have a cookout when we meet at the lake.
All four mixtures in the deep brown jug froze very quickly.
We usually vacation at a place that is south of the border.
```

Making the Connection

Mark researched United States immigration data for his history fair project. He would like to organize his information so it is easier to read.

Your Turn

1. Open the file **10-1 Project 1** from your spreadsheet software and save it as *urs*Immigration.

2. Keep the spreadsheet open for Project 1.

Country	East	Midwest	South	West
Argentina	9498	1046	15266	35855
Honduras	4233	789	28754	21743
India	15940	5821	8474	12840
Mexico	14833	52830	229731	718992
Philippines	10583	3581	1947	16884

SECTION 5.1

Format a Personal Letter

GOALS: Demonstrate the ability to:

▶ Format a block-style letter.

▶ Format and print an envelope.

▶ Work from handwritten and printed material.

▶ Spell-check, proofread, and correct errors.

PROOFREADING WARMUP

In a word processing document, key each line 3 times.
Proofread your work.

```
Janet works after school four hours a day at the town bank.
Buzz quickly designed five new projects for the wax museum.
I waited for my best friend, and she was late getting here.
```

Making the Connection

You will learn how to key and format a personal letter. You have handwritten a letter to thank Mrs. Chavez for arranging a field trip for your class. Let's put your word processing skills to work.

Your Turn

1. Open a new word processing document.

2. Press ENTER 6 times and key the following:

3. 4112 Bay View Drive
San Jose, CA 95192
Today's Date

4. Save the document as *urs*Chavez Letter. Keep the file open for Project 1.

Good Keyboarding Habits

Focus on your neck.
To avoid neck strain:

- Looking slightly downward is better for your neck than constantly looking upward.

- Do not twist your neck too far right or left.

- Position your book next to the monitor and place it on a stand.

Practice

Format a Block-Style Letter

A personal letter is a printed message addressed to a person or an organization. The parts of the letter are identified in the illustration below. In the **block-style** format, all paragraphs are positioned at the left margin.

Your Turn

1. Key and format the personal letter shown below using block style.

Return Address
Address of the writer.

4112 Bay View Drive
San Jose, CA 95192

Date
Date the letter was written.

Today's Date

← Press ENTER 4 times.

Inside Address
Name and address of the person to whom you are writing.

Ms. Maria Chavez
1021 West Palm Blvd.
San Jose, CA 95192

Salutation
Usually the word *Dear* followed by the name of the person to whom you are writing.

Dear Mrs. Chavez:

Body
Text of the letter.

I wanted to thank you for taking our class on a field trip to the Mathematics, Engineering, and Science Achievement Program at San Jose State University. I know it is a lot of work to make all the arrangements for a trip like this, especially making sure that we are all safe, have enough to eat, and arrive everywhere on time.

Continued on next page

UNIT 7

Spreadsheets

GOALS:

▶ Demonstrate how to create, edit, and format a spreadsheet.

▶ Demonstrate how to calculate in a spreadsheet using simple formulas.

▶ Demonstrate how to calculate in a spreadsheet using function formulas.

▶ Demonstrate how to copy formulas.

▶ Demonstrate how to create a spreadsheet chart.

=SUM(B2:B10)

Format a Block-Style Letter

Body
Text of the letter.

I never thought about majoring in math and science in college, but now I think that is what I want to do. I really like the idea of being able to earn a scholarship to a MESA summer camp. I love spending time on my computer, and I want to try to compete for this scholarship.

The counselor said that part of the camp would be spent panning for gold in the American River! Maybe next year we can go to another great spot! Thank you again for opening up a whole new world to me.

Closing
Final words of the letter, followed by a comma.

Sincerely,

← Press ENTER 4 times.

Your Name

2. Identify the parts of a personal letter to be sure you have included each part.

3. Save the changes. Keep the file open for Project 2.

ENRICH

Curriculum Portfolio

MATH:

Create geometrical art.

Shapes are in everything around us. Using a digital camera, capture images of the following shapes that you can find in objects around your school.

a. Triangle
b. Hexagon
c. Trapezoid
d. Pentagon
e. Rectangle
f. Square
g. Octagon
h. Parallelogram
i. Quadrilateral
j. Diamond

Create a presentation to illustrate the shapes. Use the arrow draw tool to point to the shape in the photo.

LANGUAGE ARTS:

Create an autobiography.

An autobiography is the life story a person has written about himself or herself. Create an autobiography presentation to tell your life story. Include at least six of the following points about yourself in the presentation:

1. Your name and age (mandatory)
2. Where you were born
3. Where you grew up
4. Your interests
5. Your goals
6. A person or experience that influenced you
7. Interesting places to which you have traveled
8. Favorite sports or hobbies
9. Books you read and liked
10. How you spend your spare time

Format an Envelope

Your word processing software will help you create an envelope. Format a return address unless your envelope has a preprinted return address.

Your Turn

1. **Create** a size $6\frac{3}{4}$ **envelope** for the letter you completed in Project 1.

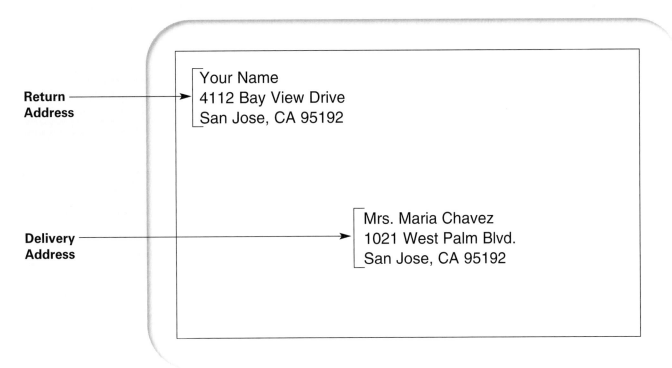

Return Address →

Your Name
4112 Bay View Drive
San Jose, CA 95192

Delivery Address →

Mrs. Maria Chavez
1021 West Palm Blvd.
San Jose, CA 95192

2. Print the envelope. Close the file.

COMPLETING UNIT 6

ENRICH

Curriculum Portfolio

Use the presentation skills you have learned to help you create your curriculum portfolio project. Choose from any of the following to help you illustrate your presentation:

a. Clip art
b. Scanned pictures
c. Digital photos
d. Sound/narration
e. Animation
f. Internet photos/images

Choose from one of the following topics:

SCIENCE:

Create a timeline.

Have you ever wondered who invented the Frisbee® Flying Discs or who invented blue jeans? Use the Internet to research about an invention. The invention can be from ancient times to the present. Create a timeline presentation of your findings. Be sure to cite your sources at the end of the presentation.

SOCIAL STUDIES:

Create a geography presentation.

Create a presentation about a country of your choice. You should illustrate and tell about the major cities, rivers, landforms, surrounding bodies of water, and any interesting geographical landmarks. Use the Internet to research the country you chose. Be sure to cite your sources at the end of the presentation.

Continued on next page

Reinforce

Format a Personal Letter With Envelope

Your Turn

1. Key and format the letter below in block-style as shown.

4112 Bay View Drive
San Jose, CA 95192
Today's Date

Mr. Ron Ashton
321 Park Avenue
San Jose, CA 95192

Dear Ron:

It was great meeting you during our class field trip to the Mathematics, Engineering, and Science Achievement Program at San Jose State University.

I am very interested in competing for the scholarship to the summer camp. Since the counselor said that we could have several people on the team, I was wondering if you would be interested in being on a team that I am organizing. There will be a total of four of us, and I think we would have a great chance at winning the scholarship.

Continued on next page

APPLY

Presentation Review

7. Use the Spelling feature to identify any errors; then correct them.

8. Apply an appropriate design template.

9. Change the slide layout, and choose appropriate clip art or photos as shown.

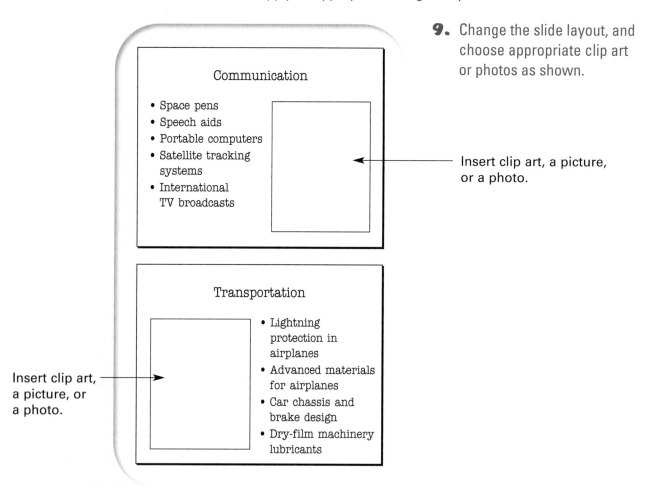

Communication

- Space pens
- Speech aids
- Portable computers
- Satellite tracking systems
- International TV broadcasts

Insert clip art, a picture, or a photo.

Transportation

- Lightning protection in airplanes
- Advanced materials for airplanes
- Car chassis and brake design
- Dry-film machinery lubricants

Insert clip art, a picture, or a photo.

10. Choose an animation and sound effect for each slide.

11. Change to Slide show view, and preview the presentation.

12. Save the changes. Print and close the file.

Format a Personal Letter With Envelope

If you are interested, please call me at 805-555-3496.
I am looking forward to hearing from you.

Your friend,

Your Name

2. Change the font style to give your letter a personal touch.

3. Save the document as *urs*Ron's Letter.

4. Spell-check, proofread, and correct errors. Save the changes.

5. Print the letter and envelope. Close the file.

Presentation Review

4. After Slide 7, add two new slides as shown.

```
Transportation

• Lightning protection in airplanes
• Advanced materials for airplanes
• Car chassis and brake design
• Dry-film machinery lubricants
```
Slide 8

```
General

• Shock-absorbing        • Polarized
  football helmets         sunglasses
• Ski boots              • Aerodynamic
• Fail-safe                golf balls
  flashlights            • Firefighter
• Joystick game            breathing systems
  controllers            • Bar coding
• Infrared cameras       • Thermal gloves
• Digital clocks           and boots
```
Slide 9

5. **Change** the **slide order** as follows:

a. Move Slide "Transportation" to come after Slide "Communication."

b. Move Slide "Home" to come after Slide "Food and Nutrition."

6. Edit Slide 3 as shown.

```
Types of Spin-Offs

• Communication
• Transportation      ←————————— Add text.
• Food–Nutrition
• Home                ←————————— Add text.
• Health–Medicine
• Home                ←————————— Delete text.
• General             ←————————— Add text.
```

Continued on next page

Check Your Understanding

1. Open a new word processing document.
2. List the parts of a personal letter.
3. What information is included in the salutation of a personal letter?
4. What information is included in the closing of a personal letter?
5. Describe the formatting for a block-style letter.
6. Save the document as *urs*Letter Parts. Print and close the file.

interNET CONNECTION

1. Open your Web browser and search for information on "spoken and written forms of address." Find the appropriate salutation you would use if you were to write a personal letter to the following individuals:
   - Governor of your state
   - President of the United States
   - Foreign ambassador
   - Judge
   - King or queen

2. Open a word processing document and create a two-column table. In the first column, key the names of the individuals listed above. In the second column, key the appropriate salutation for each.

3. Save the document as *urs*Salutation. Print and close the file.

APPLY

Presentation Review

3. Edit the slides as shown.

Communication

- Space pens
- Speech aids
- Portable computers
- Satellite tracking systems
- Satellite dishes ◄——————————— Add text.
- International TV broadcasts

Food–Nutrition

- Food additives
- Food packaging ◄——————————— Delete text.
- Heat-resistant substances
- Aluminum foil for preserving food
- Freeze-dried foods ◄——————————— Add text.
- Plastics for food and beverages

Home

- Home insulation materials
- Cordless tools
- Water purification systems
- Flat-panel televisions
- Wireless alarms ◄——————————— Delete text.
- Energy-saving air conditioners
- Safe sewage treatments

Continued on next page

SECTION 5.2

Format a Business Letter With Envelope

GOALS: Demonstrate the ability to:

▶ Format a business letter with letterhead.

▶ Format a return address and an enclosure notation.

▶ Key from printed copy.

▶ Spell-check, proofread, and correct errors.

▶ Compose at the keyboard.

PROOFREADING WARMUP

In a word processing document, key and complete the paragraph starter. Proofread your work.

```
My first day of school was one that I will never
forget. What made the greatest impact on
me was...
```

Making the Connection

A business letter should have a formal rather than a casual tone. You will learn to format a business letter. To dress up the letter and to make it more formal, you format it in a standard business-letter style.

Your Turn

1. Open the file **5-2 Project 1**. This file contains a formatted letterhead.

2. Save the file as *urs*Computer Donation Letter.

3. Keep the file open for Project 1.

LINCOLN MIDDLE SCHOOL

6021 Brobeck Street • Flint, MI 48532

Phone: 810-555-9001 • Fax: 810-555-9004

Presentation Review

Communication

- Space pens
- Speech aids
- Portable computers
- Satellite tracking systems
- International TV broadcasts

Slide 4

Food–Nutrition

- Food additives
- Food packaging
- Heat-resistant substances
- Aluminum foil for preserving food
- Plastics for food and beverages

Slide 5

Health–Medicine

- Programmable heart pacemaker
- EZ chair lift
- Digital image processing
- Cancer detection
- Invisible braces
- Ear thermometer
- Heart monitoring techniques
- Movable artificial limbs
- Lasers for eye and brain surgery
- Robotic surgery
- Computer reader for the blind

Slide 6

Home

- Home insulation materials
- Cordless tools
- Water purification systems
- Flat-panel televisions
- Wireless alarms
- Energy-saving air conditioners
- Safe sewage treatments

Slide 7

Continued on next page

Practice

Format a Business Letter in Block Style With Enclosure Notation

As you can see in the illustration below, a business letter has more parts than a personal letter.

Your Turn

1. The document you opened contains a preformatted letterhead.

2. Key and format the letter shown below.

Letterhead
The name, address, and other information about the sender.

LINCOLN MIDDLE SCHOOL
6021 Brobeck Street • Flint, MI 48532
Phone: 810-555-9001 • Fax: 810-555-9004

Date
Date the letter was written.

Today's Date

——————— Press ENTER 2–4 times.

——————— Press ENTER 4 times.

Inside Address
Name and address of the person to whom you are writing.

Mr. Anthony Martinez
Cyber Foundation
4092 Barnes Avenue
Burton, MI 48529

Salutation
Usually the word *Dear* followed by the name of the person to whom you are writing and a colon.

Dear Mr. Martinez:

Body
Text of the letter.

My friends and I at Lincoln School want to help your organization.

Our district is replacing our computers with new ones. Our computer technology teacher Mrs. Jones explained that your

Continued on next page

APPLY

Presentation Review

In this project, you will apply the skills you have learned to create a presentation. You will also edit slides and enhance the presentation with clip art and animations.

Your Turn

1. Open a **new presentation**, and create the slides as shown.

2. Save the presentation as *urs*Spin-Offs.

Spin-Offs From Space

Your name

Slide 1

What Are Spin-Offs?

- Technology originally developed for space
- Space technology adapted and used to make our lives better

Slide 2

Types of Spin-Offs

- Communication
- Food–Nutrition
- Health–Medicine
- Home

Slide 3

Continued on next page

Format a Business Letter in Block Style With Enclosure Notation

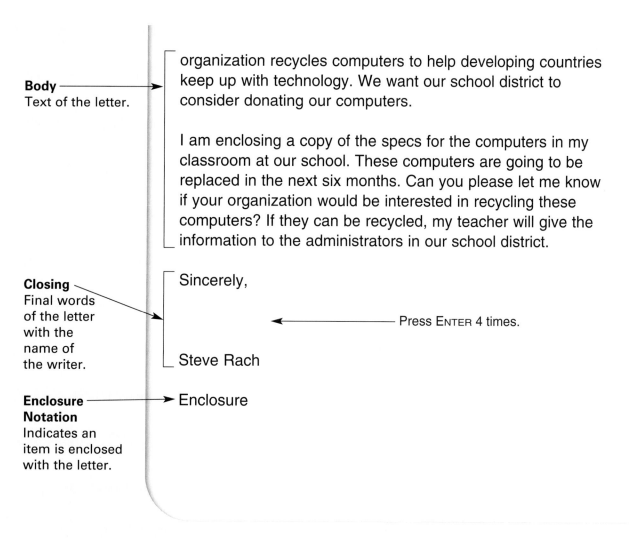

Body
Text of the letter.

organization recycles computers to help developing countries keep up with technology. We want our school district to consider donating our computers.

I am enclosing a copy of the specs for the computers in my classroom at our school. These computers are going to be replaced in the next six months. Can you please let me know if your organization would be interested in recycling these computers? If they can be recycled, my teacher will give the information to the administrators in our school district.

Closing
Final words of the letter with the name of the writer.

Sincerely,

← Press ENTER 4 times.

Steve Rach

Enclosure Notation
Indicates an item is enclosed with the letter.

Enclosure

3. Spell-check, proofread, and correct errors.

4. Save the changes to the file.

5. Print the file. Keep the file open for Project 2.

1. Open a new word processing document, and save it as *urs*Adding Animation.
2. Explain the purpose of adding animation and sound to a presentation.
3. Describe when you would want to change the animation order.
4. Save the changes. Print and close the file.

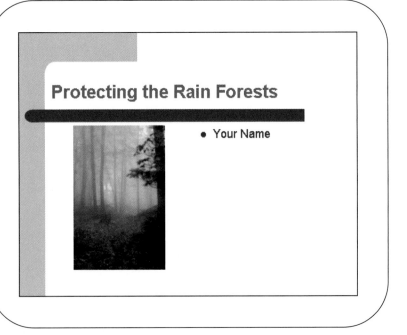

Protecting the Rain Forests

• Your Name

*inter*NET CONNECTION

1. Open one of your previous presentations ("Alexander the Great" or "Protecting the Rain Forests").
2. Explore the Clips Online and/or the Motion Clips feature of your software.
3. Look for additional clips and motion clips to enhance your presentation.
4. Add your new clips to one of the slides.
5. Save the changes, view the presentation, and close the file.

Format a Business Envelope

Your word processing software will help you create a business envelope. If your envelope has a preprinted return address, or if you plan to apply a preprinted return address label, you don't need to format a return address on the envelope.

Your Turn

1. Create a size 10 **envelope** for the letter you completed in Project 1.

Preprinted Return Address → LINCOLN MIDDLE SCHOOL
6021 Brobeck Street • Flint, MI 48532

Delivery Address →
Mr. Anthony Martinez
Cyber Foundation
4092 Barnes Avenue
Burton, MI 48529

2. Print the envelope. Close the file.

Animation

In this project you will reinforce what you have learned by adding animation to a presentation.

Your Turn

1. Open the file *urs*Rain Forest-Art you created in Section 9.3, and save it as *urs*Rain Forest-Animation.

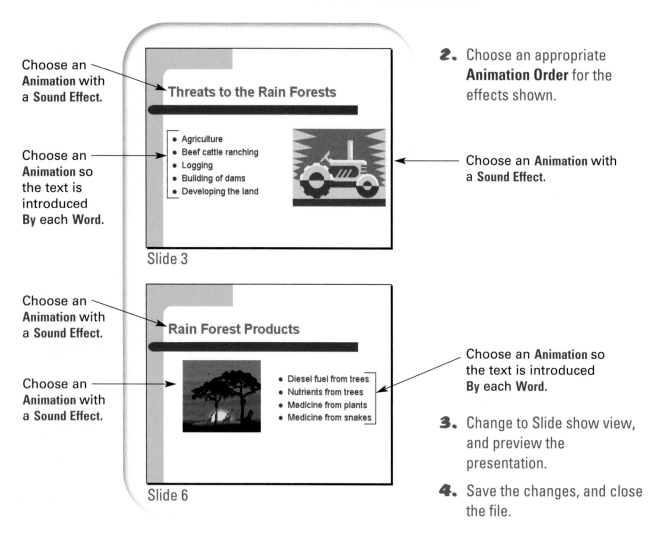

Choose an Animation with a Sound Effect.

Choose an Animation so the text is introduced By each Word.

Threats to the Rain Forests

- Agriculture
- Beef cattle ranching
- Logging
- Building of dams
- Developing the land

Slide 3

2. Choose an appropriate **Animation Order** for the effects shown.

Choose an **Animation** with a **Sound Effect.**

Choose an Animation with a Sound Effect.

Choose an Animation with a Sound Effect.

Rain Forest Products

- Diesel fuel from trees
- Nutrients from trees
- Medicine from plants
- Medicine from snakes

Slide 6

Choose an **Animation** so the text is introduced **By each Word.**

3. Change to Slide show view, and preview the presentation.

4. Save the changes, and close the file.

Practice

Format a Business Letter With a Return Address

If you are not printing your letter on letterhead stationery, you will want to include your mailing address at the top of the letter, just above the dateline. That way the person who receives the letter will know how to contact you.

Your Turn

1. Key and format the letter shown below using block style.

←————————— Press ENTER 6 times.

Route 14, Denman Road
Lexington, OH 44904
Today's Date

←————————— Press ENTER 4 times.

Mrs. Celia Wingler, Principal
East Elementary School
123 Yorkshire Road
Lexington, OH 44904

Dear Mrs. Wingler:

Hi, Mrs. Wingler. Maybe you remember me. I used to attend East Elementary.

Continued on next page

Practice

Add Sound and Change the Animation Order

You can add additional special effect animations to create more interest in your presentation.

Your Turn

1. Go to Slide 3 of the presentation, and choose an **Animation** for each part of the slide as shown.

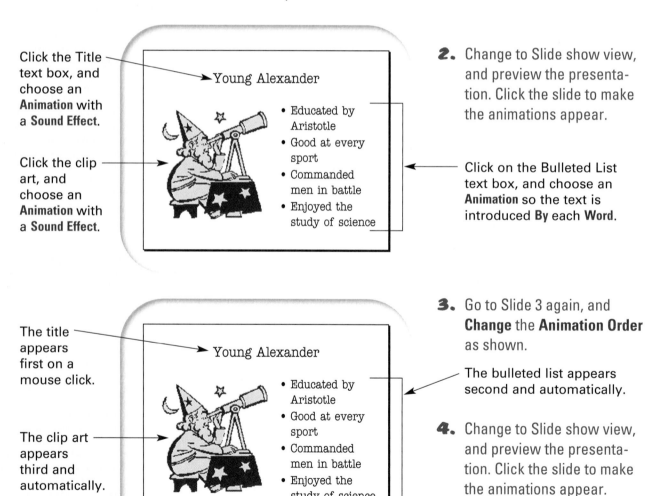

Click the Title text box, and choose an **Animation** with a **Sound Effect**.

Click the clip art, and choose an **Animation** with a **Sound Effect**.

Young Alexander

- Educated by Aristotle
- Good at every sport
- Commanded men in battle
- Enjoyed the study of science

2. Change to Slide show view, and preview the presentation. Click the slide to make the animations appear.

Click on the Bulleted List text box, and choose an **Animation** so the text is introduced **By** each **Word**.

The title appears first on a mouse click.

The clip art appears third and automatically.

Young Alexander

- Educated by Aristotle
- Good at every sport
- Commanded men in battle
- Enjoyed the study of science

3. Go to Slide 3 again, and **Change** the **Animation Order** as shown.

The bulleted list appears second and automatically.

4. Change to Slide show view, and preview the presentation. Click the slide to make the animations appear.

5. Save the changes, and close the file.

Format a Business Letter With a Return Address

I really enjoy working with small children, and I would like to volunteer at your school to work with kindergarten and first grade students. I can read to them and listen to them read. I can also help the teacher with activities in the classroom. I would also like to assist Mrs. Karnes in the media center if I can be of some help there.

I am available to help on Mondays and Wednesdays. My school day ends at 2:30 and I can be at your school by 2:45 p.m. That means I could be there for the last hour of your school day.

Please call me at 555-8807 and let me know if I may volunteer in one of your classrooms or in the media center.

Sincerely,

⟵———————— Press ENTER 4 times.

Caitie O'Neil

2. Identify the parts of a business letter to be sure you have included each part.

3. Save the document as *urs*Volunteer Letter.

4. Spell-check, proofread, and correct errors. Save the changes.

5. Print the letter and an envelope. Close the file.

Add Animation

You can animate any of the objects on your slides. **Animation** is how text and graphics appear on a slide.

Your Turn

1. Open the file ***urs*Alexander-C** you created in Section 9.3, and save it as ***urs*Alexander-Animation**.

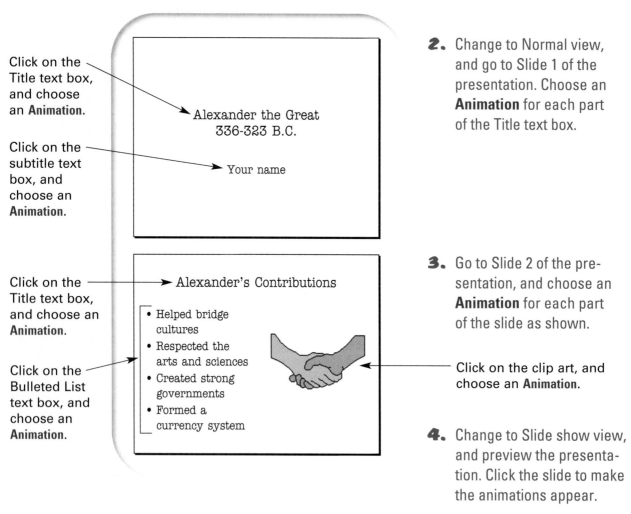

Click on the Title text box, and choose an **Animation**.

Click on the subtitle text box, and choose an **Animation**.

Alexander the Great
336-323 B.C.

Your name

Click on the Title text box, and choose an **Animation**.

Click on the Bulleted List text box, and choose an **Animation**.

Alexander's Contributions

- Helped bridge cultures
- Respected the arts and sciences
- Created strong governments
- Formed a currency system

Click on the clip art, and choose an **Animation**.

2. Change to Normal view, and go to Slide 1 of the presentation. Choose an **Animation** for each part of the Title text box.

3. Go to Slide 2 of the presentation, and choose an **Animation** for each part of the slide as shown.

4. Change to Slide show view, and preview the presentation. Click the slide to make the animations appear.

5. Save the changes, and keep the presentation open for Project 2.

Format a Business Letter With a Return Address

Reinforce the word processing features you learned by keying and formatting another business letter with a return address, an enclosure notation, and an envelope.

Your Turn

1. Open the file **5-2 Project 4**, and save the document as *urs***Complaint Letter**.

2. Edit the body of the letter using proofreaders' marks as shown.

Add the letter ────▶
parts shown.

5419 Mirra Loma Drive
Reno, NV 89502
Today's Date

Mainstream Music, Inc.
270 Clara Street
San Francisco, CA 94107

Ladies and Gentlemen:

About a month ago, I mailed you an order for a DVD movie package. I ordered DVD package #41-809 from page 5 of your catalog. The cost of the DVD package with shipping and handling was $47.35.

four weeks (inserted above "a month")
purchased (inserted below "ordered")
total (inserted below "cost")

Continued on next page

Add Animation

GOALS: Demonstrate the ability to:
▶ Add animation to slides.
▶ Add sounds.
▶ Change the animation order.

PROOFREADING WARMUP

In a word processing document, key each line 3 times.
Proofread your work.

```
A strong dollar makes it easier for interest to be lowered.
An aqueous liquid was used externally to prevent abscesses.
We bought seven pies and seven dozen cookies for the party.
```

Making the Connection

Are you familiar with the poet Shel Silverstein? One way you can find out about him is by reading the information on the jacket of one of his books.

Let's look at another way to learn about Shel Silverstein. Open the file **9-4 Project 1** and view the presentation about the poet Shel Silverstein. Think about your responses to the questions that follow.

Shel Silverstein

• Born in 1932
• Couldn't play ball
• Couldn't dance
• Liked to draw
• Liked to dance

Your Turn

1. When you viewed the presentation about Shel Silverstein, what held your attention?
2. What did you learn about Shel Silverstein?
3. Was the information interesting?
4. Is viewing the presentation more effective than reading the book jacket?
5. Which method helped you remember the information?
6. Close the presentation without saving.

Format a Business Letter With a Return Address

Today, I saw a package at my door, I was so excited that my ^order package had finally arrived. But I was really disappointed when I opened it and saw that you sent me the wrong DVDs.

I am returning the DVD package with this letter, and I am enclosing the order return form. I am asking for a full refund. ^of $47.35 And I also want to be reimbursed for the $5.00 it cost me to ship the DVD package back to you. ^Please send the refund to me at the above address.

Sincerely,

Martine Pico

Enclosure

Add the closing letter parts shown.

3. Identify the parts of a business letter to be sure you have included each part.

4. Spell-check, proofread, and correct errors.

5. Save the changes. Print the file.

6. Create and print an envelope. Be sure to include the return address on the envelope. Close the file.

Check Your Understanding

1. Open a new word processing document, and save it as *urs*Adding Art.
2. Describe when it would be necessary to change the slide layout.
3. Describe the purpose of adding clip art and pictures to a presentation.
4. Save the changes, print, and close the file.

*inter*NET CONNECTION

1. Open one of your previous presentations ("Alexander the Great" or "Protecting the Rain Forests").
2. Open your Web browser, and search for free clip art on the Internet.
3. When you find a free clip art site, look for additional clip art to enhance your presentation.
4. Add your new clip art to one of the slides.
5. Save the changes, view the presentation, and close the file.

Check Your Understanding

1. Open a new word processing document.
2. Describe how a business letter differs from a personal letter.
3. Describe the parts of a business letter that are different from those of a personal letter.
4. Explain why your return address is included at the top of a business letter.
5. Explain the purpose of an enclosure notation.
6. Save the document as *urs*Letterinfo. Print and close the file.

inter**NET** CONNECTION

In this lesson you learned to format a business letter to be mailed within the United States. What if your letter were to be mailed outside of the United States? What information would you need to include on the envelope? Would you need to format the envelope differently?

1. Open your Web browser and search for information on how to address envelopes for international addresses properly. Choose an international location.
2. Open a new word processing document and key an example of the inside address you would create for the letter. Then add any additional information that should be included on the envelope.
3. Save the document as *urs*International Addresses. Print and close the file.

Write On!

1. Open your journal and position the insertion point at the end of the document. Enter today's date to create a new journal entry.
2. Write at least one paragraph about a formal event that you have attended or wish you could attend (a wedding, an awards banquet, or a social event in your community). Describe how you would dress for the event and the proper etiquette that would be expected of you.
3. Save the changes to your journal. Close the file.

Reinforce

Add Clip Art and Pictures

Reinforce what you have learned by enhancing a presentation with clip art and pictures.

Your Turn

1. Open the file **_urs_Rain Forest-Edits**, and save it as **_urs_Rain Forest-Art**.

2. Change the slide layout; then choose an appropriate clip art layout as shown.

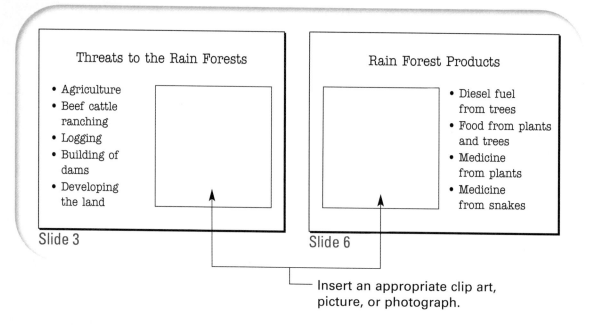

Threats to the Rain Forests

- Agriculture
- Beef cattle ranching
- Logging
- Building of dams
- Developing the land

Slide 3

Rain Forest Products

- Diesel fuel from trees
- Food from plants and trees
- Medicine from plants
- Medicine from snakes

Slide 6

Insert an appropriate clip art, picture, or photograph.

3. Save the changes, view the presentation, and close the file.

Format an E-Mail Message

GOALS: Demonstrate the ability to:

▶ Format an e-mail message.
▶ Attach a document to an e-mail message.
▶ Key from printed copy.

▶ Spell-check, proofread, and correct errors.
▶ Compose at the keyboard.

PROOFREADING WARMUP

In a word processing document, key each line 3 times.
Proofread your work.

```
Building typing skill seems easier if you type short words.
Maxine will become eloquent over a zany gift like jodhpurs.
Evi went to math, history, and art; but she missed English.
```

Making the Connection

Keith and his classmates correspond with pen pals regularly about a variety of topics. Generally, the pen pals communicate via e-mail, so they like to call themselves key pals! This month Keith is contacting his key pal to collect data so the class can compare the prices of pizza.

Your Turn

1. Open **5-3 Project 1**. Notice that the document contains a table for collecting data about the prices of pizza.

2. Close the file without making any changes.

From: [ ]

To: [J_Jaimeson@Hartland.k12.ak.us.edu]

Add Pictures and Clip Art

Pictures and photographs can also be used to communicate your message. Remember the picture you choose will likely be what your audience looks at first.

Your Turn

1. Change to Normal view, and go to Slide 3 of the presentation.

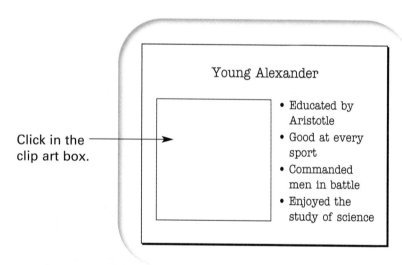

Click in the clip art box.

2. Choose the **Slide Layout** command; then choose an appropriate clip art and text layout as shown.

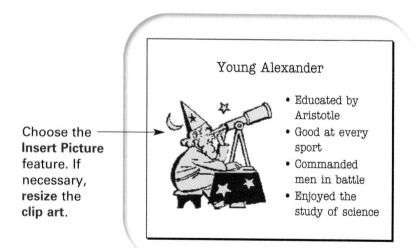

Choose the **Insert Picture** feature. If necessary, **resize the clip art**.

3. Search for an appropriate picture or photograph as shown.

4. Save the changes, view the presentation, and close the file.

Practice

Create an E-Mail Message With Attachment

Your e-mail format will vary depending on the e-mail software you are using. However, your e-mail header form will probably include all the parts illustrated below.

Your Turn

1. Create the **e-mail message** illustrated below. Note that you will probably not need to enter your e-mail address in the From: box.

Sender's e-mail address, filled in automatically.

Recipient's e-mail address. If message is to multiple recipients, separate by a semicolon or comma.

E-mail address of recipient(s) receiving a copy of message.

Descriptive name for the message.

Name of file sent with e-mail, filled in automatically when document is attached.

From:

To: J_Jaimeson@Hartland.k12.ak.us.edu

Copy:

Subject: Pizza Survey

Attach:

Hi, Joel. How's it going? Is it cold there in Alaska?

This month our math class is doing a survey on the prices of pizza. We want to see if there is a difference in pizza prices across the nation. It would really help us a lot if you would participate in this survey.

Continued on next page

Change the Slide Layout and Add Clip Art

You can add clip art to help make your presentation more interesting and entertaining. The clip art you choose should match your message.

Your Turn

1. Change to Normal view, and go to Slide 2 of the presentation.

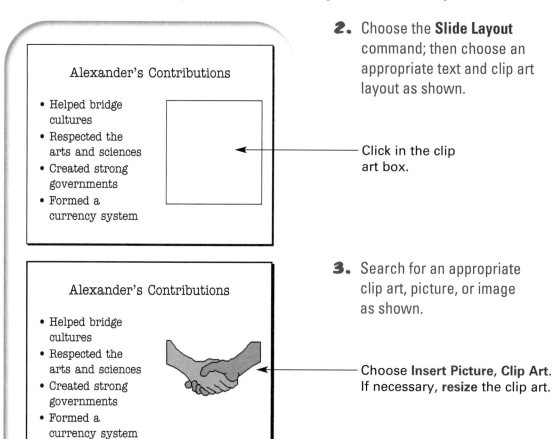

2. Choose the **Slide Layout** command; then choose an appropriate text and clip art layout as shown.

Click in the clip art box.

3. Search for an appropriate clip art, picture, or image as shown.

Choose **Insert Picture, Clip Art**. If necessary, **resize** the clip art.

4. Save the changes, and keep the presentation open for Project 2.

Practice

Create an E-Mail Message With Attachment

All we need you to do is to tell us how much you have to pay for a large take-out pizza with one, two, and three toppings. I'm attaching a document that will help you provide the information we need. The document has a table that will make it easy for you. Please enter prices in the table and send the document back to me. I need this information by next Friday.

When we get all the data, our class will graph the information. We'll let you know the results.

E-mail shorthand. This means "Talk to you later." ——→ TTYL
Keith :)

Emoticons help express your feelings. This key combination means "happy."

2. **Attach** the **file 5-3 Project 1**.

3. Spell-check, proofread, and correct errors.

4. Print the e-mail and close it without saving. Do not attempt to send this e-mail.

SECTION 9.3

Add Clip Art to Slides

GOALS: Demonstrate the ability to:
- ▶ Change the slide layout.
- ▶ Insert clip art and pictures.
- ▶ Resize clip art and pictures.

Making the Connection

Have you ever given a report and wanted to use a visual display to help your audience understand what you were talking about? By adding clip art and pictures to your presentation, you can help communicate your message. The images will help your audience remember the information you present.

Your Turn

1. Open the file **ursAlexander-B** you created in Section 9.2, and save it as *ursAlexander-C*.

2. Keep the presentation open for Project 1.

Alexander's Contributions

- Helped bridge cultures
- Respected the arts and sciences
- Created strong governments
- Formed a currency system

Reinforce

Create an E-Mail Message With Attachment

Practice what you have learned by creating a new e-mail message and attaching a document to be sent with the message.

Your Turn

1. Create the **e-mail message** illustrated below.

From:	
To:	CityCouncil@Fenton.gov
Copy:	
Subject:	River Relief Project
Attach:	

My neighbor told me about the annual River Relief project for the Shiawassee River. I am interested in helping clean up the streambank this year and so are some of my friends. However, we don't know any of the details. We need to know what days are scheduled, what time we should be there, and if we need to bring anything such as trash bags, rakes, etc.

Continued on next page

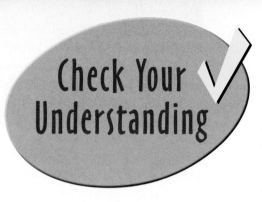

Check Your Understanding

1. Open the presentation *urs*Alexander-Edits.
2. Does your presentation match the illustration shown?
3. Make any necessary corrections.
4. Print and close the file.

*urs*Alexander-Edits

Alexander the Great
336-323 B.C.

Your name

1

Alexander's Contributions

- Helped bridge cultures
- Respected the arts and sciences
- Created strong governments
- Formed a currency system

2

Young Alexander

- Educated by Aristotle
- Good at every sport
- Commanded men in battle
- Enjoyed the study of science

3

Old and New World Empires

Macedon	Turkistan	Persian
Greece	Russia	Syria
Bulgaria	Afghanistan	Israel
Macedonia	China	Lebanon

4

Reinforce

Create an E-Mail Message With Attachment

I am attaching a list of names, phone numbers, and e-mail addresses so someone can contact my friends and me.

Nik Klopf :)

2. **Attach** the **file 5-3 Project 2** so it will be sent with the e-mail message.

3. Spell-check, proofread, and correct errors.

4. Print the e-mail and close it without saving. Do not attempt to send this e-mail.

Reinforce

Edit the Presentations

3. After Slide 4, add two **New Slides** as shown.

Rain Forest Foods

- Bananas
- Pineapples
- Coconuts
- Papayas
- Lemons
- Peppers
- Avocados
- Sugarcane

Threats to the Rain Forests

- Agriculture
- Beef cattle ranching
- Logging
- Building of dams
- Developing the land

---

4. Change the **slide order** as follows

 a. Move Slide 6 ("Threats to the Rain Forests") to come after Slide 2 ("Rain Forest Facts").

 b. Move Slide 4 ("Rain Forest Products") to the end of the presentation.

5. Use the **Spelling** feature to identify any errors; then correct them.

6. Change to Slide show view, and preview the presentation.

7. Save the changes, and close the file.

1. Open a new word processing document. Save the file as *urs*Email.
2. Describe the information that goes in each of the following e-mail header boxes.
   From:
   To:
   Copy:
   Subject:
   Attach:
3. Explain how to send an e-mail to more than one recipient.
4. Save the changes. Print and close the file.

Write On!

Imagine that you do not have access to telephone or e-mail. The only way you can keep in touch with your friends or relatives who live in a different neighborhood, city, state, or country is by writing letters.

1. Open your journal and position the insertion point at the end of the new document. Enter today's date to create a new journal entry.
2. Write a paragraph or two in your journal responding to the above scenario. How often do you think you would write a letter? Would you be able to communicate as well? Why or why not? Do you think your relationship with your friends and relatives would change? Why or why not?
3. Save the changes to the journal. Close the file.

inter**NET** CONNECTION

When you communicate via e-mail, you cannot use facial expressions or your tone of voice to let your reader know how you feel. Therefore, you must follow some common courtesies (etiquette) when writing your messages.

1. Open your Web browser and research information on "netiquette" for e-mail.
2. Research the Web for e-mail shorthand and emoticons. Describe how you can use e-mail shorthand and emoticons to help express how you feel.

Reinforce

Edit the Presentations

Reinforce what you have learned by editing a presentation.

Your Turn

1. Open the file *urs***Rain Forest** you created in Section 9.1, and save it as *urs***Rain Forest-Edits**.

2. Edit the slides as shown.

Add new bulleted text. ———

Delete text. ———
Add new text. ———

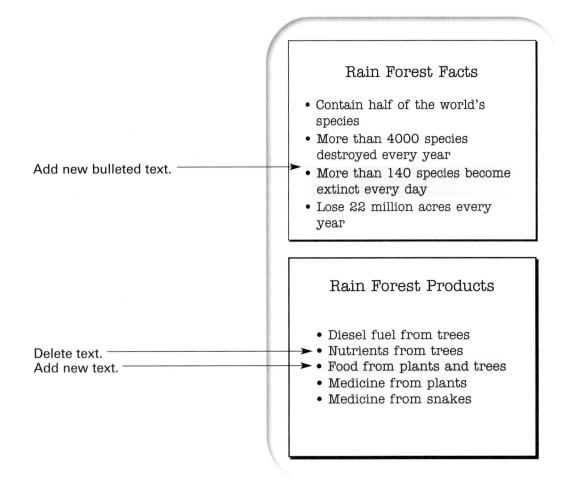

Rain Forest Facts

- Contain half of the world's species
- More than 4000 species destroyed every year
- More than 140 species become extinct every day
- Lose 22 million acres every year

Rain Forest Products

- Diesel fuel from trees
- Nutrients from trees
- Food from plants and trees
- Medicine from plants
- Medicine from snakes

Continued on next page

APPLY

Word Processing Review

You will apply the word processing skills you have learned to create and format a business letter. Refer to previous projects as needed.

Your Turn

1. Open a new word processing document.

2. Format a letter in block style.

3. Use the following information to key and format the letter.

The writer's return address is:
1113 Grand Avenue
Wausau, WI 54403

Use Today's Date.

Send the letter to:
Flagstaff Area National Monuments--WACA
6400 N. Hwy 89
Flagstaff, AZ 86004

For the salutation, key Gentlemen:.

For the closing, key Sincerely,.

The writer's name is Kevin Tolzmann.

This summer, I will be visiting my grandparents in Flagstaff. I am very interested in learning more about Native Americans. I was browsing the Web, and I learned that the ancestors of Native Americans lived in cliff dwellings in the Walnut Canyon. Then I learned that the Walnut Canyon is close to where my grandparents live in Flagstaff.

I want to ask my grandparents to take me to the Walnut Canyon National Monument. Please send me some information about the Walnut Canyon National Monument. I need to know how to get to the park, and I need to know the cost of admission. I also would like information about park activities and any special programs for the month of July.

Please send the information to me at the above address. Thank you.

4. Save the document as *urs*Walnut Canyon letter.

5. Spell-check, proofread, and correct errors.

6. Save the changes.

7. Create a No. 10 envelope for the letter. Print and close the file.

Change the Slide Order

4. Choose the Paste command. The slide order is rearranged as shown.

Alexander the Great
336-323 B.C.

Your name

1

Young Alexander

- Educated by Aristotle
- Good at every sport
- Commanded men in battle
- Enjoyed the study of science

2

Alexander's Contributions

- Helped bridge cultures
- Respected the arts and sciences
- Created strong governments
- Formed a currency system

3

Old and New World Empires

Macedon	Turkistan	Persian
Greece	Russia	Syria
Bulgaria	Afghanistan	Israel
Macedonia	China	Lebanon

4

5. Change the **Slide Order** again by moving Slide 2 ("Young Alexander") after Slide 3 ("Alexander's Contributions").

6. Change to Slide show view, and preview the presentation.

7. Save the changes, and close the file.

COMPLETING SECTION 5

ENRiCh

Curriculum Portfolio

Choose one of the following topics or use a topic assigned by your teacher. Research the topic and compose correspondence to communicate your thoughts on the issue. You can create a personal letter or you can create an e-mail message. Proofread your work carefully and save the document as *urs*Letter Portfolio. Print an envelope if you create a letter.

SCIENCE:

Compose a personal or business letter.

Select an endangered animal. Research what has caused the animal to become endangered, the status of the animal, and what can be done to save the animal from extinction.

Write a letter to a U.S. senator or representative. In your letter, express how you feel about the endangered species and why you feel it is important to protect it. You can find the names and addresses of senators and representatives on the Web or at your local library. Be sure to use the proper greeting in your letter.

SOCIAL STUDIES:

Compose a personal or business letter.

Think about a service project you can do for your community. For example, you could help to clean up the local park. You could organize a group of youths and adults to pick up the litter, improve the landscaping, and paint some of the equipment.

Once you have a plan, determine whom you should contact in your community to help plan and carry out your service project. For example, you may need to write the mayor, the city council, or the city parks and recreation department. Write a letter that defines your goals and explains why your plan is good for the community. Be sure to use the proper greeting in your letter. You can find the names and addresses of community officials and departments on the Web or at your local library.

Continued on next page

Change the Slide Order

If you want to change the order of your presentation, you can quickly rearrange the slides.

Your Turn

1. Change to Slide sorter view, and click on Slide 4 ("Alexander's Contributions") to select it.

2. Choose the Cut command.

3. Place the insertion point between Slides 2 and 3 as shown.

Alexander the Great
336-323 B.C.

Your name

1

Young Alexander

- Educated by Aristotle
- Good at every sport
- Commanded men in battle
- Enjoyed the study of science

2

Old and New World Empires

Macedon	Turkistan	Persian
Greece	Russia	Syria
Bulgaria	Afghanistan	Israel
Macedonia	China	Lebanon

3

Insertion Point

Continued on next page

ENRICH

Curriculum Portfolio

MATH:

Compose a personal or business letter.

Suppose you belong to a service club at your school. The club has 88 members. Your club has decided to sponsor a fundraiser to raise money for a family that lost its home and all personal belongings in a recent fire.

The club has decided to sell community discount cards for $10 each, and the club will keep $5 for every card sold. You estimate that 65 percent of the members will participate in the project, and you think they can each sell 10 cards. Calculate the potential profit your club can make with this project.

Write a letter to your principal asking for approval of the fundraiser. Explain why the club wants to participate in this project and describe the details. Be sure to mention how much profit your club is anticipating.

LANGUAGE ARTS:

Compose a personal letter.

Do you have a favorite book or poem? Have you ever thought about the author who created the story or the poem? For example, you might be curious about how old the author was when he or she wrote the story or poem. You may wonder where the author was born and grew up, or you may want to know why the author wrote the story or poem. Gather information and learn as much as you can about the author.

Write a letter to the author expressing why you enjoy reading the author's work. If the author is no longer living, or if you are unable to find an address for the author, create a fictitious address to use in your letter.

Add and Delete Slides

You can easily change the content of your presentation by adding and deleting slides.

Your Turn

1. Change to Slide sorter view, and delete the slide shown.

Alexander the Great
336-323 B.C.

Your name

1

Young Alexander

- Educated by Aristotle
- Good at every sport
- Commanded men in battle
- Enjoyed the study of science

2

Alexander's Empire
336-323 B.C.

- Macedonia   • China
- Greece   • Syria
- Bulgaria   • Israel
- Russia   • Iran
- Lebanon   • Afghanistan

3

Alexander's Contributions

- Helped bridge cultures
- Respected the arts and sciences
- Created strong governments
- Formed a currency system

4

Click on Slide 3 to select it, and press DELETE.

2. Change to Normal view, **add a new slide**, and choose a Table layout.

Old and New World Empires

Macedon	Turkistan	Persian
Greece	Russia	Syria
Bulgaria	Afghanistan	Israel
Macedonia	China	Lebanon

Create a table with 3 columns and 5 rows. Then key the text.

3. Save the changes, and keep the presentation open for Project 3.

SECTION 6.1

Format a One-Page Report

GOALS: Demonstrate the ability to:

- ▶ Format a one-page report.
- ▶ Format margins, paragraph alignment, and line spacing.
- ▶ Copy and paste text between documents.
- ▶ Find and replace text.
- ▶ Proofread and correct errors.

PROOFREADING WARMUP

In a word processing document, key and complete the paragraph starter. Proofread your work.

```
If I could plan a school lunch menu, I
would have. . .
```

Making the Connection

You're probably familiar with the saying, "Work smarter, not harder." That's what word processing is all about. The more features you learn, the smarter you can work. In this section you will learn some features that will make your work easier.

Your Turn

1. Open a new word processing document.
2. Key the text as shown.
3. Save the document as *urs*Charlie.
4. Keep the file open for Project 1.

ALL THE CHOCOLATE YOU CAN EAT!

By Rachelle Cantin

I read the book Charlie and the Chocolate Factory. The author of the book is Roald Dahl. The book is 155 pages long, and it was published by Puffin.

Practice

Edit Text and Use Proofing Tools

3. Go to Slide 2 and edit as shown.

Young Alexander

- Educated by Aristotle
- Good at every sport
- Loved poetry and music ◄————————— Delete the third bulleted line.
- Commanded men in battle
- Enjoyed the study of science ◄————— Key the new line of text.

4. Use the **Spelling** feature to identify any errors; then correct them.

5. Save the changes, and keep the presentation open for Project 2.

Change the Margins and Format the Report

The blank space around the edges of the page is called the **margin**. When you create a new document, the margins are already set. However, you can change those margins. Use 1-inch margins for full-page or multi-page reports.

Your Turn

1. Edit and key the remaining text in the document as shown.

Title
Center, bold, and all-capital letters.

Byline
Center.

Format Charlie and the Chocolate Factory in **italic**.

ALL THE CHOCOLATE YOU CAN EAT!

By Rachelle Cantin

I read the book *Charlie and the Chocolate Factory*. The author of the book is Roald Dahl. The book is 155 pages long, and it was published by Puffin.

Charlie Bucket is a poor boy who lives in a tiny house with his parents. Both sets of grandparents also live with Charlie in that tiny house. Charlie didn't have any money, but he found a dollar bill in the street. He used the money to buy a Wonka candy bar. The Willy Wonka Chocolate Company held a contest. When Charlie opened the candy bar, he found a golden ticket. He was one of five winners.

Change the line spacing to double.

Change the left and right **margins** to 1 inch.

Body
Press TAB to indent the first line of each paragraph.

2. Spell-check and proofread the file. Make any necessary corrections and save the changes.

3. Keep the file open for Project 2.

Practice

Edit Text and Use Proofing Tools

You can easily edit and correct your text.

Your Turn

1. Go to Slide 1 and edit as shown.

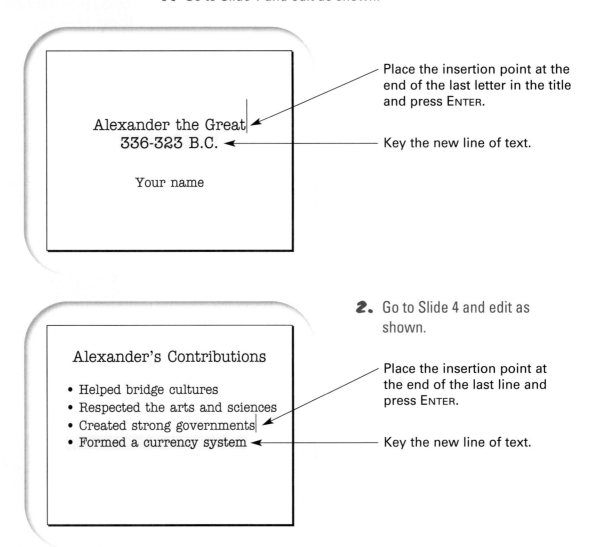

Alexander the Great|
336-323 B.C.

Your name

— Place the insertion point at the end of the last letter in the title and press ENTER.

— Key the new line of text.

2. Go to Slide 4 and edit as shown.

Alexander's Contributions

• Helped bridge cultures
• Respected the arts and sciences
• Created strong governments|
• Formed a currency system

Place the insertion point at the end of the last line and press ENTER.

— Key the new line of text.

Continued on next page

Practice

Copy and Paste Text Between Documents

You already know how to copy and paste text within the same document. Did you know you can copy and paste text from one document to another? With both documents open, you simply copy the text in one of the documents, switch to the second document, and paste the text you copied.

Your Turn

1. Open the file **6-1 Project 2**. You now have two files open, but the file you see on the screen is the one you just opened. See the illustration below.

The other four winners were Augustus Gloop, Violet Beauregarde, Veruca Salt, and Mike Teavee. Charlie went on the tour of the chocolate factory with his Grandpa Joe. The other four winners were there with their parents. They saw lots of amazing things, and they met the Oompa-Loompas. The Oompa-Loompas were the tiny people who lived and worked in the factory.

The other four kids behaved very badly on the tour. When they didn't follow directions, Willy Wonka punished them and funny things happened to them that made them disappear. But Charlie was kind and polite. Willy Wonka liked Charlie and he knew he could trust Charlie. At the end of the tour, Charlie was

Continued on next page

Edit Slides

GOALS: Demonstrate the ability to:

▶ Edit slide text.

▶ Use proofing tools.

▶ Add and delete slides.

▶ Change the slide order.

PROOFREADING WARMUP

In a word processing document, key each linc 3 times.
Proofread your work.

Four students from our school will run in the state finals.
The quadrant has been a survey device since medieval times.
The accountant had 100 five-column pads in his desk drawer.

Making the Connection

When you prepare an oral report, you
may need to make some corrections and
changes on your notes. You can easily
make changes or correct your mistakes
without starting over with presentation software.

Your Turn

1. Open the file *urs*Alexander
   you created in Section 9.1, and
   save it as *ursAlexanderEdits*.

2. Keep the file open for Project 1.

Alexander the Great
336-323 B.C.

Your name

Copy and Paste Text Between Documents

the only kid left and Willy Wonka gave him the chocolate factory. Charlie and his family could live at the factory and Charlie could have all the chocolate he could eat!

My favorite part about this book was that when the other four kids didn't follow directions, Willy Wonka punished them. Charlie followed directions and Willy Wonka rewarded him for that.

2. **Select** the entire file, and **copy** the selected text to the **Clipboard**.

3. Close the file **6-1 Project 2** without saving any changes. The file *urs*Charlie is still displayed.

4. Position the insertion point at the end of the file, and **paste** the contents from the **Clipboard**.

5. Save the changes. Keep the file open for Project 3.

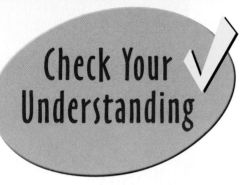

Check Your Understanding

1. Open a word processing document, and save it as *urs*Presentation Basics.
2. Describe the difference between Outline view and Normal view.
3. Describe the difference between Slide Sorter view and Slide show view.
4. Describe three types of slide layouts.
5. Describe the purpose of using a design template.
6. Save the changes.
7. Print and close the file.

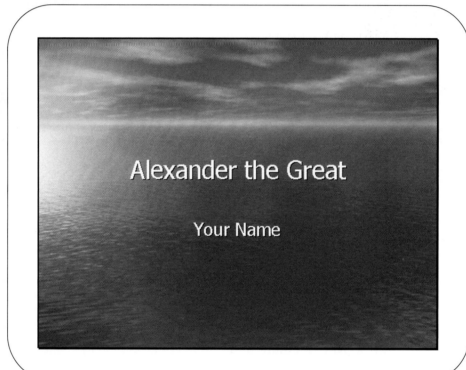

Alexander the Great

Your Name

Practice

Find and Replace Text

The Find feature enables you to quickly locate a word or a group of words. The Replace feature enables you to find and replace the word or group of words with a different word or group of words.

Your Turn

1. Use the file **ursCharlie**. Position the insertion point at the beginning of the third paragraph.

2. Edit the file as indicated in the illustration below.

3. **Find and replace** "Willy" with "Mr." in the last two paragraphs of the file.

The other four kids behaved very badly on the tour. When they didn't follow directions, Willy Wonka punished them and funny things happened to them that made them disappear. But Charlie was kind and polite. Willy Wonka liked Charlie and he knew he could trust Charlie. At the end of the tour, Charlie was the only kid left and Willy Wonka gave him the chocolate factory. Charlie and his family could live at the factory and Charlie *they* could have all the chocolate *they* he could eat!

My favorite part about this book was that when the other four kids didn't follow directions *and* Willy Wonka punished them. Charlie followed directions and Willy Wonka rewarded him for that.

4. Save the changes. Print and close the file.

Create a Basic Presentation

Reinforce what you have learned by creating a presentation.

Your Turn

1. Open a **new presentation**.

2. Create the slides shown using appropriate **slide layouts**.

3. Save the presentation as *urs*Rain Forest.

Protecting the Rain Forests

Your name

Slide 1

Rain Forest Facts

- Contain half of the world's species
- More than 4000 species destroyed every year
- Lose 22 million acres every year

Slide 2

Rain Forest Products

- Diesel fuel from trees
- Nutrients from trees
- Medicine from plants
- Medicine from snakes

Slide 3

Rain Forest Animals

- Spider Monkeys   • Scarlet Macaws
- Sloths   • Boas
- Jaguars   • Ocelots
- Iguanas   • Harpy eagles

Slide 4

---

4. **Apply** a **design template**.

5. Change to **Slide show view** and preview the presentation.

6. Save the changes. Print and close the file.

Reinforce

Format a One-Page Report

Reinforce the word processing features you learned by keying and formatting another one-page report.

Your Turn

1. Open the document **6-1 Project 4**, and save it as *urs*Crabtree.

2. Format the document as indicated.

Select the entire document and change the **line spacing** to double.

Center the title and subtitle. **Bold** the title.

LOTTA CRABTREE
By Alexa Aroyo

My report is about *Lotta Crabtree Gold Rush Girl.* The book was written by Marian T. Place, and it was illustrated by Gary Morrow. The Bobbs-Merrill Company, Inc., published the book in 1958 and in 1962, and the total number of pages is 200.

The story took place in the 1840s. The main character is Lotta Crabtree, a girl who likes to sing and dance. Lotta's mother is a very good mother, but she can't cook. Lotta's dad, who says he is going to strike it rich one day, owns a bookstore.

Change the left and right **margins** to 1 inch.

3. Open the file **6-1 Project 4b**. Select the entire document and copy the contents to the Clipboard.

4. Close the file **6-1 Project 4b**. Paste the contents in the Clipboard at the end of the document named *urs*Crabtree.

5. Save the changes. Keep the file open for the next step.

Continued on next page

Apply a Design Template

You can choose from many design templates to give the slides in your presentation a professional look.

Your Turn

1. Choose **Normal view**, and go to Slide 1.

2. Choose the **Apply Design Template** command.

3. Browse through the design templates, and apply an appropriate design.

A sample design template →

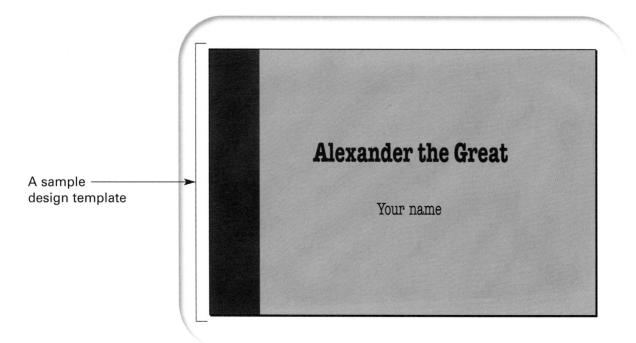

Alexander the Great

Your name

4. Change to **Slide show view**, and preview the presentation.

5. Save the changes. Print and close the file.

Format a One-Page Report

6. Complete the report by keying the final paragraphs shown in the illustration below.

> When Lotta was sixteen, she returned to New York and became America's favorite comedienne. For twenty-two years, Lotta was the star actress in light comedy. She was often called "The California Diamond." Some of her friends had a statue made of her, and they put it in the center of Portsmouth Square in San Francisco. Then in 1891, Lotta retired and gave up acting.
> The thing I liked about Lotta Crabtree was that she did a lot of things with very little money.

7. Find and replace all occurrences of "New York" with "New York City."

8. Spell-check and proofread the document. Make any necessary corrections.

9. Save the changes. Print and close the file.

Practice

Create a New Presentation

Young Alexander
336–323 B.C.

- Macedonia
- Greece
- Bulgaria
- Russia
- Lebanon

- China
- Syria
- Israel
- Iran
- Afghanistan

4. **Insert a new slide**, and choose a Two-Column layout.

Click in the text box; then key each bulleted line.

5. **Insert a new slide**, and choose a Bulleted List layout.

Alexander's Contributions

- Helped bridge cultures
- Respected the arts and sciences
- Created strong governments

Click in the text box; then key each bulleted line.

6. Save the presentation as *urs*Alexander.

7. Keep the presentation open for Project 3.

Write On!

In this lesson, you learned to locate specific text in a word processing document and replace it with new text. There are many more ways you can use the Find command to work smarter. For example, if you want to review journal entries that you have previously written about a particular subject or experience, you can use the Find command to locate quickly those entries.

1. Open your journal and use the Find command to locate all the entries that contain the word "letter." Your results should include entries about personal letters and business letters.
2. Position the insertion point at the end of the new document. Enter today's date to create a new journal entry.
3. Think about other ways you could use the Find command to work smarter, and describe them in your new journal entry. If you cannot think of other ways to use the Find command, write a paragraph describing how you used the Find command to work smarter in this lesson.
4. Save the changes to your journal. Close the file.

interNET CONNECTION

Did you know that you can use the Find command to locate specific text in Web pages? Let's see how it works.

You want information about the best roller coasters in the world. You want to know how high they are and how fast they are.

1. Open your Web browser, and search for the keywords "*roller coasters + amusement parks*."
2. When you locate a Web page that looks like it contains the information you are looking for, choose the Find command in your browser to search for the specific details. (The Find command is usually in the Edit menu.)
3. Search for keywords like "feet" or "mph." These searches may take you directly to the details you are looking for.
4. Make a list of the three highest roller coasters and the three fastest roller coasters. Compare your results with those of a classmate.

Create a New Presentation

When you create a slide, you can choose the type of layout to best match the information you want to put on the new slide. For example, a Title slide layout will guide you in creating the first slide in your presentation.

Your Turn

1. Open a **New Presentation** and choose a **Title Slide layout** similar to the one below.

2. Create the slides as shown.

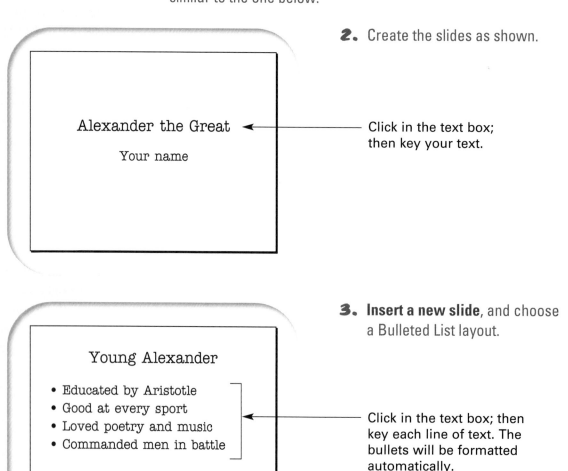

Alexander the Great

Your name

Click in the text box; then key your text.

3. **Insert a new slide**, and choose a Bulleted List layout.

Young Alexander

- Educated by Aristotle
- Good at every sport
- Loved poetry and music
- Commanded men in battle

Click in the text box; then key each line of text. The bullets will be formatted automatically.

Continued on next page

Format a Report With a Bibliography

GOALS: Demonstrate the ability to:

▶ Format a multipage report.
▶ Format margins, side headings, page numbers for a report.
▶ Insert a new page.

▶ Create and format a bibliography.
▶ Work from rough-draft copy material.
▶ Spell-check, proofread, and correct errors.

PROOFREADING WARMUP

*In a word processing document, key each line 3 times.
Proofread your work.*

```
James was not here when all of us signed the card for Rita.
Jacqueline was glad her family took five or six big prizes.
Will students use the SHIFT LOCK to type in SOLID CAPITALS?
```

Making the Connection

In this section you will learn how to create and format a multipage report. You will learn how to make an adjustment to the left margin so that the left and right margins look even when the report is bound on the left.

Your Turn

1. Open the file **6-2 Project 1**. Save the document as *urs*Banner.

2. Keep the file open for Project 1.

THE STAR-SPANGLED BANNER
By Hallie Thompson

During the War of 1812, Americans knew that the British would likely attack the city of Baltimore. In the summer of 1813, Major George Armistead was the commander at Fort McHenry at the Baltimore harbor. He asked Mary Young Pickersgill to make a flag for the fort. Armistead wanted the flag to be

Change Views and Navigate Through a Presentation

3. Change to **Slide sorter view**, and click on slide 5.

Slide sorter view lets you see miniatures of all the slides in the presentation.

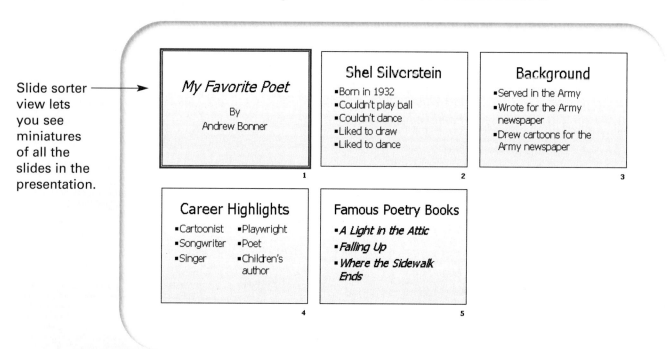

4. Change to **Slide view**, and go to the first slide.

Slide view lets you edit and work on each slide.

5. Change to **Outline view**.

Outline view lets you organize all the text in your presentation.

6. Close the presentation without saving.

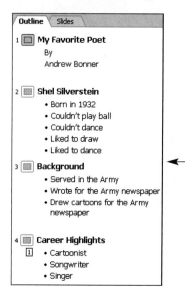

Practice

Format a Bound Report With Side Headings and Page Numbers

Side headings are the major subdivisions or major topics of a report. Side headings help to emphasize the main ideas in your report. Multipage reports are often bound or stapled on the left side of the page. You need to leave a larger left margin to allow room for the binding. Because your report has more than one page, use the page number feature to automatically number each page.

Your Turn

1. Edit the report as indicated in the illustration.

Center and bold.

Center.

Select the entire document and change the **line spacing** to double.

Add **side headings** and format **bold**.

Format 1.5-inch left margin.

Format 1-inch right margin.

THE STAR-SPANGLED BANNER
By Hallie Thompson

The Story Behind the Flag

During the War of 1812, Americans knew that the British would likely attack the city of Baltimore. In the summer of 1813, Major George Armistead was the commander at Fort McHenry at the Baltimore harbor. He asked Mary Young Pickersgill to make a flag for the fort. Armistead wanted the flag to be so big that the British would be sure to see it from a distance.

Mary's 13-year-old daughter Caroline helped her make the flag. They cut 15 stars. Each star was two feet long from point to point. They also cut eight red stripes and seven white stripes. Each stripe was two feet wide. It took them several weeks to make the flag. When they sewed everything together, the flag measured 30 feet by 42 feet. The flag weighed 200 pounds.

Francis Scott Key's Point of View

Francis Scott Key was 35 years old, and he was a well-known and successful lawyer in Georgetown, Maryland. He opposed the War of 1812, but in 1814 he had to get involved. His long-time friend Dr. William Beanes was being held prisoner on a British warship.

On September 3, 1814, Key and a government agent named John S. Skinner boarded a ship that flew a flag of truce. They went to the British warship and negotiated the release of Beanes. On September 7, the British agreed to let Beanes go, but by

Continued on next page

Change Views and Navigate Through a Presentation

Normal view lets you work on the presentation slides, outline, and notes.

In a presentation, each display is called a **slide**. You use **views** to look at the presentation and to work on your presentation.

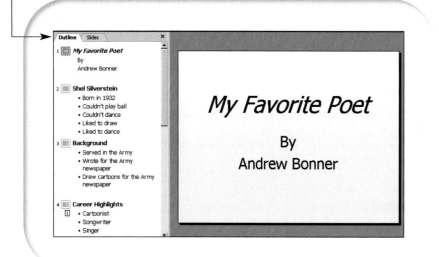

Your Turn

1. Change to **Normal view**, and use the scroll bar to move to each slide.

Slide show view lets you preview your presentation.

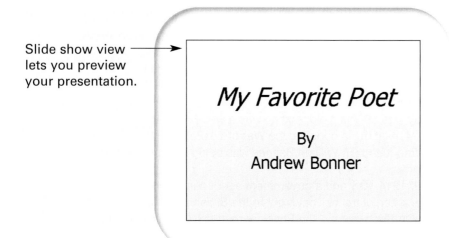

2. Change to **Slide show view**. Click the mouse, or use the right or left arrow keys to view each slide.

Continued on next page

Format a Bound Report With Side Headings and Page Numbers

then Key, Skinner, and Beanes knew too much about the planned attack on the city of Baltimore. So the British held all three Americans as prisoners on the warship while they attacked Baltimore.

On September 13, the three American prisoners watched from the warship as the British battleships fired upon Fort McHenry. They knew it would be difficult for the American soldiers to fight off the British. The battle continued through the night, and they feared the American soldiers would surrender.

Add **side headings** and format **bold**. ──► **The Story Behind the Song**

When the sun rose the next morning, they saw a big American flag flying over the fort. It was the flag Pickersgill had made. The Americans had survived the battle.

Insert page number. ──────────►

Oh! Say, can you see, by the dawn's early light,

What so proudly we hailed at the twilight's last gleaming?

Whose broad stripes and bright stars, through the perilous fight.

O'er the ramparts we watched were so gallantly streaming?

And the rocket's red glare, the bombs bursting in air,

Gave proof through the night that our flag was still there.

Oh! Say, does that Star-Spangled Banner yet wave

O'er the land of the free and the home of the brave?

2. Save the changes.

3. Position the insertion point at the end of the document, and key and format the first verse of the *Star-Spangled Banner* as shown at left.

4. Save the changes. Keep the file open for Project 2.

Format all the text **italic**.   **Center** each line of text.

SECTION 9.1

Presentation Basics

GOALS: Demonstrate the ability to:

- ▶ Change slide view of a presentation.
- ▶ Navigate through a presentation.
- ▶ Create a new presentation.
- ▶ Apply a design template.

PROOFREADING WARMUP

In a word processing document, key each line 3 times.
Proofread your work.

```
The little black puppy ran to the door to greet his master.
Jeff amazed the audience by quickly giving six new reports.
Terry is taking English Literature 215 on Tuesday mornings.
```

Making the Connection

When you give an oral report, what speaking and visual aids do you use? Do you use index cards or a poster? Do you keep everyone's attention?

Using presentation software, you can easily create a professional-looking presentation that will keep your audience's attention.

Your Turn

1. Launch your presentation software and open the file **9-1 Project 1**.

2. Save the presentation as *urs*Favorite Poet.

3. Keep the presentation open for Project 1.

My Favorite Poet

By

Andrew Bonner

Practice

Format a Bibliography

A **bibliography** is an alphabetical list of the sources of information you used in writing a report. The sources are single-spaced and formatted with a hanging indent. In a **hanging indent**, the first line of the paragraph begins at the left margin and all other lines in the paragraph are indented.

Your Turn

1. Position the insertion point at the end of the document, and then **insert a new page break**.

2. Key and format the bibliography as illustrated.

Single-space the sources, and leave a blank line between the sources.

Internet reference.

Format with **hanging indent**.

Online encyclopedia reference.

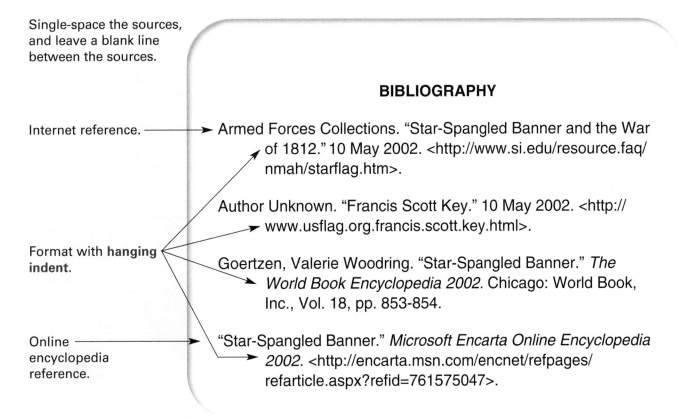

BIBLIOGRAPHY

Armed Forces Collections. "Star-Spangled Banner and the War of 1812." 10 May 2002. <http://www.si.edu/resource.faq/ nmah/starflag.htm>.

Author Unknown. "Francis Scott Key." 10 May 2002. <http:// www.usflag.org.francis.scott.key.html>.

Goertzen, Valerie Woodring. "Star-Spangled Banner." *The World Book Encyclopedia 2002.* Chicago: World Book, Inc., Vol. 18, pp. 853-854.

"Star-Spangled Banner." *Microsoft Encarta Online Encyclopedia 2002.* <http://encarta.msn.com/encnet/refpages/ refarticle.aspx?refid=761575047>.

3. Save the changes. Print and close the file.

Good Keyboarding Habits

Focus on your wrists.
To avoid wrist strain:

- Make sure your wrists do not rest on anything.

- Keep your wrists straight, not bent.

- Never curve your wrists right or left.

Format a Multipage Report With a Bibliography

Reinforce the word processing features you learned by keying and formatting another multipage report with a bibliography.

Change the left **margin** to allow for the space needed for binding on the left side.

Your Turn

1. Key and format the report as illustrated.

Add the side — heading **Borders** and format **bold**.

ARGENTINA

By Nathan Chin

Argentina is the world's eighth-largest country, and its land varies greatly. It has some of the world's tallest mountains, and it also has grassy plains and deserts.

Argentina is bordered by Chile, Uruguay, Brazil, Paraguay, and Bolivia on its northern borders. Argentina is also bordered by the Pacific and Atlantic Oceans. Its southern tip reaches almost to the continent of Antarctica.

Continued on next page

UNIT 6

Presentations

GOALS:

▶ Demonstrate the ability to create and navigate through a new presentation.

▶ Demonstrate correct use of presentation editing and proofing tools.

▶ Demonstrate how to enhance a presentation with clip art and photos.

▶ Demonstrate how to enhance a presentation with animation and sounds.

Format a Multipage Report With a Bibliography

Add the side heading **Terrain** and format **bold**.

Argentina's varied geography includes the Perito Moreno glacier in the southern Andes. This is one of the few glaciers in the world still advancing.

Argentina has 1,056,640 square miles. It is South America's second-largest country, after Brazil. Argentina is about one-third the size of the United States.

Copy and paste all the content from the file **6-2 Project 3**.

Insert page number.

2. Save the document as *urs*Argentina.

3. Spell-check and proofread the file. Save any changes.

4. Position the insertion point at the end of the file, and insert a new page break.

Continued on next page

COMPLETING UNIT 5

ENRICH

Curriculum Portfolio

Choose one of the following topics or one assigned by your teacher:

MATH:

Create a math facts Web page game.

Create a math game Web page for your peers. The purpose of the site is to review math concepts and to have fun. Organize the information on the Web page by topics, such as fractions, geometry, percentages, and so forth. Write a brief introduction to each topic and then provide links to other Web pages that offer math games, math quizzes, and homework helpers.

SOCIAL STUDIES:

Create and format a historical newsletter.

Create a historical newsletter about the Roman Empire. Format the newsletter in columns, create a masthead, and format headlines. Enhance the newsletter with pictures and objects and a divider. Consider the following suggestions for determining the content: facts and details about events, an editorial about an event, advertisements, and classified ads.

SCIENCE:

Create a science Web page game.

Create a science trivia quiz. Research fascinating facts about the world of science and then write 10–20 questions about the trivia. Your Web pages should provide links to other pages with the answers to the questions.

LANGUAGE ARTS:

Create and format a biographical newsletter.

Create a biographical newsletter about an author and the author's notable works. Format the newsletter in columns, create a masthead, and format headlines. Enhance the newsletter with pictures and objects and a divider.

Formatting a Multipage Report With a Bibliography

5. Create and format the bibliography illustrated below.

BIBLIOGRAPHY

"Argentina." *Microsoft Encarta Online Encyclopedia 2002*. 3 May 2002. <http://encarta.msn.com/find/Concise>.

"CIA—The World Fact Book 2002—Argentina." 3 May 2002. <http://www.odci.gov/cia/publications/factbook/geos/ar.html>.

Wilkie, Richard W. "Argentina." *The World Book Encyclopedia 2002*. Chicago: World Book, Inc., Vol. 1, pp. 646-660.

---

6. Proofread the bibliography page, and make any necessary corrections.

7. Save the changes. Print and close the file.

APPLY

Review Project

7. Group the objects as a single unit.

8. Save the changes.

9. Complete the flyer by adding the graphics shown in the illustration below. Resize and position the graphics to fill the page.

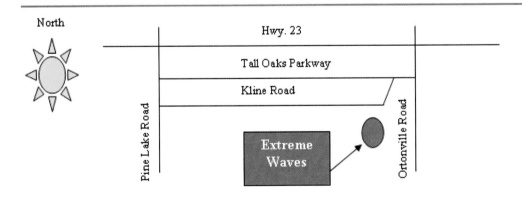

Extreme Waves

The Ultimate Skateboard Park!

This park is for all ages and all skill levels. It is very family oriented, and it is the local skaters' pride and joy.

An enormous effort was put into constructing this park. There are both metal ramps and wood ramps. The entire park has great coping and clean-finished edges. You'll really

enjoy the ramps and courses. You can also practice your technical tricks in the 15,000-square-foot concrete area.

This park has it all, and you can ride year round. Catch all the action at Extreme Waves! Helmets are required. Sorry, no bikes or scooters.

North

Hwy. 23

Tall Oaks Parkway

Kline Road

Pine Lake Road

Ortonville Road

Extreme Waves

10. Save the changes. Print and close the file.

1. Open a new word processing document.
2. If you are binding multiple pages of a report on the left side, how much extra space should you add to the left margin?
3. Explain the benefit of adding side headings to a report.
4. What is the purpose of a bibliography?
5. What is a hanging indent?
6. Save the document as *urs*Report. Print and close the file.

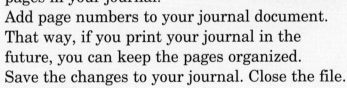

Write On!

In this section you learned to add page numbers to your report. By now, you must have multiple pages in your journal. Add page numbers to your journal document. That way, if you print your journal in the future, you can keep the pages organized. Save the changes to your journal. Close the file.

inter**NET** CONNECTION

Did you know that you can tell what country a Web site is from by looking at its URL? Domain names for sites within the United States usually include *.net, .com, .edu,* and *.org.* Domain names for sites outside the United States have two-letter extensions that identify the country. For example, the letters *"uk"* in a URL indicate that the Web site is from the United Kingdom.

1. Open your Web browser and locate a site that will help you identify "Internet country abbreviations."
2. Identify the countries for the following two-letter abbreviations: *bz, ma,* and *aq.*
3. Bookmark the site.

APPLY

Review Project

In this project, you will apply the desktop publishing skills you have learned to create and format a flyer. Refer to previous projects as needed.

Your Turn

1. Open a new document. Change to landscape orientation, and change all the margins to 1 inch.

This park is for all ages and all skill levels. It is very family oriented, and it is the local skaters' pride and joy.

An enormous effort was put into constructing this park. There are both metal ramps and wood ramps. The entire park has great coping and clean-finished edges. You'll really enjoy the ramps and courses. You can also practice your technical tricks in the 15,000-square-foot concrete area.

This park has it all, and you can ride year round. Catch all the action at Extreme Waves! Helmets are required. Sorry, no bikes or scooters.

2. Key the text shown.

3. Format the text in 2 columns.

4. Save the document as *urs*Extreme Waves.

5. Spell-check, proofread, and correct errors.

6. Below the columns of text, use drawing tools to create the map shown.

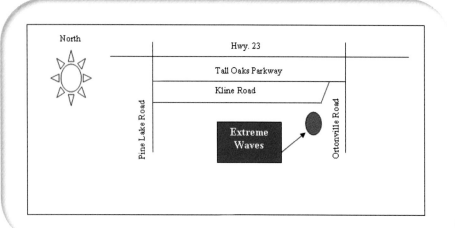

Continued on next page

SECTION 6.3

Format a Title Page

GOALS: Demonstrate the ability to:

▶ Key and format a title page.

▶ Center text vertically on a page.

▶ Enhance appearance of a title page.

PROOFREADING WARMUP

In a word processing document, key each line 3 times.
Proofread your work.

```
The Sun is the closest star in our very large solar system.
The Aztecs built Tenochtitlan on an island in Lake Texcoco.
A number of students were excused from their science class.
```

Making the Connection

The hard part is done. You have keyed your report, formatted it, proofread it, and corrected all errors. Now it's time for the finishing touch—creating a title page. Not only do you want the title page to include all the necessary information, but also you want it to make a good first impression!

Your Turn

1. Open a new word processing document.

2. Key the information for a title page.

3. Save the document as *urs*Title Page.

4. Keep the file open for Project 1.

Press ENTER
6x

THE STAR-SPANGLED BANNER

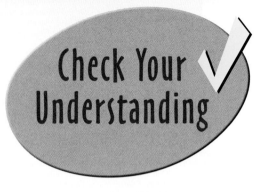

Check Your Understanding

1. Open a new word processing document.
2. Key the answer to each question using a complete sentence.
3. What is the purpose of a hyperlink?
4. Explain why you would create a link to another location on the same page.
5. How can you tell that text has been formatted to link to another location?
6. How can you tell that a graphic has been formatted to link to another location?
7. Why should you preview a Web page in your Web browser?
8. Save the document as *urs*Hyperlinks. Print and close the file.

8th Grade American History

On April 27, the 8th Grade American History students went on their annual field trip. They traveled by charter bus to Washington, D.C. The field trip was fantastic. Every one had fun and learned a lot.

Click on the link below to see pictures from the interesting sites we visited.

Photos of Landmarks

Top of the Document

**Copyright 20--
Pleasant Valley Middle School Tech Team**

Compare the illustration with urs*Field Trips.*

Format a Title Page

A title page gives a formal, finished look to the report. It identifies what the report is about. You can enhance the appearance of the title page by adding graphics and borders and by changing the font style, size, and color.

Your Turn

1. Key and format the title page as indicated.

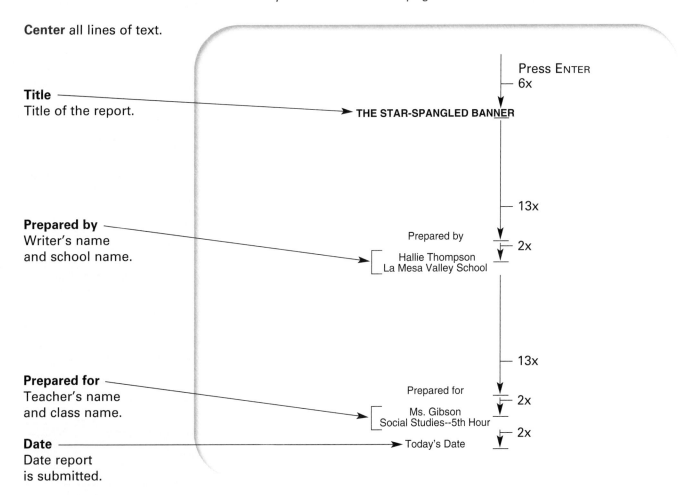

Center all lines of text.

Press ENTER 6x

Title
Title of the report.

THE STAR-SPANGLED BANNER

13x

Prepared by
Writer's name and school name.

Prepared by

2x

Hallie Thompson
La Mesa Valley School

13x

Prepared for
Teacher's name and class name.

Prepared for

2x

Ms. Gibson
Social Studies--5th Hour

2x

Date
Date report is submitted.

Today's Date

2. Change the **vertical alignment** of text to **center**.

3. Save the changes. Print and close the file.

Create Hyperlinks

8th Grade American History

On April 27, the 8th Grade American History students went on their annual field trip. They traveled by charter bus to Washington, D.C. The field trip was fantastic. Everyone had fun and learned a lot.

Click on the link below to see pictures from the interesting sites we visited.

Photos of Landmarks

Top of Document

Insert this new line of **text** and **create a hyperlink** to the Web page **Landmarks**.

Create a hyperlink to go to the top of the document.

Did you know?
* The White House was built between 1792 and 1800.
* John Adams was the first president to move in.
* Although it has been called the President's House and the President's Palace, it was officially designated the White House when Theodore Roosevelt put the name on his stationery in 1901.

Top of Document

Insert an appropriate **clip art** image representing the home page, and then **create a hyperlink** from the graphic to the Web page **Field Trips**.

5. Open the Web page **Landmarks** that you created in Section 8.2.

6. Create the hyperlinks described at the left.

Create a hyperlink to go to the top of the document.

7. Add the following copyright notice at the bottom of each Web page.

Copyright 20--
Pleasant Valley Middle School Tech Team

8. Save the changes to each document.

9. Preview the Web page in your browser and test all the hyperlinks. Make any necessary corrections.

10. Save any changes. Print and close both files.

Reinforce

Format a Title Page

Your Turn

1. Create and format the title page illustrated below.

Change the vertical alignment of text to Center.

ARGENTINA

Prepared by

Nathan Chin
Notre Dame Academy

Prepared for

Mr. Jorgensen
Social Studies—3rd Hour

Today's Date

2. Save the document as *urs*Argentina Title Page.

3. Print and close the file.

Create Hyperlinks

In this project you will reinforce the skills you have learned by creating internal and external hyperlinks to Web pages from Sections 8.1 and 8.2.

Your Turn

1. Open the Web page document *urs*Field Trips that you created and saved in Section 8.1, Project 4.

2. Format the two side headings with heading styles.

3. Create the hyperlinks described below. Note that your Web page theme will probably be different from the pages illustrated.

Insert these new lines of **text** to create a list of contents.

Select each topic, and **create a hyperlink** to the heading with the same name.

Pleasant Valley Middle School
Field Trip Memories

7th Grade World History
8th Grade World History

7th Grade World History

On September 28, 7th Grade World History students took a journey back with wizards, peasants, nobles, and the royal court. They watched a play watching knights compete in a jousting event, and visited shopkeepers. T shopkeepers demonstrate glass blowing, armor making, and calligraphy.

4. Save the changes. Keep the file open.

Continued on next page

1. Open a new word processing document.
2. List the information that you should include on a title page.
3. Describe how you can enhance the appearance of a title page.
4. Save the document as *urs*Title Page Notes. Print and close the file.

Write On!

The student forum wants to sponsor Crazy Hat Day. If students donate 25 cents, they will be permitted to wear silly hats throughout the school day. The money collected will be used to purchase a new flag for the school. As president of the student forum, it is your job to persuade the principal to approve this event. How will you convince the principal that sponsoring Crazy Hat Day would be good for the school?

1. Open your journal and position the insertion point at the end of the new document. Enter today's date to create a new journal entry.
2. Write a paragraph or two describing the main points you will make to persuade the principal to approve Crazy Hat Day.
3. Save the changes to your journal. Close the file.

inter NET CONNECTION

As you know, the World Wide Web is a source for lots of information. However, not all the information you find on the Web is accurate. Just because you read it at a Web site does not mean that it is true. Before you rely on information that you find on the Web, you should evaluate the source.

1. Open your Web browser and search for a site that provides suggestions or guidelines for evaluating Web pages.
2. Open a new word processing document. Create a list to identify the questions you should ask and the information you should look for to verify that you can trust the source.
3. Save the document as *urs*Evaluation. Print and close the file.

Test Hyperlinks

As you create your Web pages, you can open them in your Web browser to see what they will look like on the World Wide Web. Text and graphics sometimes align differently when displayed in a Web browser, so you should always preview your Web pages. When you preview the pages in a Web browser, you can also test your hyperlinks.

Your Turn

1. **Preview** the **Web page** in your browser. If necessary, change the text and graphic formats so that the information is displayed correctly in your Web browser.

2. Test all the hyperlinks. When you click the link for the Venus Fun Facts page, the page should open—even though you just closed the document. Make any necessary changes so all the hyperlinks work correctly.

3. Save the changes. Print and close each file.

Format a Report With a Reference Page

GOALS: Demonstrate the ability to:

▶ Key and format a multipage report in MLA style.

▶ Cite sources in a report.

▶ Format a header.

▶ Create a works cited reference page.

▶ Proofread and correct errors.

PROOFREADING WARMUP

In a word processing document, key and complete the paragraph starter. Proofread your work.

```
If I could go back in time and meet just one person,
I would want to meet _____
because...
```

Making the Connection

When you don't put your name on your assignments, your teacher does not know who did the work. Multipage reports that follow the MLA style have a header that contains the writer's name and the page number. Some teachers ask you to include the hour of your class and/or the date. That information makes the teacher's recordkeeping tasks easier.

In this section, you will learn to format your document so your name will automatically appear on every page of the document.

Your Name
Your Teacher's Name
Class
Today's Date

The Roman Empire Under Augustus

Roman power was crumbling and would likely have ended had it not been for two great statesmen: Gaius Julius Caesar and

Your Turn

1. Open the file **6-4 Project 1**, and save the document as *urs*Roman Empire.

2. Keep the file open for Project 1.

PROJECT 2 Continued Practice

Create a Hyperlink to Another Web Page

4. If necessary, open the Web page **Venus** that you created in Section 8.1.
5. Create the hyperlink shown below.

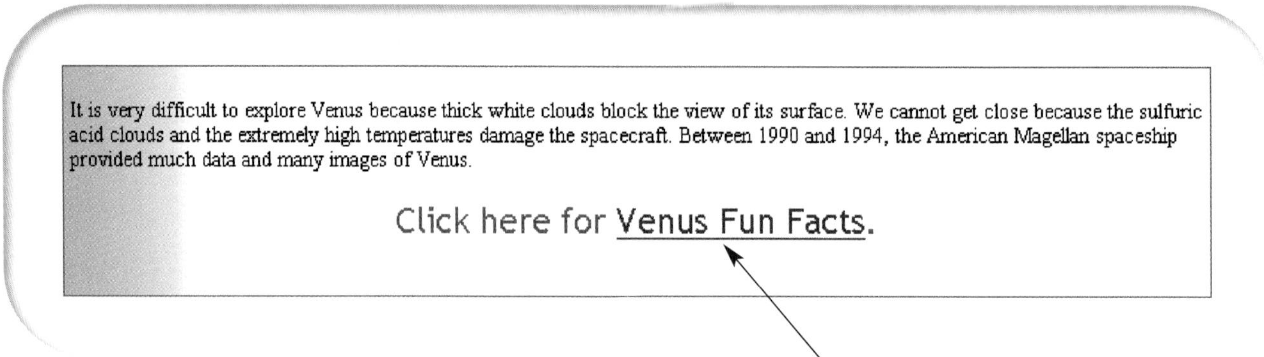
It is very difficult to explore Venus because thick white clouds block the view of its surface. We cannot get close because the sulfuric acid clouds and the extremely high temperatures damage the spacecraft. Between 1990 and 1994, the American Magellan spaceship provided much data and many images of Venus.
Click here for Venus Fun Facts.

Insert this new line of text and **create a hyperlink** to the Web page **Venus Fun Facts**.

6. Save the changes. Keep the file open for Project 3.

Practice

Format a Report With Citations

When you format a report, your name, teacher, class, and the date appear on the first page at the beginning of the report.

When you format your report in MLA style, you cite briefly each source by giving the author's name and the page number in a **citation** in the body of the report. The reader can get more specific details about the source in a section at the end of the report called *Works Cited*.

Your Turn

1. Edit the document as indicated below.

2. **Change** left and right **margins** to one inch.

A **heading** replaces the need for a title page in a report.

Your First and Last Name

Your Teacher's Name

Enter this information, double-spaced and aligned at the left margin.

Class

Today's Date

The Roman Empire Under Augustus

Roman power was crumbling and would likely have ended had it not

been for two great statesmen: Gaius Julius Caesar and his great-nephew

Key the citations as shown.

Augustus, also known as Octavian. In 27 B.C., Octavian told the Senate that
(Cavazzi, "Emperor Augustus")
∧

he had restored the republic. When he offered to give up his job, the Senate

gave him several offices. It named him "first citizen" and "Father of the
(Augustus)
∧

Continued on next page

Create a Hyperlink to Another Web Page

A **Web site** is two or more related Web pages. When you click on a hyperlink to another Web page, the second page is opened. Create a hyperlink for a graphic the same way you create a hyperlink for text—select the graphic and apply the hyperlink format.

Your Turn

1. Create the hyperlinks described below.

Weather

- The temperature on the surface of Venus is about 900 degrees. That is hot enough to melt lead.
- The atmosphere consists of mostly carbon dioxide, with some nitrogen and sulfuric acid. The atmospheric pressure on Venus is about 90 times greater than on Earth. You would have to dive down nearly a half mile in the ocean to experience this pressure.
- Winds are very strong, and sometimes the winds are over 200 mph. On Earth, weather with 74 mph wind is classified as a hurricane.

More Information on Venus

Top of the Document

Copyright 20--
Pleasant Valley Middle School Tech Team

Insert an appropriate **clip art** image representing the home page, and then **create a hyperlink** from the graphic to the Web page **Venus**.

Create a hyperlink to this Web address: http://www.nasa.gov

2. Apply a theme, add graphics, and change fonts to enhance the appearance of the Web page.

3. Save the changes to the file.

Continued on next page

Format a Report With Citations

(Cavazzi, "The Late Roman Republic")

Country". He took for himself the title of Augustus, or revered one. Octavian then became the first Roman emperor, or absolute ruler of an empire.

Augustus was a clever politician. He held the offices of consul, tribune, high priest, and senator all at the same time. However, he refused to be crowned emperor. Augustus knew that most Romans would not accept one-person rule unless it took the form of a republic.

Open the file **6-4 Project 1b**. Copy and paste the contents of the file.

3. Close the file **6-4 Project 1b**.

4. Save the changes. Keep the file open for Project 2.

Practice

Create a Hyperlink

4. Edit the bottom of the page as shown below.

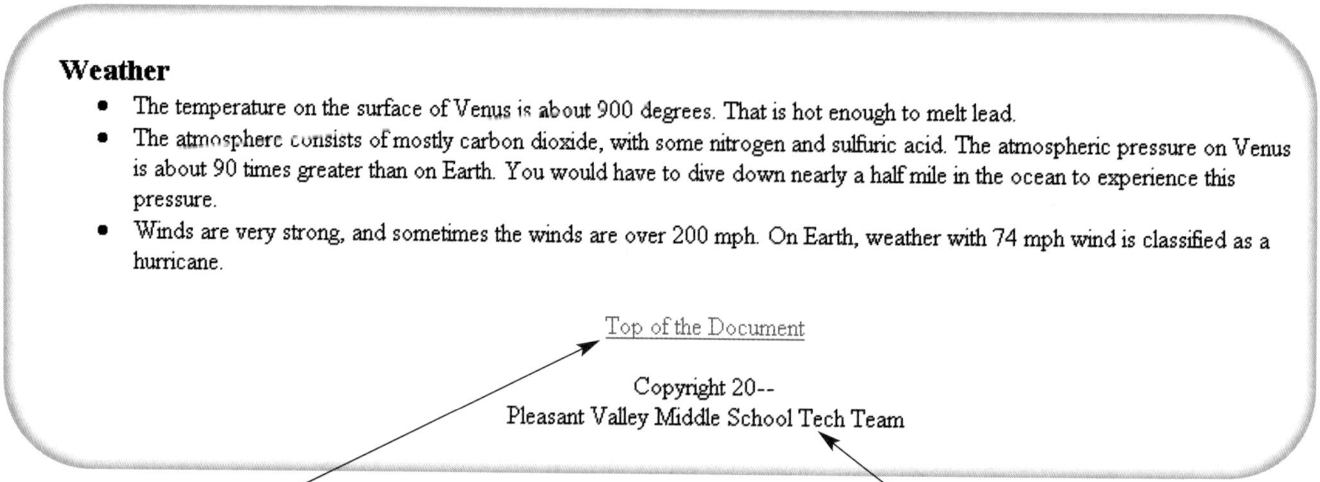

Weather

- The temperature on the surface of Venus is about 900 degrees. That is hot enough to melt lead.
- The atmosphere consists of mostly carbon dioxide, with some nitrogen and sulfuric acid. The atmospheric pressure on Venus is about 90 times greater than on Earth. You would have to dive down nearly a half mile in the ocean to experience this pressure.
- Winds are very strong, and sometimes the winds are over 200 mph. On Earth, weather with 74 mph wind is classified as a hurricane.

Top of the Document

Copyright 20--
Pleasant Valley Middle School Tech Team

Create a hyperlink to go to the top of the document.

Insert this copyright notice at the end of the Web page.

5. Save the changes. Keep the document open for Project 2.

Format a Header

A **header** is information that appears at the top of each page in a document. A **footer** is information that appears at the bottom of each page in a document. Include your name and the page number in a header.

Your Turn

1. Format a header as shown below.

Create a **header** with your last name at the right margin and the page number at the right.

Format the **header** to appear on all pages.

Your Last Name #

Augustus wanted boundaries that would be easy to defend. So he rounded out the empire to natural frontiers--the Rhine and Danube rivers in the north, the Atlantic Ocean in the west, and the Sahara in the south. Augustus also stationed soldiers there.

Augustus was not interested in gaining new territory for Rome. Instead, he worked on governing the existing empire. He paid provincial governors large salaries so that they would not feel the need to overtax the people or keep public money for themselves.

To make sure that people did not pay too much or too little tax, Augustus ordered a census, or population count, to be taken from time to time. He made Rome more beautiful. He wrote strict laws to govern the way people behaved in public. He protected the city by

Continued on next page

Create a Hyperlink

2. **Create a hyperlink** to a place in the current document.

Select one of the words in the list, and **create a hyperlink** to the heading with the same name.

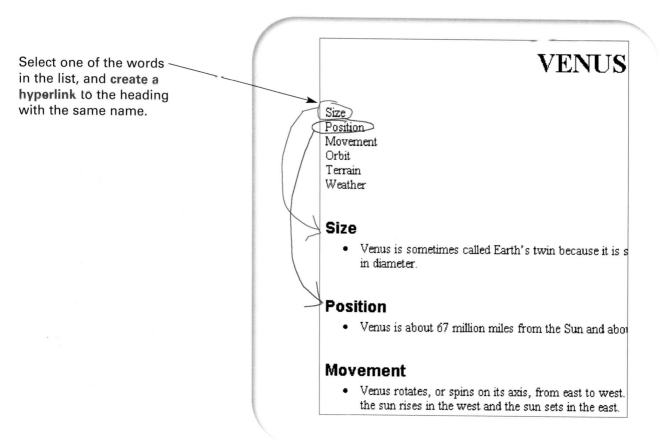

3. Create hyperlinks for each of the remaining words in the list of contents.

Continued on next page

Format a Header

setting up a fire brigade and a police force and encouraged learning

by building Rome's first library. *(Cavazzi, "Roman Society")*

Augustus ruled for 41 years and brought peace to Rome. He

gave Romans a new sense of pride and reorganized the government

of Rome so that it ran well for more than 200 years. *(Cavazzi, "The Late Roman Republic")* The peace that

he brought to Rome was called the Pax Romana. For the most part,

Rome and its people prospered, civilization spread, and cultures mixed.

In the early years of the empire, about 1 million people lived in

Rome. It suffered from many of the same problems as cities today--too

little housing, air pollution, crime, unemployment, and a high cost of

living. Many Romans could not find jobs and had to pay taxes on

almost everything.

2. Save the changes. Keep the file open for Project 3.

Create a Hyperlink

To help viewers quickly and easily navigate through the information on your Web page, you can create hyperlinks. A **hyperlink** is text or a graphic that you click to go to a file, to a location on the same Web page, or to a different Web page. Text with a formatted hyperlink is usually displayed in a different color and underlined.

In this section, you will learn to create shortcuts that will save you time navigating your Web pages by creating hyperlinks.

Your Turn

1. Edit the document as shown below.

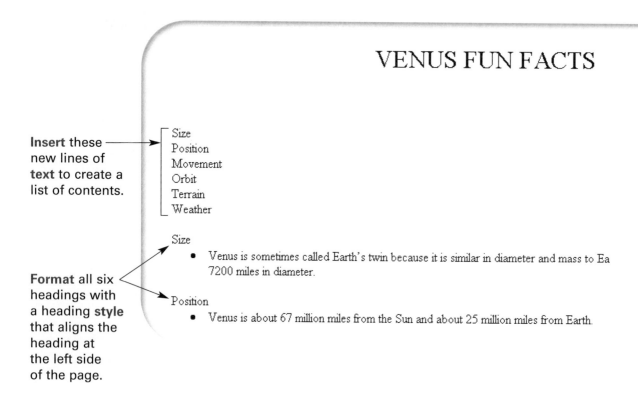

VENUS FUN FACTS

Insert these new lines of **text** to create a list of contents.

Size
Position
Movement
Orbit
Terrain
Weather

Format all six headings with a heading **style** that aligns the heading at the left side of the page.

Size

● Venus is sometimes called Earth's twin because it is similar in diameter and mass to Ea 7200 miles in diameter.

Position

● Venus is about 67 million miles from the Sun and about 25 million miles from Earth.

Continued on next page

Practice

Format a Works Cited Reference Page

A **Works Cited** page is a common type of reference page. This page is a list of all the sources you cited in the report.

Your Turn

1. **Insert** a **page break** at the end of the document.

Select the entire document and change the **line spacing** to **double**.

2. Create the works cited page as shown in the illustration below.

Works Cited

"Augustus." *Microsoft Encarta Online*. 10 Dec. 2002. <http://

Format each source with a hanging indent.

encarta.msn.com>.

Cavazzi, Franco. "Emperor Augustus." *Illustrated History of the Roman Empire*. 10 Dec. 2002. <http://www.roman-empire. net/emperors/augustus-index.html>.

Cavazzi, Franco. "Roman Society." *Illustrated History of the Roman Empire*. 10 Dec. 2002. <http://www.roman-empire. net/society/society.html>.

Cavazzi, Franco. "The Late Roman Republic." *Illustrated History of the Roman Empire*. 10 Dec. 2002. <http://www.roman-empire.net/republic/laterep-index.html>.

3. Proofread and make any necessary corrections.

4. Save the changes. Print and close the file.

SECTION 8.3

Create Hyperlinks for Web Pages

GOALS: Demonstrate the ability to:
- ▶ Create hyperlinks.
- ▶ Preview a Web page.

PROOFREADING WARMUP

In a word processing document, key each line 3 times.
Proofread your work.

These short, easy words help you when you build your speed.
Even Jacques may gaze up to find six crows in the blue sky.
James and I grew up in Montana; we always go home in March.

Making the Connection

Navigating to different parts of a Web page or to other Web pages can be time consuming. See how long it takes you to find some information about Venus.

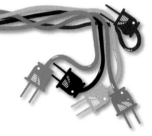

Your Turn

1. Open the Web page ***urs*Venus Fun Facts** that you saved in Section 8.2, Project 1.

2. Look at a clock, and write on a sheet of paper what time it is.

3. Now complete the steps to the right:

4. Look at the clock, and record the time. Calculate how much time you spent navigating the Web pages.

5. Keep the Venus Web page and the Venus Fun Facts Web page open for Project 1.

1. Scroll down to the bottom of the Web page and go to the facts on weather.
2. Go back to the top of the Web page.
3. Go to the facts on Terrain.
4. Go to the facts on Size.
5. Open the Web page document Venus that you saved in Section 8.1.
6. Go back to the Venus Fun Facts page and go to the facts on Movement.
7. Open your Web browser and go to this URL: http://www.nasa.gov.

Create a Multipage Report With Citations

Create another multipage report with citations.

Your Turn

1. Open a new word processing document.

2. Key the first part of the report as indicated.

Change the left and right **margins** to one inch.

Create a header with your name and the page number for all pages.

Your Last Name #

Your First and Last Name

Your Teacher's Name

Class

Today's Date

King of the Wild Frontier

"Be always sure you are right, then go ahead" (Lofaro 1148d). You're probably wondering what that means. Well, a guy named Davy Crockett used to say that. It is one of his best-known quotes. Read on to find out more about this legendary person.

Actually, his name was David Crockett. He was born in a small cabin in Tennessee on August 17, 1786 (*Davy Crockett*). His family lived in a cabin on the banks of the Nolichucky River. Davy had eight brothers and sisters. Four were older and four were younger.

Continued on next page

Check Your Understanding

1. Open a new word processing document.
2. Compose complete sentences to respond to the following:
   a. Describe how you can position a table in the middle of a page.
   b. Describe the steps for removing table borders.
   c. Describe the steps for automatically adjusting the widths of the table columns.
3. Write a paragraph explaining how formatting a table is similar to formatting a graphic.
4. Save the document as *urs*Table Formats. Print and close the file.

Weather

- The temperature on the surface of Venus is about 900 degrees. That is hot enough to melt lead.
- The atmospheric pressure on Venus is about 90 times greater than on Earth. You would have to dive down nearly a half mile in the ocean to experience this pressure.
- Winds are very strong, and sometimes the winds are over 200 mph. On Earth, weather with 74 mph wind is classified as a hurricane.

MORE VENUS DATA

Diameter	Approximately 7200 miles
Atmosphere components	Carbon dioxide, nitrogen, sulfuric acid
Distance from the Sun	About 67 million miles
Distance from Earth	About 25 million miles
Landscape	Mountains, canyons, volcanoes, and plains filled with lava

Compare the illustration with urs*Venus Fun Facts.*

Create a Multipage Report With Citations

Davy lived with his family in Tennessee until he was 13. He went to school, but he didn't like it. He skipped school a lot. He ran away from home because he knew his dad was going to punish him for playing hooky. He joined a cattle drive to make money. He drove the cattle to Virginia almost 300 miles away. He stayed in Virginia and worked a lot of jobs for over two years. He returned to his family in Tennessee when he was 16 (*Davy Crockett Biography*).

Copy and paste the entire contents of file **6-4 Project 4**.

3. Close the file 6-4 Project 4.

4. Proofread and make any necessary corrections.

5. Save the document as *urs*Davy Crockett. Keep the file open for the next step.

Continued on next page

Reinforce

Create a Table

The Lincoln Memorial

We had many stairs to climb to reach the Lincoln Memorial.

Did you know?
* The Lincoln Memorial is a tribute to Abraham Lincoln.
* There are 36 columns - each column represents a state in the union at the time of Lincoln's death.
* It took about eight years to build the monument, and it cost about three million dollars.
* The memorial was dedicated in 1922 on Lincoln's birthday, February 12.

← Insert the file photo **Lincoln**, and resize as needed.

← Key this caption below the photo.

The White House

The President was not at the White House when we visited.

Did you know?
* The White House was built between 1792 and 1800.
* John Adams was the first president to move in.
* Although it has been called the President's House and the President's Palace, it was officially designated the White House when Theodore Roosevelt put the name on his stationery in 1901.

← Insert the file photo **White House**. Resize the photo as needed.

← Key this caption below the photo.

5. Save the changes. Print and close the file.

Create a Multipage Report With Citations

6. **Insert a new page break** at the end of the document, and create a Works Cited page using the references shown below.

Works Cited

Author Unknown. "Davy Crockett Biography." 6 April 2002.

<http://www.infoporium.com/heritage/crockbio.shtml>.

"Davy Crockett." *Microsoft Encarta Online Encyclopedia 2002.*

<http://encarta.msn.com>.

Davy Crockett Birthplace Association. "American West-Davy

Crockett." 6 April 2002. <http://www.americanwest.com/

pages/davycroc.htm>.

Lofaro, Michael A. "Davy Crockett." *The World Book Encyclopedia*

2002. Chicago: World Book, Inc., Vol. 14, pp. 1148d-1149.

The Texas State Historical Association. *The New Handbook of*

Texas-Online. "Davy Crockett (1786-1836)-Biography."

6 April 2002. <http://www.alamo-de-parras.welkin.org/

history/bios/crockett/crockett.html>.

7. Save the changes. Print and close the file.

Create a Table

4. Enhance the Web page by adding the photos and captions identified in the illustrations below.

The Capitol Building

Insert the file photo **Capitol**, and resize as needed.

Key this caption below the photo.

We were lucky to visit the Capitol Building when the Senate was in session.

Did you know?

* President Washington selected the site for the building of the Capitol building.
* The cornerstone was laid in September 1793, and the construction began. The building was completed in 1807, but there have been many additions and renovations since then.
* The building has five levels and more than 500 rooms. The Senate and the House of Representatives are on the second floor.

History of Construction

1791	Construction begins
1793	Cornerstone laid
1800	Building not complete, but Congress occupies building
1812	British troops set Capitol on fire
1815	Restoration begins
1818	Construction of the Rotunda begins
1824	Original dome completed
1826	Original structure completed
1851	Library of Congress burned by fire
1856	Old dome removed
1859	New House and Senate chambers completed
1863	New dome completed

Continued on next page

1. Open a new word processing document. Answer the following using complete sentences.
2. What is a citation?
3. Define a header and explain what information is included in the header.
4. What is a works cited page?
5. What is the difference, if any, in how a works cited page is formatted compared with a bibliography page?
6. Save the document as *urs*Citations. Print and close the file.

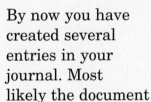

Write On!

By now you have created several entries in your journal. Most likely the document contains multiple pages. Formatting a header for the document will help you identify the pages of the document if you should ever print all or part of your journal.

1. Open your journal and create a header with your name and the page number.
2. Position the insertion point at the end of the journal. Enter today's date to create a new journal entry.
3. Think of a situation when you (or maybe one of your classmates) did not receive credit for a classroom assignment because you forgot to put your name on your work or because some of the pages were misplaced or lost. What did you learn from that experience? Write about the experience in your journal.
4. Save the changes to your journal. Close the file.

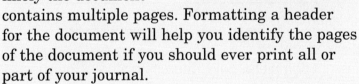

inter**NET** CONNECTION

In this lesson, you formatted a report about Davy Crockett. An image would help the reader understand more about your report.

1. Open your file *urs*Davy Crockett and save the document as *urs*Davy Crockett2.
2. Open your Web browser, and search the Internet for an image of Davy.
3. Copy the image into the document. Resize and position the image within the document.
4. Save the changes. Print and close the file.

Create a Table

In this project you will reinforce the skills you have learned and create and format a table on a Web page.

Your Turn

1. Open the file **8-2 Project 2**, and save the document as a Web page. Name the document *urs***Landmarks**.

2. Apply a theme of your choice.

3. In the section about the Capitol Building, under the bulleted list, create and format the table shown below.

Bold this column of text. ⟶

First, create a title above the table.

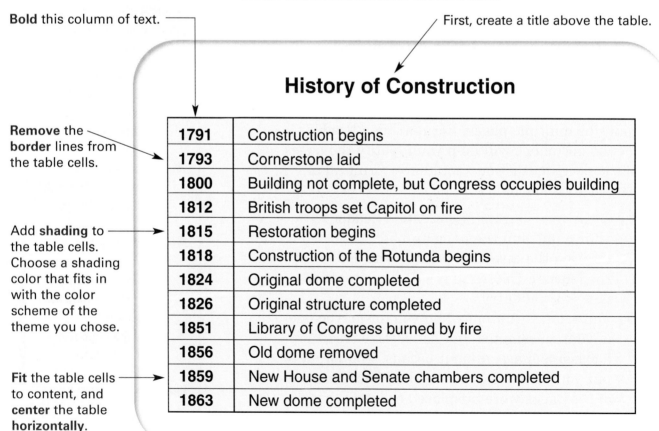

Remove the **border** lines from the table cells.

Add **shading** to the table cells. Choose a shading color that fits in with the color scheme of the theme you chose.

Fit the table cells to content, and **center** the table horizontally.

History of Construction

1791	Construction begins
1793	Cornerstone laid
1800	Building not complete, but Congress occupies building
1812	British troops set Capitol on fire
1815	Restoration begins
1818	Construction of the Rotunda begins
1824	Original dome completed
1826	Original structure completed
1851	Library of Congress burned by fire
1856	Old dome removed
1859	New House and Senate chambers completed
1863	New dome completed

Continued on next page

SECTION 6.5

Format a Report With Footnotes or Endnotes

GOALS: Demonstrate the ability to:

▶ Key and format footnotes and endnotes.

▶ Convert footnotes to endnotes.

▶ Work from printed and unarranged material.

▶ Spell-check, proofread, and correct errors.

PROOFREADING WARMUP

In a word processing document, key each line 3 times.
Proofread your work.

```
I could not read the small print on the map she sent to me.
A dozen jumpy zebras quickly zipped over the six big gates.
Because I had good grades, my scholarship has been renewed.
```

Making the Connection

When you work really hard on an assignment, you like to take credit for your time and efforts. Sometimes you even feel proud of your work, and you probably like it when people notice what you have done.

When you research a topic for a report, most likely you will gather your information from a magazine, a newspaper, an encyclopedia, or a Web site. Did you ever stop to think who organized and reported that information?

In this section you will learn about giving credit to the sources of information you use in your reports.

bad bacteria. The good bacteria produce natural antibiotics, which fight the bad bacteria. Friendly bacteria can promote good health.[1]

As Pat Kendall, a food science and human nutrition specialist, says, "Yogurt

Your Turn

1. Open the file **6-5 Project 1**, and save the document as *urs*Yogurt1.

2. Keep the file open for Project 1.

Create and Format a Table on a Web Page

You can position a table anywhere on a Web page. You can also add fill colors (called **shading**), and you can even add or remove table cell borders.

You will save a document as a Web page, and then you will create and format a table on the Web page.

Your Turn

1. Position the insertion point at the bottom of the Web page.

2. Create and format the table shown below.

Add **shading** to the table cells. Choose a color.

Bold this column of text.

Create a title above the table.

Adjust the table cells to content.

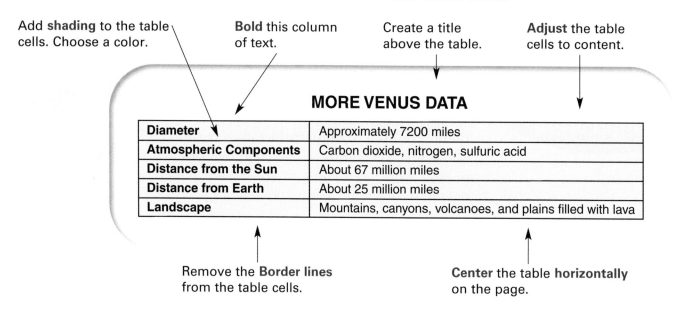

MORE VENUS DATA

Diameter	Approximately 7200 miles
Atmospheric Components	Carbon dioxide, nitrogen, sulfuric acid
Distance from the Sun	About 67 million miles
Distance from Earth	About 25 million miles
Landscape	Mountains, canyons, volcanoes, and plains filled with lava

Remove the **Border lines** from the table cells.

Center the table **horizontally** on the page.

3. Save the changes. Print and close the file.

Insert a Footnote

Footnotes are notes at the bottom of a page that provide references for text on the same page. You can use a footnote to give credit to the source by telling the reader where you found the information. If you quote from a source word for word, you need to format the information as a direct quotation and cite the source. When you put someone else's ideas into your own words (paraphrase), you must also give credit by citing the source.

Your Turn

1. This report already contains three footnotes. Take some time to look through the report and locate the footnotes. The first footnote is on page 2. See the illustration below.

Footnote reference mark.

bad bacteria. The good bacteria produce natural antibiotics, which fight the bad bacteria. Friendly

bacteria can promote good health.[1]

As Pat Kendall, a food science and human nutrition specialist, says, "Yogurt deserves its

reputation as a healthful food." Yogurt contains protein, potassium, magnesium, vitamin B-12,

riboflavin, and zinc. It is low in fat and it helps the immune system. The good bacteria in yogurt

aid digestion. It can even help fight acne.

Footnote.

[1] Dannon Yogurt Products. *The History of Cultures*. 13 May 2002. <http://www.dannon.com/pages/dannon_browser.cfm/mode.article/>.

2

2. Locate the main topic, RESEARCH, and edit the document as indicated on the following page.

Continued on next page

Create a Table in a Web Page

GOALS: Demonstrate the ability to:

▶ Create a table in a Web page.

▶ Add shading to the table cells.

▶ Remove table border lines.

▶ Center a table horizontally on the page.

PROOFREADING WARMUP

In a word processing document, key and complete the paragraph starter. Proofread your work.

```
If I could travel into the future, this is how far I
would go and why.
```

Making the Connection

Tables are useful for organizing information on Web pages. When you add a table to a Web page, you can enhance the table with various formats.

Your Turn

1. Open the file **8-2 Project 1** and Save As a Web page. Name the document *urs*Venus Fun Facts.

2. Keep the file open for Project 1.

VENUS FUN FACTS

Size

• Venus is sometimes called Earth's twin because it is similar in diameter and mass to Earth.

Insert a Footnote

Insert a footnote for paraphrased material:
Sullivan, James A. Bacterial Growth Cam. "Bacteria Cam: Growth of *Streptococcus pneumoniae.*" 14 May 2002. <http://cellsalive.com/ecoli.htm>.

RESEARCH

In my research I learned that bacteria grow, eat, and then reproduce. If the conditions are right (such as the right temperature and the right environment), each bacterium grows slightly in size or length. A new cell wall grows through the center of the bacterium, and then the bacterium splits into two identical daughter cells. I found a Web site that showed real E.coli bacteria growing and splitting. First there was one. After about 20 minutes there were two. Then after 20 more minutes there were four. Then there were eight, then sixteen, then thirty-two, and so on. Within just a few hours there was a colony of hundreds of bacteria.

I also learned that not all bacteria are bad. Some bacteria can cause disease, but others can cure. For example, antibiotics are made from bacteria. We also use bacteria to make several foods. We use bacteria to make cheese and buttermilk from milk. We use bacteria to make vinegar from alcohol.

Insert a footnote for paraphrased material:
Dairy Research and Information Center. "An Introduction to Bacteria."
14 May 2002. <http://drinc.ucdavis.edu/html/dairyb/index.shtml>.

Continued on next page

1. Open a new word processing document.

2. Key the answer to each question using a complete sentence.

3. List three or more examples of visuals that are common to Web pages.

4. What is the purpose of a theme?

5. How is it different inserting photos and clip art images on a Web page?

6. Save the document as *urs*Web Pages. Print and close the file.

interNET CONNECTION

After you create a Web page you may decide to publish it on the Web. That means that persons who have access to the Internet will be able to view your Web page.

1. Open your Web browser and research the Web to find out how you can publish your Web page.

2. Some Web hosts allow students to publish their Web pages at no cost. See if you can find any of these Web hosts. Bookmark the pages for future use.

Insert a Footnote

3. Locate the paragraph that begins "As Pat Kendall, . . ."

4. Edit the paragraph as indicated below.

Insert a footnote for a direct quotation:
Kendall, Pat. PENpages College of Agricultural Sciences. "Live, Active, and Probiotic: Yogurt Culture." 14 May 2002.
<http://www.penpages.psu.edu/penpages_reference/12101/121012735.html>.

As Pat Kendall, a food science and human nutrition specialist, says, "Yogurt deserves its reputation as a healthful food." Yogurt contains protein, potassium, magnesium, vitamin B-12, riboflavin, and zinc. It is low in fat and it helps the immune system. The good bacteria in yogurt aid digestion. It can even help fight acne.

Insert a footnote for paraphrased material:
pageWise, Inc. "Benefits of Yogurt." 14 May 2002.
<http://mimi.essortment.com/yogurtbenefits_oex.htm>.

5. Proofread and make any necessary corrections.

6. Save the changes. Keep the file open for Project 2.

Create a Web Page

4. Add clip art as shown below.

Pleasant Valley Middle School
Field Trip Memories

7th Grade World History

On September 28, 7th Grade World History students took a journey back in time. They spent the day with peasants, nobles, and the royal court. They watched a play by Shakespeare, enjoyed watching knights compete in a jousting event, and visited shopkeepers. They also watched shopkeepers demonstrate glass blowing, armor making, and calligraphy. This happened just 33 miles away at the annual Renaissance Festival. What a great experience it was to go back to the medieval times and experience life as it was in the 16th century.

Insert a clip art image.

8th Grade American History

On April 27, the 8th Grade American History students went on their annual field trip. They traveled by charter bus to Washington, D.C. The field trip was fantastic. Everyone had fun and learned a lot.

5. Save the changes. Print and close the file.

Practice

Convert Footnotes to Endnotes

Endnotes are another common type of reference page at the end of the document that provide references for text within the document. Endnotes are the same as footnotes—they just appear in a different location in the report. Sometimes the endnotes are inserted on a page by themselves as the last page in the document.

When you cite a source in a document, you choose between the footnote and the endnote format. However, if you change your mind, you can convert footnotes to endnotes and vice versa.

Your Turn

1. **Save** the document *urs*Yogurt1 as *urs*Yogurt2. Use F12 to save.

2. Position the insertion point at the end of the document and insert a new page break.

3. Key, **center**, and **bold** the title ENDNOTES. Then press ENTER.

4. **Convert** all **the footnotes to endnotes**.

5. Keep the file open for the next step.

Continued on next page

Create a Web Page

In this project you will reinforce the skills you have learned by creating and formatting a Web page for Pleasant Valley Middle School. The purpose of the Web page is to communicate information about class field trips.

Your Turn

1. Open the file **8-1 Project 4** and save the document as a Web page. Name the document *urs*Field Trips.

2. Format the Web page as shown below.

Format a horizontal line border.

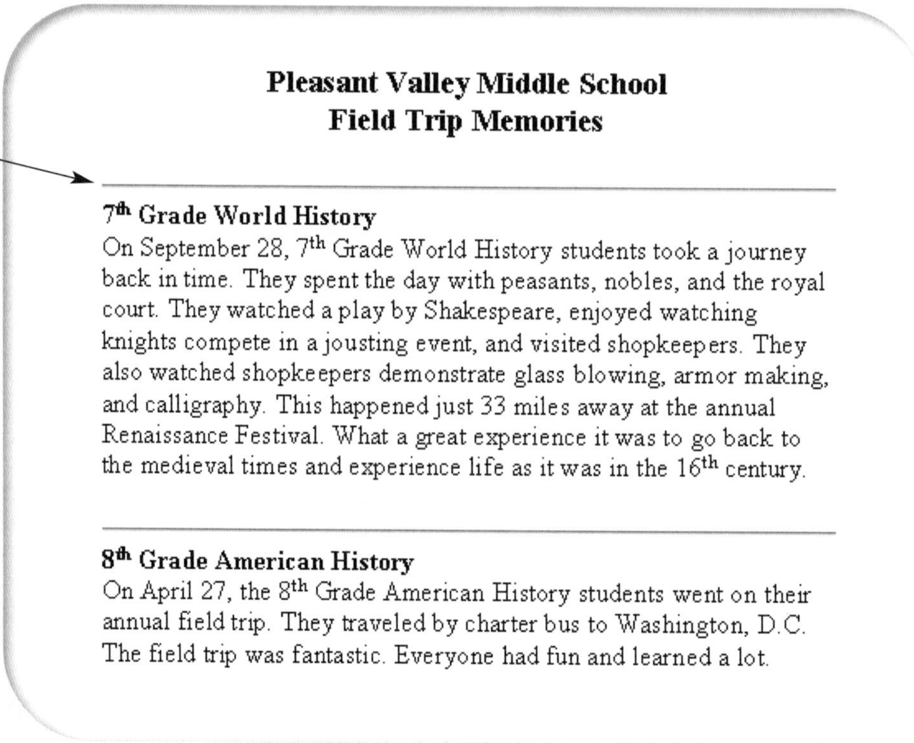

**Pleasant Valley Middle School
Field Trip Memories**

7th Grade World History
On September 28, 7th Grade World History students took a journey back in time. They spent the day with peasants, nobles, and the royal court. They watched a play by Shakespeare, enjoyed watching knights compete in a jousting event, and visited shopkeepers. They also watched shopkeepers demonstrate glass blowing, armor making, and calligraphy. This happened just 33 miles away at the annual Renaissance Festival. What a great experience it was to go back to the medieval times and experience life as it was in the 16th century.

8th Grade American History
On April 27, the 8th Grade American History students went on their annual field trip. They traveled by charter bus to Washington, D.C. The field trip was fantastic. Everyone had fun and learned a lot.

3. Choose and apply a theme.

Continued on next page

Convert Footnotes to Endnotes

6. Compare your endnotes page with the one shown below.

ENDNOTES

———————————

[1] Sullivan, James A. Bacterial Growth Cam. "Bacteria Cam: Growth of *Streptococcus pneumoniae*." 14 May 2002. <http://cellsalive.com/ecoli.htm>.

[2] Dairy Research and Information Center. "An Introduction to Bacteria" 12 May 2002. <http://drinc.ucdavis.edu/html/dairyb/index.shtml>.

[3] Dannon Yogurt Products. "The History of Cultures." 13 May 2002. <http://www.dannon.com/pages/dannon_browser.cfm/mode.article/jid.15/aid.182/>.

[4] Kendall, Pat. PENpages College of Agricultural Sciences. "Live, Active, and Probiotic: Yogurt Culture." 14 May 2002. <http://www.penpages.psu.edu/penpages_reference/12101/121012735.html>.

[5] PageWise, Inc. "Benefits of Yogurt." 13 May 2002. <http://mimi.essortment.com/yogurtbenefits_oex.htm>.

[6] Manning, Edna. *Natural Life Magazine #43*. "Yogurt—Food of Centenarians." 14 May 2002. <http://www.life.ca/nl/43/yogurt.html>.

[7] Author Unknown. "Cheap-Quick_&-Easy Homemade Yogurt." <http://surfboard.surfside.net/prussell/Yogurt.htm#ingredients>.

---

7. Save the changes. You may need to manually insert some page breaks so that side headings are not separated from the first paragraph of text below the heading.

8. Create a title page for this report.

9. Print and close the file.

Practice

Insert Photos and Graphics on a Web Page

You can insert photos and clip art images on a Web page just as you do in the documents you create.

Your Turn

1. Insert clip art as indicated below.

VENUS

‡Viewing Venus

Venus, the sixth largest planet, was named for the Roman goddess of love and beauty. Venus is Earth's closest neighbor. It is visible with the naked eye during daytime and nighttime. Only two objects are brighter than Venus—the sun and the moon.

VENUS

Insert clip art about Venus. Resize as necessary.

2. Save the changes. Print and close the file.

Reinforce

Format Footnotes and Endnotes

Reinforce the word processing features you learned by creating another multipage report with footnotes and endnotes.

Your Turn

1. Open the file **6-5 Project 3**. Save the file as *urs***Rockets**.

2. Locate the first paragraph on the history of rocketing and edit the document as indicated below.

HISTORY OF ROCKETING

The Chinese were the first on record to launch a rocket in the thirteenth century. They used something called a "fire arrow" against the attack of the Mongols. Then as technology grew, the Chinese began experimenting with gun-powder rockets. They attached bamboo tubes to arrows and launched them with bows. Soon they figured out when they used gun-powder, the rockets could launch themselves. Then because of war, the use of rockets spread quickly across Asia and Europe. Italy designed a rocket-powered running surface torpedo to set other ships on fire. Many other uses of rockets were known because of war. For example, each side used rockets in the American Civil War.

Insert a footnote for paraphrased material:
Cliff, Eugene M. "Rocket." *The World Book Encyclopedia 2002.* Chicago: World Book, Inc., Vol. 16, p. 384.

3. Keep the file open for the next step.

Continued on next page

Practice

Apply a Visual Theme to a Web Page

Web pages are often displayed with many visual elements. You can apply a theme to give your Web page a decorative look. A **theme** is a set of unified design elements and color schemes that include a background design, customized bullets, and borders. When you apply a theme to your Web page, the bullet symbols and the borders are formatted to the theme you have chosen.

Your Turn

1. Choose and apply a **theme** to your Web page.

2. Notice that the text, bullets, and borders are now formatted for the theme you chose. The illustration below is provided as an example. Your Web page may look much different.

The **theme** includes a background image.

VENUS

✚Viewing Venus
Venus, the sixth largest planet, was named for the Roman goddess of love and beauty. Venus is Earth's closest neighbor. It is visible with the naked eye during daytime and nighttime. Only two objects are brighter than Venus—the sun and the moon.

✚Exploring Venus
It is very difficult to explore Venus because thick white clouds block the view of its surface. We cannot get close because the sulfuric acid clouds and the extremely high temperatures damage the spacecraft. Between 1990 and 1994, the American Magellan spaceship provided much data and many images of Venus.

The bullets and border line are automatically formatted when you apply a theme.

3. Save the changes. Keep the file open for Project 3.

Format Footnotes and Endnotes

4. Locate the paragraph shown below and add another endnote.

It wasn't until 1942 that the first A4 rocket was launched. On the first try, the rocket flew only about one-half mile into the clouds and landed in the ocean. On the second try, the rocket flew about 7 miles high and then exploded. On the third try, though, the rocket flew about 120 miles and landed on target. This marked the beginning of the space age.

Insert a footnote for paraphrased material:
Benson, Tom. NASA Glenn Learning Technologies. "Brief History of Rockets." 15 May 2002. <http://www.grc.nasa.gov/WWW/K-12/ TRC/Rockets/history_of_rockets.html>.

5. Locate the paragraph on Newton's Laws and add the endnote indicated below.

will depend on the thrust created by the engine. When the thrust stops, gravity takes over and the rocket falls to the ground.

Insert a footnote for paraphrased material: Genesis Search for Origins. "Newton's Laws of Motion and Rockets." 17 May 2002. <http://www.genesismission.org/ educate/scimodule/LaunchPropulsion/L&P_PDFs/B8_STnewtonslaws.pdf>.

6. Keep the file open for the next step.

Continued on next page

Save a Document as a Web Page

Most documents you create on the computer can be displayed on Web pages. Web pages can contain text, graphics, photos, sound, and video. You will learn to insert **bullets** and save a document as a Web page.

Your Turn

1. Open a new word processing document, and key and format the paragraphs shown below.

Format a horizontal **border**.

Insert bullets.

Venus

• Viewing Venus

Venus, the sixth largest planet, was named for the Roman goddess of love and beauty. Venus is Earth's closest neighbor. It is visible with the naked eye during daytime and nighttime. Only two objects are brighter than Venus—the sun and the moon.

• Exploring Venus

It is very difficult to explore Venus because thick white clouds block the view of its surface. We cannot get close because the sulfuric acid clouds and the extremely high temperatures damage the spacecraft. Between 1990 and 1994, the American Magellan spaceship provided much data and many images of Venus.

2. **Save** the document **as a Web page**. Name the Web page *urs*Venus.

3. Keep the file open for Project 2.

Format Footnotes and Endnotes

7. Locate the second paragraph on Mass and Velocity and add the endnote shown below.

> The velocity is the speed and direction of motion. The speed is determined by the power of the engine. The direction will be the angle of the launch rod unless there is wind. The wind can change the direction of the rocket after it is launched. The velocity affects how stable the rocket is in the air.

Insert a footnote for paraphrased material:
Brain, Marshall. *Howstuffworks*. "How Rocket Engines Work."
17 May 2002. <http://www.howstuffworks.com/rocket1.htm>.

8. Save the changes. Proofread and make any necessary corrections.

9. Save a copy of the same document as *urs*Rockets2.

10. Convert all the footnotes to endnotes. Adjust the page breaks if necessary.

11. Save the changes. Print and close the file.

Create a Web Page

GOALS: Demonstrate the ability to:
- ▶ Save a document as a Web page.
- ▶ Apply a theme and bullets.
- ▶ Format a horizontal line border.
- ▶ Insert photos and graphics.

PROOFREADING WARMUP

In a word processing document, key each line 3 times.
Proofread your work.

```
We are planning to have a cookout when we meet at the lake.
All four mixtures in the deep brown jug froze very quickly.
We usually vacation at a place that is south of the border.
```

Making the Connection

When you are proud of your work, you post it where others can see it. Web pages are a good way to share your work with others. Have you ever thought about publishing your work on the Web? To do this, you need to create a Web page.

Your Turn

1. Open your Web browser and go to your school's home page.
2. Look for things you enjoy seeing on a Web page, and make a list.
3. Share your list with a partner to see if you found similar visual elements.
4. Close your Web browser.

Colors
Bullets
Borders
Background Designs

1. Open a new word processing document.
2. What is the difference between a direct quotation and a paraphrase?
3. What is the difference between a footnote and an endnote?
4. Describe the process for converting footnotes to endnotes.
5. Save the file as *urs*Footnotes. Print and close the file.

Write On!

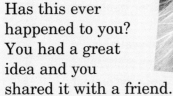

Has this ever happened to you? You had a great idea and you shared it with a friend. Later, you heard your friend sharing your idea with others. Everyone thinks your friend has a great idea. Your friend never gave you credit. How did that make you feel?

1. Open your journal and position the insertion point at the end of the document. Enter today's date to create a new journal entry.
2. Write at least one paragraph about how you did (or would) feel if someone used your ideas as his or her own and did not give you credit.
3. Save the changes to your journal. Close the file.

inter**NET** CONNECTION

Most people realize that when they quote the work of another, they must cite the source. But did you realize that you must also cite the source if you paraphrase or summarize another person's work? If you don't cite your source, you are guilty of not giving people credit for their work.

1. Open your Web browser and search for an online dictionary.
2. Find the definition for the term "plagiarism."
3. Open a word processing document. In your own words, define *plagiarism*. Then explain why it is important to give credit to others for their words and ideas.
4. Save the document as *urs*Plagiarism. Print and close the file.

Check Your Understanding

1. Open a new word processing document.
2. Key the answer to each question using a complete sentence.
3. What is the purpose of a template?
4. What are the advantages of using a template?
5. List three or more examples of templates that you can use.
6. Save the document as *urs*Templates. Print and close the file.

inter NET CONNECTION

Generally, the manufacturer of your software will provide additional document templates at its Web site. You can often download these templates at no additional cost.

1. Open your Web browser and locate the site for the manufacturer of your desktop publishing software.
2. Explore the templates that are available. Identify at least three templates that you would likely use in the future for your own projects.
3. Bookmark the Web pages for the templates you think you would use.

SECTION 6.6

Table of Contents

GOALS: Demonstrate the ability to:

▶ Key and format a table of contents.

▶ Format a tab stop with dot leaders.

▶ Spell-check, proofread, and correct errors.

PROOFREADING WARMUP

In a word processing document, key each line 3 times. Proofread your work.

```
It was a good idea to start to write your report this week.
My ax just zipped through the fine black wood quite evenly.
The accident was distressing; however, no one was impaired.
```

Making the Connection

Many newspapers provide a directory (often labeled *Index*) at the bottom of the front page of the newspaper. The directory provides an overview of the sections and topics covered in the newspaper, and it shows the page numbers for those sections and topics.

If you have a long report with several pages, you can provide a directory of the contents to help your readers identify the main ideas in your report and find information.

Your Turn

1. Open a new word processing document.

2. Key, center, and bold the title CONTENTS. Then press ENTER 2 times.

3. Save the document as *urs*Yogurt TOC.

4. Keep the file open for Project 1.

CONTENTS

INTRODUCTION 1
PROBLEM 1
HYPOTHESIS 1
RESEARCH 2
THE EXPERIMENT 5
Materials.. 5
Procedures 5
Results.. 7
CONCLUSION 8
BIBLIOGRAPHY 9

Create a New Document From a Template

Your Turn

1. Create a **new** document from a **template**. Choose a template for a calendar with photos or graphics. Be sure the calendar you choose is for the current year.

2. Locate the month when your birthday occurs.

3. Customize the calendar as indicated at left.

Insert an appropriate clip art image for the month.

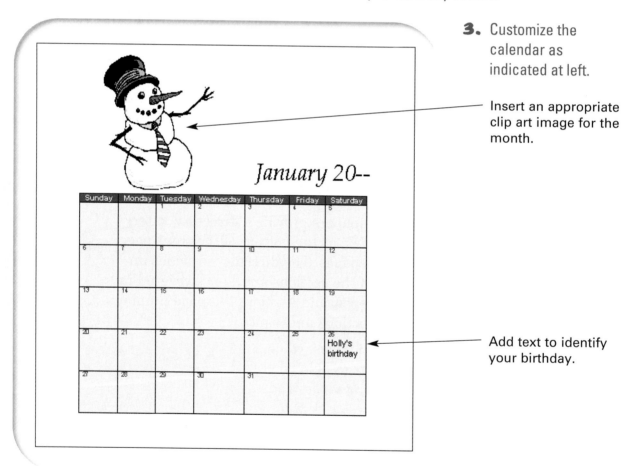

Add text to identify your birthday.

4. Save the document as *urs*Calendar.

5. Print the calendar page with your birthday and then close the document.

Practice

Create a Table of Contents

A **table of contents** is a listing of all the main topic headings and subtopic headings. A table of contents is generally used only for long reports. Sometimes, dot leaders (periods) are used to guide the reader's eyes from the section headings to the page numbers.

Your Turn

1. Complete the table of contents page by entering and formatting the information shown below.

Change the left and right **margins** to one inch.

Format a right-aligned **tab** stop **with leaders.** Set the tab stop at the right margin.

CONTENTS

INTRODUCTION... 1

PROBLEM.. 1

HYPOTHESIS 1

RESEARCH 2

THE EXPERIMENT... 5

Materials.. 5

Procedures... 5

Results 7

CONCLUSION 8

BIBLIOGRAPHY 9

2. Save the changes.

3. Spell-check, proofread, and correct errors. Print and close the file.

Practice

Use a Template to Create a Business Card

3. Customize the first business card in the template by replacing the sample information with the personal information shown below.

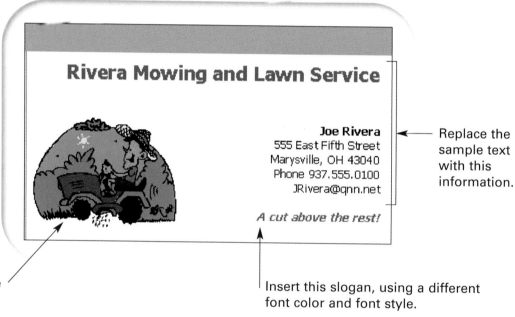

Rivera Mowing and Lawn Service

Joe Rivera
555 East Fifth Street
Marysville, OH 43040
Phone 937.555.0100
JRivera@qnn.net

A cut above the rest!

Replace the sample text with this information.

Insert an appropriate clip art image.

Insert this slogan, using a different font color and font style.

4. Copy all the content of the customized card to the Clipboard. Select the content on one of the sample cards and paste the contents from the Clipboard. Continue to select and paste until all the sample cards are replaced with the customized card contents.

5. Save the changes. Print one page of cards and close the file.

Reinforce

Create a Table of Contents

Reinforce the word processing features you learned by creating another table of contents.

Your Turn

1. Open a new word processing document and create a table of contents using the information illustrated below.

Change the left and right **margins** to 1 inch.

CONTENTS

INTRODUCTION

HISTORY OF ROCKETING

RESEARCH

Newton's Laws

Kinetic and Potential Energy

Mass and Velocity

THE ROCKET MODEL

Building the Rocket

Testing the Rocket

Rebuilding the Rocket

Safety Tips

APPLICATION

BIBLIOGRAPHY

Continued on next page

Use a Template to Create a Business Card

You can create business cards by using a business card **template** that has preformatted margins and borders for you to fill in the information you want. You can even decorate your template.

Your Turn

1. Open a new word processing document. From the New Document section, choose a **template** for business cards. Find a template that provides a framework for multiple cards on the same page.

Generally, templates for business cards provide a framework to create 6–10 cards on a page.

You can replace the sample text with your own personal information.

You can replace the graphic with one that you choose.

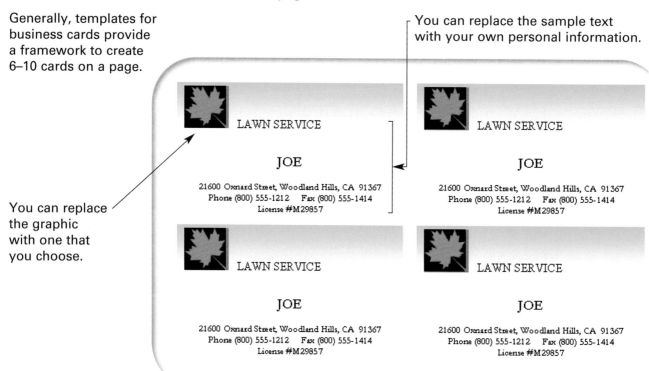

2. Save the document as *urs*Business Card.

Continued on next page

Creating a Table of Contents

2. Open the file **6-6 Project 2.** Locate each heading, and enter the appropriate page numbers in the table of contents. Align the page numbers at the right side of the page with dot leaders. Close the report document without saving any changes.

3. Save the table of contents as *urs*Rockets TOC.

4. Spell-check, proofread, and correct errors. Print and close the file.

Create Documents From Templates

GOALS: Demonstrate the ability to:

▶ Use a template to create a business card.

▶ Use a template to create a calendar.

PROOFREADING WARMUP

In a word processing document, key each line 3 times.
Proofread your work.

```
We have to learn to make introductions with poise and ease.
Mo brought back five or six dozen pieces of quaint jewelry.
The trip to Grandma's house was farther than they expected.
```

Making the Connection

Joe Rivera gets paid to mow some of his neighbors' lawns and to rake leaves in the fall. Joe believes he can increase his business by using business cards. Joe will give business cards to his current customers and also to potential new customers in his neighborhood.

In this section, you will learn how to create your own business cards.

Your Turn

1. Open a new word processing document, and create a list of information that should be included on a business card.

2. In Project 1 you will learn an easy way to create a business card.

3. Close the document without saving the changes.

Name
Telephone
Hours available for work

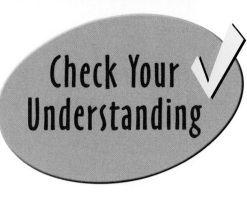

Check Your Understanding

1. Open a new word processing document.
2. Key the answer to each question, using a complete sentence.
3. What is the purpose of a table of contents? What type of information is contained in a table of contents?
4. What are dot leaders, and what is their purpose?
5. Save the file as *urs*Table of Contents. Print and close the file.

inter NET
CONNECTION

Visitors to Web sites can also find tools to help them find information within the site. Many times, the home page of a Web site provides a list of the site's main topics. When you click on the hyperlink for a main topic, a list of subtopics is displayed. The list serves the same purpose as a table of contents, but hyperlinks eliminate the need for page numbers.

1. Open your Web browser. Locate three different Web sites and make note of how the contents of the site are presented. Click on some of the links to navigate the site.
2. Open a new word processing document. Compare and contrast how the contents of the Web site are presented and how you navigate the site.
3. Save the document as *urs*Web Contents. Print and close the file.

Check Your Understanding

1. Open a new word processing document.
2. Key the answer to each question using a complete sentence.
3. What is a newsletter-style column format?
4. Describe what the text looks like when the paragraph alignment is justified.
5. What information is contained in a masthead?
6. Save the document as *urs*Newsletters.
7. Print and close the file.

inter**NET** CONNECTION

School newsletters are a great way to share information about what is going on at school. Students, teachers, parents, and community residents enjoy reading school newsletters. To make the newsletters easily accessible, many schools are now publishing their newsletters on the Web.

1. Open your Web browser and search for school newsletters.
2. Find a school newsletter that you like. For example, you might like a newsletter because of the information it contains or because of its attractive format.
3. Open a word processing document, and copy and paste the URL for the newsletter Web site. Then give the name of the newsletter, and write a paragraph describing why you think it is good.
4. Save the document as *urs*Online Newsletter. Print and close the file.

Review Project

In this project, you will apply the word processing skills you have learned to create and format a multipage report. Refer to previous projects as needed.

Your Turn

1. Open a new word processing document. Key the report shown below and on the next page.

Wild Weather

"Weather is the state of the atmosphere at some place and time." (Moran 156). Weather is important to us, each and every one of us every day. For example, we decide what clothes to wear based on the weather, and our outdoor activities are planned around the seasons and the daily forecasts. Even during warm-weather seasons, however, the weather conditions can be severe. Sometimes temperatures reach record highs, and utility companies must supply more power for air conditioning. Or high winds and storms damage trees and power lines. So I was wondering what causes the weather to go wild. Here's what I learned.

Air Masses

An air mass is a large body of air where all the air has about the same temperature and humidity. Air masses can be very cold, very hot, very dry, or very wet. An air mass that develops over land is dry compared with one that develops over water. An air mass that develops near the equator is warmer than one that develops at a higher latitude.

Air masses move and swirl over the surface of Earth. As the air mass moves, its temperature and humidity can change because of the ground conditions below. Because they move in different directions and at different speeds, they often bump into each other. Rain, thunderstorms, snow, tornadoes--all of these weather-related events can result when air masses meet (WW2010 University of Illinois).

Continued on next page

Create a Newsletter

2. Spell-check, proofread, and correct any errors.

3. Save the document as *urs*The Great Globe. Keep the file open for the next step.

4. Format the newsletter similar to the one illustrated below.

Create a
masthead.

Enhance
the headings.

Insert appropriate
clip art.

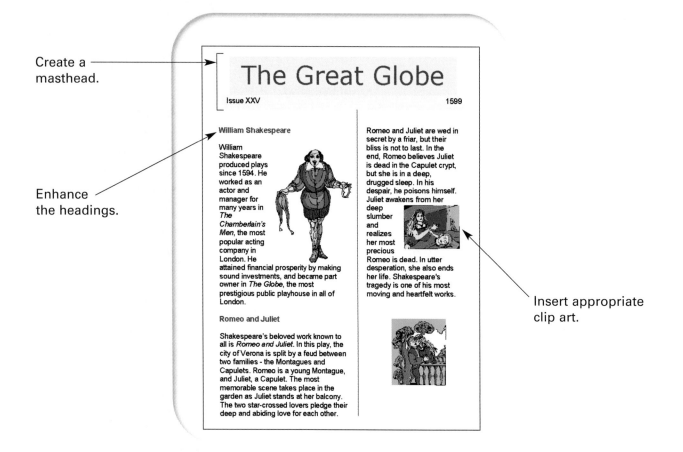

The Great Globe

Issue XXV   1599

William Shakespeare

William Shakespeare produced plays since 1594. He worked as an actor and manager for many years in *The Chamberlain's Men*, the most popular acting company in London. He attained financial prosperity by making sound investments, and became part owner in *The Globe*, the most prestigious public playhouse in all of London.

Romeo and Juliet

Shakespeare's beloved work known to all is *Romeo and Juliet*. In this play, the city of Verona is split by a feud between two families - the Montagues and Capulets. Romeo is a young Montague, and Juliet, a Capulet. The most memorable scene takes place in the garden as Juliet stands at her balcony. The two star-crossed lovers pledge their deep and abiding love for each other.

Romeo and Juliet are wed in secret by a friar, but their bliss is not to last. In the end, Romeo believes Juliet is dead in the Capulet crypt, but she is in a deep, drugged sleep. In his despair, he poisons himself. Juliet awakens from her deep slumber and realizes her most precious Romeo is dead. In utter desperation, she also ends her life. Shakespeare's tragedy is one of his most moving and heartfelt works.

5. Save the changes. Print and close the file.

Review Project

Thunderstorms

Thunderstorms are formed by the rapid upward movement of warm, humid air. As the warm, moist air is forced upward, it cools and its water vapor condenses, forming cumulus clouds. Water droplets form in the clouds and begin falling. As the droplets fall through the clouds, they collide with other droplets and become larger. Sometimes, though, the raindrops evaporate and never reach the ground.

As the thunderstorm grows, electrical charges build up in the clouds. They connect with charged particles on the ground below and complete an electrical circuit. That's when we see a bright flash of lightning. The rapid heating of the air around a lightning bolt generates shockwaves. These shockwaves become soundwaves as they travel through the air. This is how thunder is produced.

Heavy rains from thunderstorms sometimes cause flooding and mudslides. Lightning can strike trees and other objects, setting them on fire, and lightning can electrocute people and animals. Strong winds can also cause damage.

These storms often contain large hailstones that can dent cars or destroy crops in a matter of minutes. Hail forms when strong currents rise up and carry water droplets above the freezing level into the thunderstorms. The water freezes into ice. Often the hail melts before it reaches the ground, but sometimes chunks of ice the size of softballs come to the ground (Palmer).

2. Save the document as *urs*Wild Weather.

3. Format the report.

   a. Use your name and today's date in the heading on the first page. The teacher's name is Mr. Tiemann, and the class name is Science.

   b. Adjust the margins for a bound report.

Continued on next page

Reinforce

Create a Newsletter

Reinforce the desktop publishing features you have learned by creating another newsletter.

Your Turn

1. Key the newsletter article shown below.

William Shakespeare

William Shakespeare produced plays since 1594. He worked as an actor and manager for many years in *The Chamberlain's Men*, the most popular acting company in London. He attained financial prosperity by making sound investments and became part owner in *The Globe*, the most prestigious public playhouse in all of London.

Romeo and Juliet

Shakespeare's beloved work known to all is *Romeo and Juliet*. In this play, the city of Verona is split by a feud between two families—the Montagues and Capulets. Romeo is a young Montague, and Juliet, a Capulet. The most memorable scene takes place in the garden as Juliet stands at her balcony. The two star-crossed lovers pledge their deep and abiding love for each other.

Romeo and Juliet are wed in secret by a friar, but their bliss is not to last. In the end, Romeo believes Juliet is dead in the Capulet crypt, but she is in a deep, drugged sleep. In his despair, he poisons himself. Juliet awakens from her deep slumber and realizes her most precious Romeo is dead. In utter desperation, she also ends her life. Shakespeare's tragedy is one of his most moving and heartfelt works.

Continued on next page

APPLY

Review Project

   c. Create an appropriate header for all pages except the first page.

4. Position the insertion point at the end of the document and copy and paste the contents of the file **Sec6Review**.

5. Find the word "snow" and replace it with the word "hail."

6. Spell-check, proofread, and correct errors. Save the changes.

7. Insert a new page at the end of the document, and create a Works Cited page using the information provided below.

Works Cited

Brain, Marshall and Freudenrich, Craig C., Ph.D. *HowStuffWorks.* "How Hurricanes Work." 29 April 2002. <http://www.howstuffworks.com/hurricane2.htm>.

Moran, Joseph M. "Weather." *The World Book Encyclopedia 2002.* Chicago: World Book, Inc., Vol. 21, p. 156.

Palmer, Chad. *USA TODAY.* "More About Thunderstorms." 29 April 2002. <http://www.usatoday.com/weather/tg/wtsmwhat/wtsmwha1.htm>.

Williams, Jack. *USA TODAY Latest News.* "Ground, Upper-Air Combines for Tornadoes." 29 April 2002. <http://www.usatoday.com/weather/wtwist1.htm>.

WW2010 University of Illinois. "Air Masses: Uniform Bodies of Air." 29 April 2002. <http://ww2010.atmos.uiuc.edu/(Gh)/guides/mtr/af/arms/hom.rxml>.

8. Open your Web browser and search for information about the costliest hurricanes in the United States. Add some information about the hurricane costs to the report under the heading *Tropical Storms and Hurricanes.* Be sure to cite your source(s) appropriately. Don't forget to add the source(s) to the Works Cited page.

9. Save the changes. Print and close the file.

Format a Newsletter

You can make the newsletter more appealing by adding a **masthead**. The masthead displays the title of the newsletter and the issue number and date. You can make the newsletter appealing by formatting the headings and inserting clip art images.

Your Turn

1. Edit the document as shown in the illustration below.

Create a masthead by formatting the title, using clip art, and using text boxes. The issue number is 39 and the date is May 30, 20--.

Enhance the heading formats by changing the font, font size, and font color.

Insert clip art images, and format the text to wrap around the image.

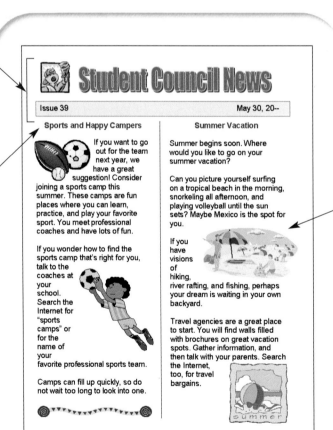

Student Council News

Issue 39   May 30, 20--

Sports and Happy Campers

If you want to go out for the team next year, we have a great suggestion! Consider joining a sports camp this summer. These camps are fun places where you can learn, practice, and play your favorite sport. You meet professional coaches and have lots of fun.

If you wonder how to find the sports camp that's right for you, talk to the coaches at your school. Search the Internet for "sports camps" or for the name of your favorite professional sports team.

Camps can fill up quickly, so do not wait too long to look into one.

Summer Vacation

Summer begins soon. Where would you like to go on your summer vacation?

Can you picture yourself surfing on a tropical beach in the morning, snorkeling all afternoon, and playing volleyball until the sun sets? Maybe Mexico is the spot for you.

If you have visions of hiking, river rafting, and fishing, perhaps your dream is waiting in your own backyard.

Travel agencies are a great place to start. You will find walls filled with brochures on great vacation spots. Gather information, and then talk with your parents. Search the Internet, too, for travel bargains.

2. Save the changes. Print and close the file.

COMPLETING UNIT 4

ENRICH

Curriculum Portfolio

Compose and format a multi-page report on one of the following topics. You can choose to format the report in MLA style or in another style. Be sure to cite your sources and provide a list of your sources at the end of the document. Use side headings to identify the main topics in your report. Your report should include a table of contents. Proofread your work carefully, and save the document with an appropriate filename. Print the documents.

SCIENCE:

Compose a report.

Earthquakes and volcanoes are among the most powerful and frightening types of change on Earth. They can cause massive damage. Still, we are often fascinated by them. Research the causes and effects of earthquakes and volcanoes.

Write a report on your findings. Explain what happens during an earthquake, and identify the locations of major earthquake and volcanic zones. Identify the three types of volcanoes, and explain what conditions might cause an eruption. Discuss the role geologists play in measuring earthquakes, collecting data, and predicting future earthquakes. You may also want to discuss some of the major earthquakes and volcanoes during the last few decades.

SOCIAL STUDIES:

Write a biographical report.

Choose an important person from the twentieth century who is no longer living. The person can be a hero or a famous person. Research and gather information about the person's childhood, education, career, and significant influences and/or contributions.

Write a biographical report about the person. Include in your report why you would have liked to meet that person.

Continued on next page

Format Text in Columns

Text in newspaper-style **columns** flows from one column to the next. To format text in newspaper-style columns, you simply select the text and apply the column format.

Your Turn

Sports and Happy Campers

If you want to try out for the team next year, we have a great suggestion! Consider joining a sports camp this summer. These camps are fun places where you can learn, practice, and play your favorite sport. You meet professional coaches and have lots of fun.

If you wonder how to find the sports camp that's right for you, talk to the coaches at your school. Search the Internet for "sports camps" or for the name of your favorite professional sports team.

Camps can fill up quickly, so do not wait too long to look into one.

Summer Vacation

Summer begins soon. Where would you like to go on your summer vacation?

Can you picture yourself surfing on a tropical beach in the morning, snorkeling all afternoon, and playing volleyball until the sun sets? Maybe Mexico is the spot for you.

If you have visions of hiking, river rafting, and fishing, perhaps your dream is waiting in your own backyard.

Travel agencies are a great place to start. You will find walls filled with brochures on great vacation spots. Gather information, and then talk with your parents. Search the Internet, too, for travel bargains.

1. Change the top **margin** to 2 inches, and change all other margins to 1 inch.

2. Select the entire document, and **format** the text in 2 **columns** with a line between the columns.

3. **Insert a column break** before the heading Summer Vacation to force the start of a new column.

4. When you've made the changes the document should look similar to the illustration on the left. Save the changes. Keep the file open for Project 2.

ENRICH

Curriculum Portfolio

MATH:

Research and report on metrics.

In the United States, we use the English system of measurement. However, most other countries of the world use the metric system.

Research the history and important dates in the chronology of the metric system. Write a report about your findings. Provide examples of why people must understand both systems, regardless of where they live. Include in your report if and when you think the United States will convert to the metric system of measurement.

LANGUAGE ARTS:

Compose a report about school dress codes.

Do you think your school should have a dress code? Now is your chance to voice your opinions to the school administration and the parent/teacher organization. Research the topic to find at least three credible sources that support your position on the issue.

Write a persuasive report that explains your views and your personal concerns. Provide facts to support your reasoning. Remember to keep your audience in mind as you write your report.

SECTION 7.3

Create Newsletters

GOALS: Demonstrate the ability to:

▶ Format text in newspaper-style columns.

▶ Format justified paragraph alignment.

▶ Format a newsletter with multiple columns and objects.

▶ Work from printed material.

PROOFREADING WARMUP

In a word processing document, key each line 3 times. Proofread your work.

```
You should always be honest with yourself about your goals.
David quickly put the frozen jars away in small gray boxes.
Although Bill said it wasn't, Jason thought it was farther.
```

Making the Connection

Have you noticed that most newspapers are formatted into columns? Using columns allows you to display the text in a more interesting way. You will learn to design a new layout and to format the next publication of a student-council newsletter.

Your Turn

1. Open the file **7-3 Project 1**, and save the document as *urs***Student Council Newsletter**.

2. Keep the file open for Project 1.

Sports and Happy Campers

If you want to try out for the team next year, we have a great suggestion! Consider joining a sports camp this summer. These camps are fun places where you can learn, practice, and play your favorite sport. You meet professional coaches and have lots of fun.

If you wonder how to find the sports camp that's right for you, talk to the coaches at your school. Search

UNIT 5

Desktop Publishing

GOALS:

▸ Use draw tools to create text boxes, lines, and shapes.

▸ Use draw tools to layer and group objects.

▸ Format text into columns.

▸ Create a Web page from a template.

▸ Create hyper-links to navigate in a Web page.

▸ Apply a theme to a Web page.

Check Your Understanding ✓

1. Open a new word processing document.
2. Key the answer to each question using a complete sentence.
3. List the drawing tools you used in this lesson.
4. Describe some shapes you can create.
5. What is the difference between a callout and a text box?
6. What is the advantage of grouping objects?
7. Save the document as *urs*Shapes. Print and close the file.

*inter*NET CONNECTION

In this lesson you created a visual timeline. There are many visual timelines published on the Web. The advantage to accessing an online timeline is that when you click on an image in the timeline, you may have access to a hyperlink. This provides details about what the image represents.

1. Open your Web browser and search for sites with visual timelines.
2. Find some sites where the images provide hyperlinks to more detailed information about the content of the timeline.
3. Bookmark two examples that you like best and share your findings with the class.

Good Keyboarding Habits

Focus on your arms and elbows.
Keep your arms and elbows:

- So that your arms move your hands.

- At a 90-degree angle.

- Close to your sides.

Create a Timeline

Reinforce the desktop publishing features you learned by creating a timeline.

Your Turn

1. Open a new document. Change the margins to 1 inch.

2. Change the **page orientation** to landscape.

3. Create a timeline similar to the one shown below.

Order and group objects.
Create the images with clip art, shapes, and callouts.

Insert a text box and use the Arrow tool to point to the timeline. **Fill** the text box with a **color**.

Create a table with 1 row and 5 columns. **Add shading** to the table cells.

Use the Line tool to draw lines above and below the table.

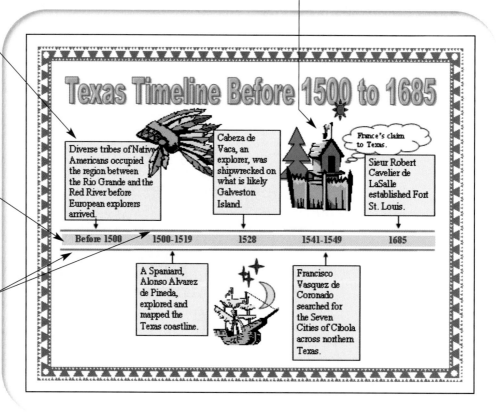

4. Save the document as *urs*Texas Timeline. Print and close the file.

Design Pages With Pictures and Objects

GOALS: Demonstrate the ability to:

▶ Format and add borders.
▶ Create text boxes.

▶ Add fill colors to text boxes.
▶ Create and format art objects.

PROOFREADING WARMUP

*In a word processing document, key each line 3 times.
Proofread your work.*

We know that a good thing to do is to rest and read a book.
The lazy judge was very quick to pay tax money for the box.
Kia understands that the classroom rules apply to everyone.

Making the Connection

After you work hard to compose and format a report, you want to make sure your report is read. Let's explore what you can do to enhance the appearance of the report and create some memorable images that will attract interest.

Your Turn

1. Open a new word processing document.
2. Key the title Volcanoes.
3. Save the document as *urs*Volcanoes Title Page. Keep the file open for Project 1.

Volcanoes

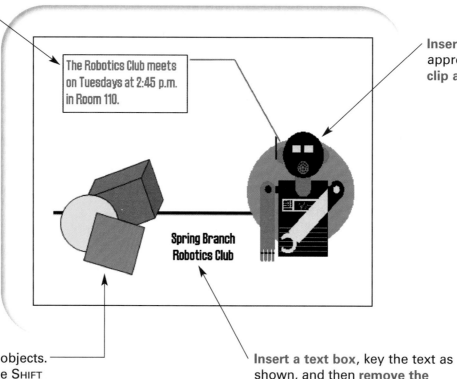

Group Objects

If you are working with multiple objects, you may find that it is often helpful to **group** objects. When you **group** objects, you create a single unit, making it is easier to resize and position the objects.

A **callout**, which is similar to a text box, includes text as well as a leader that points to something on the page.

Your Turn

1. Add the objects illustrated and described below.

Create a callout. Key the text as indicated.

The Robotics Club meets on Tuesdays at 2:45 p.m. in Room 110.

Insert an appropriate **clip art** image.

Spring Branch Robotics Club

Resize the drawing objects. Then, hold down the SHIFT key and click on each of the remaining objects. When all of the objects are selected, **group the objects.**

Insert a text box, key the text as shown, and then **remove the border** from the text box.

2. Save the changes. Print and close the file.

Create a Title Page With Enhanced Pictures and Objects

Clip art, pictures, and drawings are **objects**. You can move objects any place you choose on your page. A **textbox** is an object that holds text.

Your Turn

1. Change the margins to 1 inch, and create a title page similar to the one shown below.

Volcanoes

A Science Fair Project By Amy O'Farrell

Format a page border. Choose a color and line style.

Format the report title with a font style, font size, and color.

Insert a clip art image for volcanoes. **Resize the graphic** as needed, and **position the graphic** on the page.

Create a text box to hold the text shown here.

Select the text box, and **add a fill color** and **shadow style**.

2. Save the changes. Print and close the file.

Position Objects

In this project you will use the drawing objects you created in Project 1 to complete a flyer.

You can change the arrangement or layer the objects by changing the order of the objects. For example, you can position an object in front of or behind another object. You can also rotate and flip objects.

Your Turn

1. Arrange the objects as shown.

Layer the objects.

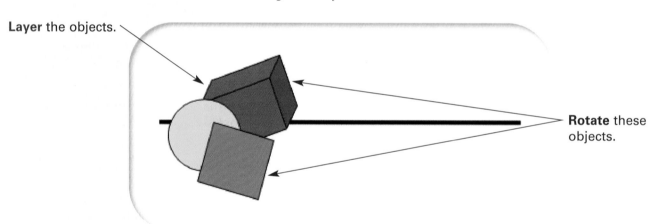

Rotate these objects.

Use the **nudge feature** to position the objects precisely.

2. Save the changes. Keep the file open for Project 3.

Reinforce

Create a Title Page

Reinforce the desktop publishing features you learned by creating another title page.

Your Turn

1. Open a new document, and change all the margins to 1 inch.

2. Create a title page similar to the one illustrated below.

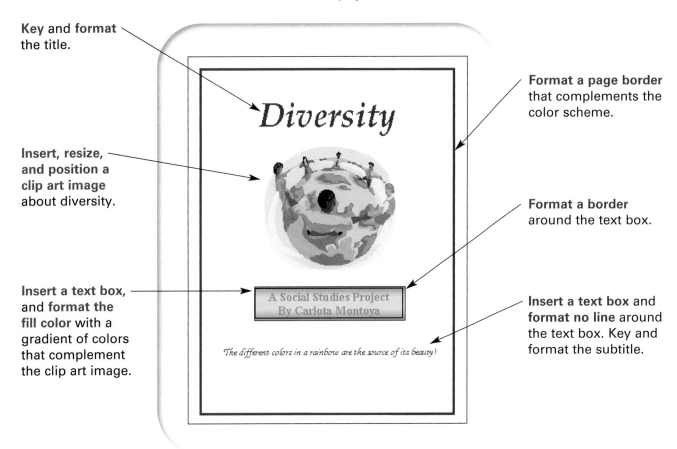

Key and format the title.

Insert, resize, and position a clip art image about diversity.

Insert a text box, and format the fill color with a gradient of colors that complement the clip art image.

Format a page border that complements the color scheme.

Format a border around the text box.

Insert a text box and **format no line** around the text box. Key and format the subtitle.

Diversity

A Social Studies Project
By Carlota Montoya

The different colors in a rainbow are the source of its beauty!

3. Save the document as *urs*Diversity Title Page. Print and close the file.

Practice

Portrait Orientation

Landscape Orientation

Change Page Orientation and Create Objects Using Drawing Tools

Page orientation determines whether the page is displayed vertically or horizontally.

A variety of **drawing tools** is available for creating your own objects. You can customize the objects by changing the size and color. You can even change the way the objects display on the page by flipping and rotating them.

Your Turn

1. **Change the page orientation** to landscape.

2. Use the **drawing tools** to create the objects illustrated below. Use the Fill Color tool to change the color of the objects to the colors shown.

Oval Tool   Rectangle Tool   Rectangle Tool   Apply 3-D

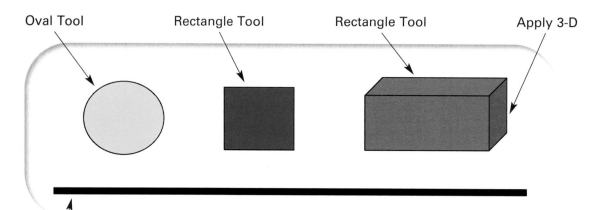

Line Tool and
Line Style Tool

3. Save the document as *urs*Robotics Flyer. Keep the file open for Project 2.

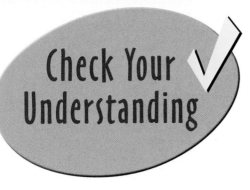

Check Your Understanding

1. Open a new word processing document.
2. Key the answer to each question using complete sentences.
3. What is the definition of an object in desktop publishing?
4. List three or more examples of objects in desktop publishing.
5. What is the purpose of a text box?
6. What are the advantages to using a text box?
7. Save the document as *urs*Objects.
8. Print and close the file.

inter**NET** CONNECTION

Oftentimes, you cannot find what you're looking for in your software's clip art gallery. As you know, you can find and download images from the Web. But how do you know you have permission to copy the image? Perhaps you have heard the term *public domain*. Items in the public domain can be used freely. This means anyone can copy and use the items as desired.

1. Open your Web browser and search for sites that provide public domain images.
2. Bookmark the sites for future use.

Design Pages With Drawing Tools

GOALS: Demonstrate the ability to:

▶ Change page orientation.
▶ Use drawing tools to create objects.

▶ Layer and group objects.
▶ Create callouts.

PROOFREADING WARMUP

In a word processing document, key and complete the paragraph starter. Proofread your work.

```
The best thing that happened recently to me was...
```

Making the Connection

Sometimes content does not fit on the page. The page is simply not wide enough.

Instead of trying to reduce the content, think about how you can better utilize the space on the page. You might be able to solve the problem by changing the page layout.

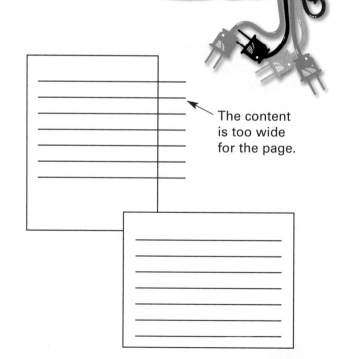

The content is too wide for the page.

Your Turn

1. Open a new document, and change all the margins to 1 inch.

2. Keep the document open for Project 1.